WALL STREET CITY

Other books by the same authors:
Cyber-Investing: Cracking Wall Street with Your Personal Computer

WALL STREET CITY: YOUR GUIDE TO INVESTING ON THE WEB

DAVID L. BROWN

AND

KASSANDRA BENTLEY

John Wiley & Sons, Inc.

New York ◆ Chichester ◆ Weinheim ◆ Brisbane ◆ Singapore ◆ Toronto

Library of Congress Cataloging in Publication Data:

Brown, David L., 1940–
    Wall Street city : your guide to investing on the web
 / David L. Brown and Kassandra Bentley.
      p.   cm.
    Includes index.
    ISBN 0-471-17878-0 (paper/cd rom : alk. paper)
    1. Finance, Personal—Computer network resources. 2. Investments—
Web Computer network resources. 3. Wall Street city. 4. World Wide
(Information retrieval system) 5. Internet (Computer network)
I. Bentley, Kassandra. II. Title.
HG179.B74638 1997
D25.06'3326—dc21   97-12706

Printed in the United States of America

10 9 8 7 6 5 4 3 2

CONTENTS

Chapter 9 The News Room   113

Part Four: Purchasing a Stock   123

Chapter 10 Technical Timing Tools on the Net   125

Chapter 11 Tricks of the Trade   143

Chapter 12 The CyberBrokers   154

Part Six: Investment Strategies   233

Chapter 17 The Ideal Portfolio   235

Chapter 18 Mutual Fund Mania   244

Chapter 19 The Game Is Bonds   265

Chapter 20 Take It to the Bank   272

Chapter 21 Global Investing   279

We dedicate this book to the Internet generation—the children who entered the world just as the Internet exploded into our collective consciousness and who will never know a world without the World Wide Web. Specifically, we dedicate it to:

> *Nicolas Tobias Navarro*
> *Jeffrey Braden Brown*
> *Courtland Walker Brown*
> *Trina Elizabeth Navarro*
> *Corrigan Alexis Brown*
>
> *Heather Michelle Weis*
> *Victoria KayAnn Wells*
> *Jacob Alan Wells*
> *Taylor Lee Mann*

Our interest in the Internet as an investing resource began when we were writing the first edition of an earlier book, *Cyber-Investing,* in late 1994. In the final editing stages, we hurriedly added three paragraphs about the Internet and listed all the Web sites we could find about investing. There were fourteen.

By the time that book was published in mid-1995, the commercial cyberquake had begun. Companies were scrambling to establish Web sites, as the Internet became the most rapidly adapted technology in history. It soon became obvious that investing resources on the Internet could fill an entire book. We didn't realize then how difficult it would be to stuff something as explosive as the Internet between the covers of a mere book.

Nevertheless, we have tried. It seemed imperative to create a structure on which to drape this kaleidoscopic medium; otherwise, the guide would be as chaotic as the Internet itself. We chose the cyber-investing process which we established in our earlier *Cyber-Investing* book.

Although the book you are holding is entitled *Wall Street City* and that Web site is featured prominently throughout the book (http://www.wall streetcity.com), it is not just a guide to that site. The Internet is brimming with investing-related sites—we spotlight more than 300 in these pages—and while we think Wall Street City is by far the most comprehensive, with many features not found anywhere else, the ultimate decision on where to go for investing resources is yours. We've tried to make it as painless for you as possible.

Wall Street City, the book, is divided into seven parts. Part One is an introduction to the investing process that will form the underlying structure for most of the book and to the Internet itself. Part Two tells you where to find prospecting tools for stocks: free lists, search engines, stock picks from market experts, and stocks unique to the Internet. Part Three discusses Web sites that offer research tools, such as company reports, earnings estimates, SEC reports, insider trading reports, and searchable news databases.

Part Four has to do with buying a stock. We offer a brief discussion of technical analysis and where to find technical timing tools on the Net. We also review 19 discount brokers who offer trading directly over the Internet. Part Five discusses how to use Web resources to monitor your portfolio, the market, and industry groups, and how to plan for the optimum time to sell a stock.

The remaining chapters take you beyond our five-step cyber-investing process. Part Six introduces you to Web sites that will help you plan an ideal portfolio through asset allocation. Then it serves up five chapters of resources for nonstock investment vehicles: mutual funds, bonds, bank CDs, global securities, and options. Part Seven presents Web sites with educational content for investors, which may be the ultimate value of the Internet to investors. An alphabetical list of Web-site addresses is found in the Appendix.

Several CyberInvesting Guides are included which give line-by-line comparisons of investing features offered by each site at the time it was reviewed. By the time you read this, however, some of the comparisons may no longer be valid. That's why we are maintaining these and other CyberInvesting Guides at our own Web site, CyberInvest.Com. For the most recent comparisons, visit us at http://www.cyberinvest.com.

The free CD-ROM in the back of the book offers several important benefits, courtesy of Sprint Corporation. It contains software for Sprint Internet Passport™ and: free online time with Sprint for 30 days; free Netscape Navigator browser; free access to Wall Street City for 30 days; preselected bookmarks (at Wall Street City) for the major Web sites in this book and access to an online guide to the Wall Street City site. Hard-wired browser buttons give you instantaneous links to CyberInvest.Com, prominent brokerage firms, and prominent on-line banks. Instructions on installing and using the Sprint Internet Passport start on page 341.

David L. Brown
Kassandra Bentley
http://www.cyberinvest.com

Houston, Texas
April 1997

ACKNOWLEDGMENTS

We have many people to thank for their help in writing this book. Richard Carlin, Tom Melton, and the Wall Street City development staff—Craig Carlin, Vivian Chow, Danny Hoover, Robert Mondshine, and Scott Wierschem—created the outstanding Web site which was the inspiration and foundation of the book. Mark Draud, Tom Melton, Craig Carlin, Mark Monbaron, Steve Adamo, and Belinda Aber contributed a great deal of time and effort to edit and proofread the manuscript. Neil Waldman made it possible to include the Sprint CD-ROM with the book.

There are others who offered assistance for which we are grateful. Paul Alvim and Greg Gensemer helped us gather material for the book; Michael Mead gave us his expertise on DPOs for Chapter 6; Douglas Graham of Macro*World Research Corporation assisted with the portfolio planning and asset-allocation material in Chapter 17; Jeff Brown, Roger Wadsworth, John Ryan, and Jonathan Squire helped us develop our own Web site and the CyberInvesting Guides. Geri Fries, as always, worked hard to schedule our time and help keep the book on track.

Finally, we want to thank Jacqueline Urinyi at John Wiley & Sons for her editorial support, and Carolyn Brown, for her encouragement and support throughout the writing of this book.

D.L.B.
K.B.

PART ONE

Introduction

Part One provides a brief introduction to investing on the Internet. It includes an overview of the cyber-investing process and just enough of the nuts and bolts of the Internet to help you get started.

CHAPTER ONE

INVESTING ON THE INTERNET

The Internet is the biggest change in human communications since the printing press.
—Vice President Al Gore

The Internet, as almost anyone who draws a breath must know, is the hottest new medium since television. Two years ago the word *Internet* wasn't even in the dictionary. Now, it is a household word. It is the frontier of the information superhighway. It is where the fallout from the information explosion ended up. It has done for cyberspace what the railroads did for the Old West: opened it up for settlement by commerce and ordinary citizens. On the Internet, you can get anything you want— and you can get it from the comfort and privacy of your home or office.

In a nutshell, the Internet is a worldwide network of millions of computers and thousands of computerized networks linked together by modems and telephone lines. Major corporations from AT&T to Xerox have home pages where they can tell the world about themselves. So do businesses like Bubbles Car Wash and Taco Bell. Celebrities such as Madonna and Howard Stern and Rush Limbaugh have home pages. So do universities and museums, the Smithsonian, and the White House. The Securities and Exchange Commission (SEC) has a presence on the Internet. So does the IRS. The FBI. The CIA (yes, the CIA). So do ABC, CBS, CNN, NBC, PBS, MTV, and the rest of the alphabet soup. Some ten million of us—including ordinary people—have homes on the Internet where it is open house, day or night, seven days a week, fifty-two weeks a year.

As an interactive medium, the Internet is changing the way we live and the way we do business. Why? Primarily because it is so easy to use. It is literally a follow-your-nose medium, or more accurately, a follow-your-mouse medium. Point and click your mouse, and you can jump instantly from your travel agent to your stockbroker, from a bookstore to a shopping mall. In less time than it takes to read this paragraph, you can point-and-click yourself from Atlanta to Australia, New York to New Zealand, Seattle to Singapore. The Internet is changing our expectations about the quantity of information available, the timeliness of that information, and the efficiency of its retrieval.

One of the businesses it is changing the most is the business of investing. Just two years ago, the Internet was a frontier town when it came to information about stocks or mutual funds. Today, it is a virtual Wall Street with hundreds of sites that provide not only large quantities of information on stocks and the market in general but also information of the highest quality; much of it is free. You can get current and historical quotes on stocks, options, bonds, and mutual funds. You can find stock picks and market commentary from dozens of experts. You can see research reports that used to be available only to the professionals and corporate profiles that once required a trip to your broker's office or the library. You can find out which insiders are buying and selling their company's stock. You can obtain copies of 10Qs and 10Ks from the SEC's own database. You can trade stocks or stories over the Internet and track your portfolio on a real-time basis. You can even create a customized stock ticker that scrolls across your computer screen and displays current prices on just the stocks that you want to see!

We'll be talking about all this and more in these pages, but understand that it is impossible to write a lasting, definitive guide to investing on the Internet. We reviewed more than 200 Web sites in writing this book. A good portion of them completely changed their appearance and content during the last weeks of our review, and new sites appeared faster than buds in the early spring. How many will blossom and bear fruit remains to be seen, but the point is, the Internet is constantly changing. It is the most fluid and dynamic medium in the world, and *that* is both its beauty and its challenge.

We will meet that challenge in this book in two ways. First, we will introduce you to an investing process and tell you where you can find the current resources on the Internet to implement each step of the process. Second, we'll introduce you to several Web sites, including our own, that will serve as beacons to guide you to new and better sites as they are developed in the months and years to come.

FYI   We will not attempt to cover the on-line services, such as America Online, CompuServe, Prodigy, or Microsoft Network. Their financial content is concentrated in well-defined areas, which makes it easy to see exactly what they offer. For more information, visit their home pages which are listed in the Appendix.

The Five-Step Cyber-Investing Process

As you may know, stocks have the highest historical return of any investment. Over the past 70 years, a random selection of stocks would have averaged 10 to 12 percent compounded annually. The average return increases dramatically when one uses even the simplest selection method. In an earlier book about cyber-investing, we talked at length about the benefits of computerized investing.[1] Suffice to say here that with the information and research available on the Internet—and a systematic investing process such as the one described in this book—you should be able to boost those average returns to 15 to 20 percent or more per year. In his book *One Up on Wall Street,* Peter Lynch affirms: "The amateur investor has numerous built-in advantages that, if exploited should result in his or her outperforming the experts, and also the market in general."

One way to organize the incredible amount of investing information on the Internet is to superimpose on it an investing process and show you where to find information for each step of the process. We will use the five-step cyber-investing process developed in our Cyber-Investing book (see Exhibit 1.1). This process does not involve a specific investing strategy; it is simply a process for successful investing. So regardless of your investment style, regardless of whether you agree with ours, the process should serve you well.

---

[1] David L. Brown and Kassandra Bentley, *Cyber-Investing: Cracking Wall Street with Your Personal Computer,* Second Edition (New York: John Wiley & Sons, 1997).

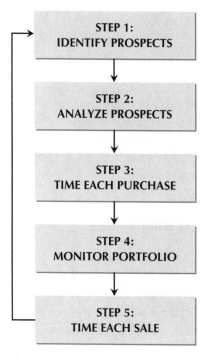

Exhibit 1.1   The cyber-investing process.

Step 1: Identify the Prospects

Whatever you choose to invest in—whether stocks, bonds, mutual funds, houses, race horses, fine art, or baseball cards—you must first identify the prospects. (Hot tips and rumors are one way but clearly not the best!) Out of all possible prospects, only a handful will meet your specific needs. Take stocks, for example. Value investors will look at the long-term potential of a stock. Momentum investors will want to find high momentum stocks. Technicians will be concerned chiefly with price patterns and technical breakouts. We'll show you where on the Internet to identify prospects for possible purchase.

Step 2: Evaluate the Prospects

Once you've identified a list of prospects, you have to narrow them down to the one or several that you want to buy. Even with a list of stocks that meet your basic criteria, some are going to have more potential reward and less potential risk than others. There are two basic ways to evaluate stocks (and one of them is not to ask your friends!). A *technical* evaluation reveals the current and historical price pattern of the stock. A *fundamental* evaluation takes a close look at the company's earnings, price-to-earnings ratio, and other fundamentals. A fundamental evaluation looks at earnings estimates made by research analysts and company profiles put together by independent services. It examines the company's balance sheet and news reports about events that might affect the company's future.

We'll show you where on the Internet to find information for both technical and fundamental evaluations. For those who prefer to have the Internet do the work for them, we'll point to a site that provides a combined technical and fundamental evaluation for every stock in an easy-to-read percentile ranking chart.

Step 3: Purchasing the Stock

There are two steps in the purchase of a stock. The first is to buy it at the right time, when it is technically positioned to go up. This does not mean, of course, that the stock *will* go up, but our research indicates that you can increase your potential profits by using technical signals to time your purchase. (Even if you are concerned only with a company's fundamentals, it has been proven that technical timing can add from one to three or more percentage points to your returns.[2]) We'll show you what the Internet has to offer in this regard.

The second step is the actual purchase of the stock. On the Internet, you can enter your own trades and significantly reduce even discounted brokerage commissions by doing so (to as low as $10 a trade). You can enter the trade from home, anytime of the day or night and never talk to a broker. This is called *on-line trading,* and it is one of the fastest growing aspects of investing on the Internet.

At this writing, there are approximately 20 brokerage firms on the Internet that offer on-line trading. We'll visit all of them.

---

[2] See *Cyber-Investing: Cracking Wall Street with Your Personal Computer* (Chapter 1).

Step 4: Managing Your Portfolio

Managing a portfolio is an ongoing job. It starts the minute you buy your first stock and continues until you sell your last holding. It involves monitoring your portfolio so that you'll know when it is time to sell a stock, buy more of it, or perhaps trade it for a better one. It involves setting up *alerts* to advise you of events that affect your holdings. It involves reviewing industry groups so you'll be able to stay invested in the top-performing groups. It involves keeping an eye on market conditions so you will know whether or when to reallocate your assets. Finally, it involves reviewing your performance. All of these components of managing a portfolio can be done with resources on the Internet.

Step 5: Timing the Sale

The last step in the five-step investing process is the actual sale of a stock based on its risk/reward potential. Although this step is technically part of portfolio management, we will consider it separately to acquaint you with both positive and negative reasons to sell a stock and how to use Internet resources to accomplish this.

Some topics that we will cover do not fit neatly within these five steps, so we have given them their own chapters. Those who prefer mutual funds, options, bonds, bank CDs, or global investing will find those subjects in Chapters 18 through 22; Chapter 23 is devoted to educational material for investors on the Web.

The Last Word

In his book *Market Wizards,* Jack D. Schwager noted that *discipline* was the word mentioned most frequently by the world's top traders he had interviewed.[3] A methodology and the discipline to stick with it made those traders, *super*traders. They would never dream of basing an investment decision on *emotion.* But emotion is the main reason ama-

---

[3] Jack Schwager, *Market Wizards: Interviews with Top Traders* (New York: New York Institute of Finance, a division of Simon & Schuster, 1989).

teur investors tend to lose money in the stock market. If you can estab-lish a systematic investing process—and find the discipline to stick with it—you can improve upon the average returns of the marketplace.

The systematic five-step process we've described is just one approach to investing—one that allows us to organize a wide assortment of Web sites into a coherent guidebook. You may wish to add steps of your own to this process or develop a different process entirely. It really doesn't matter what kind of system or method you use, as long as you funnel your prospects through a rigorous evaluation to eliminate the emotional factor.

With the Internet, you can now do it faster, easier, and better.

CHAPTER TWO

The Nuts and Bolts of the Internet

You have more power on your desk (today) than Merrill Lynch had on its mainframe 20 years ago.

—Junius Peake
Professor of Finance
University of Northern Colorado

A proper introduction to the Internet would require a whole book. Bookstores are filled with such books, and you should take a look at some of them if you are new to the Internet. All we want to do in this chapter is to cover the nuts and bolts, so to speak, to give the novices among you the confidence to venture onto the Net. Seasoned surfers should skip to the next chapter.

The Internet, as mentioned earlier, is a rapidly growing worldwide network of interconnected computers. The World Wide Web, which some think *is* the Internet, is a communication method that allows computers of all makes and models to utilize the Internet's infrastructure to communicate with one another. (The Internet existed a long time before the World Wide Web as a communications network between the government and universities, but that's another story you can read about in another book.) The *Web,* as it is called, is not the only interface to the Internet, but it is the only one you need to concern yourself with at the moment.

Browsers and ISPs

To get on the Internet, you will need a computer, a modem, a phone line, and a browser. A *modem* is a communications device that allows a computer to transmit data over a phone line. A *browser* is a software program that can read the common language in which World Wide Web documents are written (HyperText Markup Language or HTML) and translate it into graphics and text.

Two of the most popular browsers are *Netscape Navigator* and *Microsoft Internet Explorer,* whose home pages are shown in Exhibits 2.1 and 2.2. They can be purchased at a software store or downloaded free on the Internet if you already have Internet access. Most of the

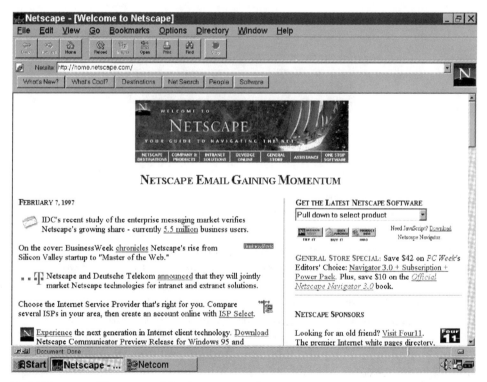

Exhibit 2.1 Netscape Navigator 3.0: home page.

Exhibit 2.2   Microsoft Internet Explorer 3.0: home page.

investing Web sites we will be talking about require the use of secure browsers. (*Secure* browsers can read specially encrypted language in which secure pages are written.) Versions 2.0 of both Netscape Navigator and Microsoft Internet Explorer are secure, but many sites require versions 3.0 or higher to take advantage of certain features on that site.

You'll also need an Internet service provider (ISP), which is the communications carrier that transmits the data between your computer and the Internet. There are dozens of ISPs, three of the largest being AT&T, Netcom, and Sprint. You will be asked to choose an ISP at the time you install your browser. The ISP charges a monthly fee for Internet access (currently about $20) for unlimited hours.

Web Sites and URLs

The location of a business or service on the Internet is called a *Web site* or *Web page.* A Web site can contain many pages or documents linked to one another; the *home page* is the primary document, the one you usually see first when you arrive at the site. The address of the Web site is a *URL* (pronounced you-are-el) which stands for Uniform Resource Locator. Think of a Web site as the building where a company is located for which the URL is the street address. The home page then would be the reception area and the other pages or sections at that Web site would correspond to the different departments of the company. Exhibit 2.3 shows the home page for Wall Street City.

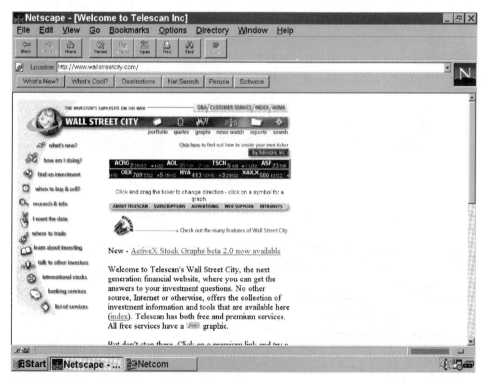

Exhibit 2.3   Wall Street City: home page.

URLs consist of several usually standard elements. Look at the URL for Wall Street City: http://www.wallstreetcity.com, for example.

- *Prefix.* On the World Wide Web, URLs begin with the prefix *http://.* HTTP stands for Hypertext Transfer Protocol, the method by which Web documents are transferred across the Internet.
- *Service type.* Next is the type of service, in this case *www* which stands for World Wide Web. (Others that you'll see in these pages are *pawws* and *pathfinder*.)
- *Domain name.* After that comes the company name or *domain name.*
- *Zone.* At the end is a three-letter code for the zone. Exhibit 2.4 shows the current zones; there will be more in the future.
- Each of these elements except the prefix is separated by a dot.

You can go to a specific page within a Web site if you add the location of that page to the URL, such as: http://www.wallstreetcity.com/newsletters.

ZONE	DESCRIPTION
com	Commercial sites
edu	Educational sites
gov	Government sites
int	International organizations
mil	Military sites
net	Networking organizations, such as service providers
org	Professional organizations and societies

Exhibit 2.4   Current zones of the Internet.

If you visit any international Web sites, you will notice they have a two-letter country code just before the zone. There is a move afoot to require a country code for U.S. sites, but that is not official at this writing.

F^{YI}   There are no spaces in URLs, and they are usually written in lowercase letters. Also, the slashes in the URL are *forward* slashes, not back slashes.

By the way, if you're looking for a specific company on the Web, try entering the URL as http://www.nameofcompany.com. Sometimes it works. If it doesn't, try one of the Internet's massive search engines.

Internet Search Engines

Search engine is another term for the several *indexers* of the Web, such as Alta-Vista, Excite, InfoSeek, Lycos, Magellan, and Yahoo. (Yahoo's home page is shown in Exhibit 2.5.) These are the Internet scouts that visit new Web sites and catalogue information under *keywords* and *phrases* so that ordinary people like us can find our way in the wilderness. Thanks to their Herculean efforts, you can simply enter a keyword or key phrase to locate a Web site or the information you desire. The indexer will scour the Internet and return in seconds with a list of *hits*—sometimes thousands of URLs whose Web site contains the matching word or phrase. If your keywords are unique, chances are the URL you're looking for will be in the top ten because they're listed in order of most relevant.

Learning to use these search engines is a good way to navigate in cyberspace. How do you learn? By practicing.

Hot Links Are Cool

The navigational tactic that makes the Internet such a cool place to do business is hypermedia or hyperlinks. *Hyperlinks* (or *links*) allow you to move instantaneously (jump) from one place to another on the Internet just by clicking on specially designed graphics (hot graphics) or highlighted words (hypertext or hot text) that are linked to a destination site.

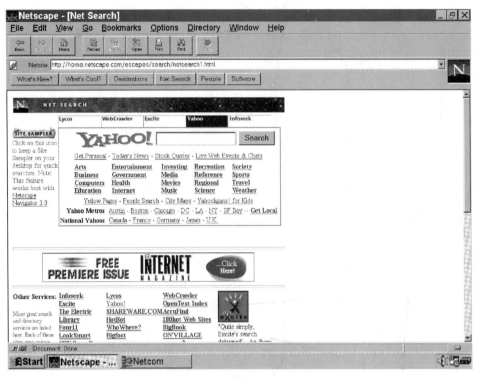

Exhibit 2.5   The search engine page for Yahoo!

Hot text is usually differentiated from ordinary text with an underline and color or bold highlight. How can you tell if a graphic is hot? Move the mouse pointer over it. If the pointer arrow changes shape, the graphic or text is hot.

Hyperlinks can take you to a destination within the same Web site, which is sort of like standing in the accounting department on the 4th floor of XYZ Corporation and beaming yourself up to the executive suite on twelve. Links can also transport you in seconds to a totally different Web site in another city, another state, or another country.

Neither Snow nor Rain nor Heat . . .

An important part of the Internet is *electronic mail,* or *e-mail.* E-mail is the cyberspace version of the U.S. Postal Service, with an e-mail address equivalent to a post office box number. An e-mail address is not the same thing as a URL or a Web site. To continue the postal analogy, you can have a box at the post office without having a physical location for a business. If Netcom is your service provider, your Internet e-mail address will look something like this: jjdoe@ix.netcom.com. You will have an opportunity to establish an Internet e-mail address when you set up an Internet account with your ISP.

An e-mail address is required for some of the investing features we will be talking about (such as portfolio alerts). Some Web sites require an e-mail address before they will allow you to register at their site. (See Exhibit 2.6.)

A Few Surfing Tips

If you are just learning to crawl on the Net, here are a few tips to help you stand upright and surf.

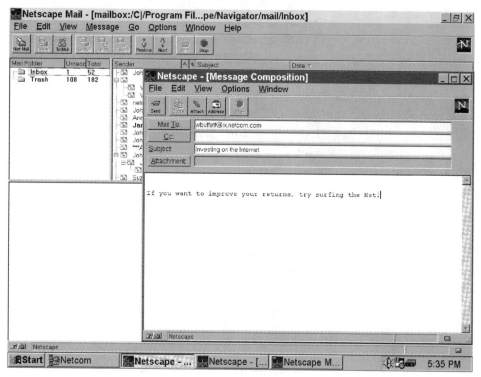

Exhibit 2.6   The electronic alternative to the U.S. Postal Service.

Back/Forward.   Move back and forth between sites or pages that have been downloaded by using the ◄ Back and ► Forward buttons on your browser toolbar.

Frames.   Frames are a formatting technique that allow part of a Web page to remain stationary as a user moves to other pages within the Web site. To move back and forth among pages in a frame, don't use the Back/Forward buttons. Instead, click the *right* mouse button to open a menu which will give you a selection of Back in Frame or Forward in Frame. Otherwise, if you click the Back button, you may leave that section altogether. Fidelity Investments, shown in Exhibit 2.7, makes good use of frames.

Printing frames.   When printing frames, click inside the frame window that contains the data you wish to print *before* you click Print. Otherwise, the browser may select the wrong information to print.

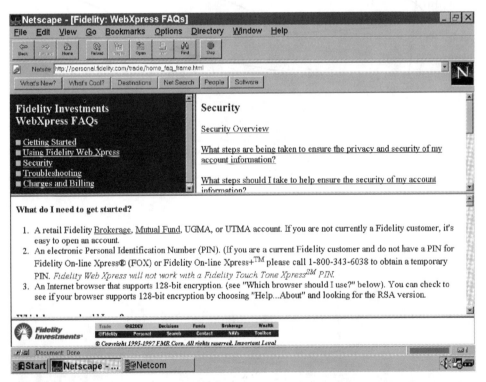

Exhibit 2.7   Fidelity Investments uses four frames for its FAQ page.

Tables.   Much of the data on the investing Web sites use tables, so you will need a browser that supports tables, such as Netscape 2.0 or higher or Microsoft Internet Explorer 2.0 or higher.

Bookmarks.   Use the Bookmark or Favorites feature of your browser to save URLs for quick recall the next time you visit a site (Exhibit 2.8). To save time, you can bypass preliminary pages by bookmarking special destination pages within a site, such as the account page at a broker Web site.

Webmaster's e-mail.   The manager of a Web site is called the *Webmaster.* (This seems to be a genderless word, although *The New York Times* "Glossary of Internet Terms" calls a female Webmaster a Webgoddess!) Most Web sites have a hyperlink to the Webmaster's e-mail for your questions and comments.

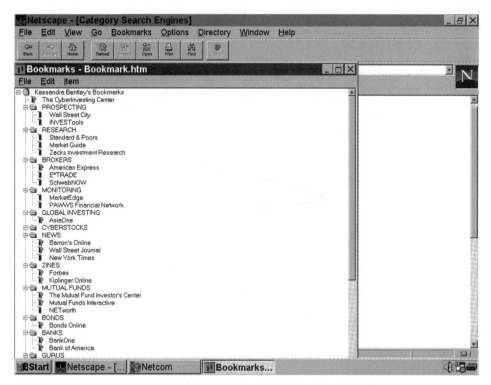

Exhibit 2.8   Netscape's Bookmark page, categorized for the investing process.

Customized home page. Both Netscape Navigator and Microsoft Internet Explorer allow you to specify the default home page. In other words, you can choose which Web site you want to see first when you load the browser software.

Turning off graphics. Exciting graphics can make the difference between a cool and a mediocre Web site. But the snazzier the graphics, the longer it may take to download them. If you're the impatient type you might want to disconnect the graphics feature of your browser. (Some sites list an option for "no graphics.") Be forewarned, however, that some sites depend on a graphic toolbar for navigation.

Clearing your cache. A Web page is stored in a *cache file* on your hard disk and/or memory the first time you request it. If you request it again during the same session, the browser will first check the memory or disk cache, and if the page is there, will display that one rather than retrieving it anew. This sometimes makes for stale pages. To avoid this, clear the cache every now and then. (Use the Clear Memory Cache Now and Clear Disk Cache Now buttons in the Network Preferences section of your browser.)

By the way, the Reload or Refresh button on the browser toolbar will retrieve a fresh page for the displayed URL, but it won't clear the cache.

FAQ. Most sites have an FAQ, a list of *Frequently Asked Questions.* This is often a good way to find out information about the site that is not readily discernible.

Guided tours. If a site has a guided tour, take it. (Some call them *demos.*) Many of them are excellent, and you can see exactly what you'll be getting if a subscription is required.

Be forewarned: You may be required to complete a simple registration form to receive a temporary ID or password. Some Web sites require your full name, address, and e-mail address before they will let you on site, and some will likely use that information for solicitation purposes. If you're interested in the site, however, it may be worth a little junk e-mail.

Free trials. Many of the investing sites mentioned in this book offer limited free trials. Again, this requires that you sign up for the service, and in some cases, submit a credit card number for future billing (you'll be given the option to phone in or fax the credit card information). Be sure to notice what happens at the end of the trial period: Some will automatically discontinue the service; some will automatically start billing you.

Plugging in plug-ins.   Some sites require the use of special software to enhance the visual or audio capabilities of your browser. For example, the Adobe Acrobat Reader enhances the appearance of newsletters and reports; Shockwave provides multimedia enhancements; and RealAudio offers broadcast- or stereo-quality sound, depending on your modem. These programs can be downloaded on the spot.

Pay-as-you-surf.   Many of the investing Web sites in this book sell reports, books, or services on a per-item basis. There are various ways to pay for these, which we'll talk about at length in Chapter 7.

Internet security.   This is a big topic which is of special interest to investors. See Chapter 11 for more information on Internet security.

A Cool-Site Sampler

If you've never surfed the Net before, the sheer quantity of Web sites that we will talk about may be overwhelming. To get you started, we've selected a few sites that are user-friendly and chock-full of investing goodies. We will be referring to many of these sites throughout the book because they offer information for more than one of the five steps of the cyber-investing process.

CNN Financial Network

http://www.cnnfn.com

CNN Financial Network has news from around the world, just like its TV counterpart; plus, you can search the news database by company name. It's all *free.*

Kiplinger Magazine

http://www.kiplinger.com

The Kiplinger Web site is a crisp, easy-to-use site that has many free articles on investing, a good glossary of investing terms, and several lists of top-performing mutual funds.

Continued

MarketEdge

http://www.marketedge.com

MarketEdge is the site of Thomson Financial Services and the home of CDA/Investnet, which tracks insider trading. The Thomson research reports and other research information are available only to subscribers, but Bob Gabele's Insider Trading tip of the day is free. Take the MarketEdge tour for a good look at the site.

The Mutual Fund Investor's Center

http://www.mfea.com

The Mutual Fund Investor's Center is a free site from the Mutual Fund Education Alliance. It offers planning tools, the ability to search more than 1,000 no-load and low-load funds, and links to funds that sell shares without brokers directly to the public. There is also a glossary and other educational material at this site.

The New York Times on the Web

http://www.nytimes.com

In one way, the electronic Times is better than the print version: Each article has links to related stories and Web sites of companies mentioned in the story. The Times also has a CyberTimes section that focuses on stories related to the Internet, a glossary of cyberspeak, and a guide to the Internet that the Times reporters themselves use to research a story. It's all free with registration.

Stock Smart

http://www.stocksmart.com

Stock Smart is a completely free site with layers and layers of stock and mutual fund data. Check out its Industry Rollup section.

Wall Street City

http://www.wallstreetcity.com

Wall Street City is the namesake of this book and one of the investing supersites on the Web. It was developed by Telescan, Inc., and the amount of information here truly boggles one's mind. We will refer to this site repeatedly throughout the book, but if you just want to sample what it has to offer, try the free Quick Search at the Find an Investment page, which is a minisearch based on Telescan's powerful ProSearch engine. Click on a stock symbol on the search report to see a stock graph and a list of company reports. There is a 30-day free trial, but the site has much that is always free.

The Wall Street Journal Interactive Edition

http://www.wsj.com

This is the cool electronic counterpart of the good gray Journal. Like the Times and CNN, the Journal also has links to related stories and/or Web sites mentioned in an article. Sign up for their free trial and customize your own Personal Journal to track news stories on your favorite stocks or companies. You can also search the Journal's archives. Take their free tour.

You'll learn about dozens of other terrific sites in the following pages. We hope you'll try them all and that you'll visit us at Cyber-Invest.Com at http://www.cyberinvest.com.

The Last Word

We've come to the end of our nuts-and-bolts intro to the Internet. You can learn more by reading one of the many books on the subject. But all you really need to do at this point is just log on to the Internet and point and click. It really is that easy.

Part Two

Finding Keepers

In Part One you learned about the cyber-investing process and acquired enough skills for a surfing permit on the Internet. Part Two will launch you into cyberspace with the first step of the cyber-investing process: *prospecting for stocks*. (Investment vehicles, such as mutual funds, CDs, bonds, options, and global securities are discussed in Part Six.) Specifically, we will show you where to find:

- Lists of stocks that meet specific criteria
- Lists of stocks making the news, including initial public offerings
- Simple screening tools that can filter stocks through successive screens
- Full-blown stock search programs that allow you to design a search
- Stock picks from the market gurus
- Prospects indigenous to the Internet, such as cyberstocks, direct public offerings, and stock tips from the chat rooms of cyberspace

CHAPTER THREE

THE A LISTS

Never invest your money in anything that eats or needs repairing.

—Billy Rose, Producer

The first step in the cyber-investing process is to identify a short list of investment prospects that are attractive to *you.* With nearly 10,000 public companies listed on the major exchanges, this could be a daunting task, but the Internet offers many tools to facilitate this task.

The simplest tools—though not the most powerful—are lists of pre-screened stocks based on performance numbers or someone's definition of *best,* or *top,* or *good.* This is a simplistic way of prospecting, but far better than relying on rumors or tips or random guesses. The key to mining such lists successfully is to find the ones that make the most sense to you and then thoroughly evaluate any stock before you purchase it.

The most ubiquitous lists on the Internet are those ranking the best and worst performing stocks in certain categories or based on specific criteria. These lists appeal to many commonsense investment philosophies. For example, a list of the largest percentage gainers for the day would appeal to investors who favor momentum stocks. The key to finding the best prospects on such a list would be to identify the stocks that still have some steam left, which you can do with the technical evaluation described in Part Four.

Other lists might present stocks with the most insider buying or highest volume or the highest upward revision in earnings estimates. And so on, ad infinitum.

There are countless screens that can be used to produce lists of best or worst stocks. Try to find a list that fits your investing philosophy and use it as a starting point in the five-step investing process.

It's Raining Quotes and Dogs

Stock quotes on the Internet are as plentiful as raindrops. Virtually every major investing Web site—INVESTools, MarketEdge, Quote.com, among others—offers free stock quotes (delayed 15 or 20 minutes). Some sites give you quotes one stock at a time; others give multiple quotes. Many serve up their quotes with price-and-volume charts. Customers of brokerage firms can get real-time quotes for placing a trade; otherwise, real-time quotes are through subscription only (about $30 a month).

Two sites that offer their quotes with a twist are:

1. *Wall Street City* (http://www.wallstreetcity.com) offers a scrolling stock ticker which can be customized with stocks of your choice, if you have Netscape Navigator 3.0 or Microsoft Explorer 3.0.

2. *Yahoo! and Net Controls* offer a customized news ticker called "My Yahoo! News Ticker" that will run on your Windows 95 task bar and with existing applications, including screen savers. In addition to stock quotes, you can get headline and industry news, sports scores, and weather reports. To set up the ticker, go to http://my.yahoo.com/ticker.html.

If you're surfing the Net and just want some quotes, check out these sites:

CNNfn   (http://www.cnnfn.com)

DBC Online   (http://mw.dbc.com) Real-time quotes available.

Continued

> *Money Magazine*   (http://www.money.com)
>
> *PC Quote*   (http://www.pcquote.com) Real-time quotes available.
>
> *Security APL*   (http://www.secapl.com)
>
> *Stock Smart*   (http://www.stocksmart.com)
>
> *StockMaster*   (http://www.stockmaster.com)

The Best- (and Worst-) Dressed Lists

Many of the lists offered by investing Web sites are free; others charge for lists that are screened by proprietary indicators or ranking systems (sometimes as part of the Web site's subscription services). Costs are listed where available, but keep in mind they could change by the time you read this book. For an up-to-date list of costs and features, visit CyberInvest.Com at http://www.cyberinvest.com.

FYI   The URL is given each time a Web site is mentioned in a section and in the CyberInvesting Guides. An alphabetical listing of URLs appears in the Appendix.

Bloomberg Personal

http://www.bloomberg.com

Bloomberg Personal is the Web site of the new *Bloomberg Personal* magazine aimed at individual investors. It has a list of the year's 100 top-performing stocks to date. Free.

CyberInvest.Com

http://www.cyberinvest.com

Investment Ideas at this site highlight the newest and hottest investing vehicles on the Web, with links to the originating Web site.

Equis International

http://www.equis.com

Technicians will love the list of "hot stocks" at the Equis International Web site (see Exhibit 3.1). Equis is the creator of the best-selling Meta-Stock technical analysis software, and these stocks are filtered through its technical screens. You don't need MetaStock to view these lists, but if you are a MetaStock user, Equis will provide you with the "exploration filters" it uses each week to come up with the lists. Categories include:

- ◆ Stocks with bullish (bearish) engulfing pattern
- ◆ Stocks up (down) >20 percent on double-average volume

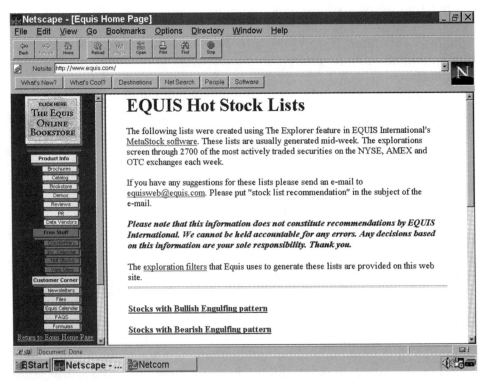

Exhibit 3.1   Equis International's Hot Stock Lists.

- Stocks crossing above (below) 200-day moving average on double-average volume
- Stocks consolidating over the last 16 weeks
- Most volatile stocks over last 16 weeks

Free.

Forbes

http://www.forbes.com

The major focus of the Forbes site seems to be mutual funds, which we'll talk about in a later chapter. For stock prospecting, there is a list of the 200 best small companies in America. Free.

Holt Stock Report

http://metro.turnpike.net/holt/curr.htm

This site offers various prospecting lists that will appeal to momentum investors. There are stocks making new highs and lows, most active stocks (by exchange), high-momentum stocks, and high EPS growth stocks with volume increases. These lists are also presented for optionable stocks. (See Exhibit 3.2.) Free.

Hoover's Online

http://www.hoovers.com

This Austin, Texas–based company publishes "The List of Lists" which covers everything from the Fortune 500 to the Forbes 200, from the 10 largest this to the 20 best of that. Some of the lists could be used for prospecting. They are at the Who's on Top page. Free.

Macro*World @ Wall Street City

http://www.wallstreetcity.com

This developer of a well-known and highly respected forecasting tool can be found at the Wall Street City site. We recommend it primarily for

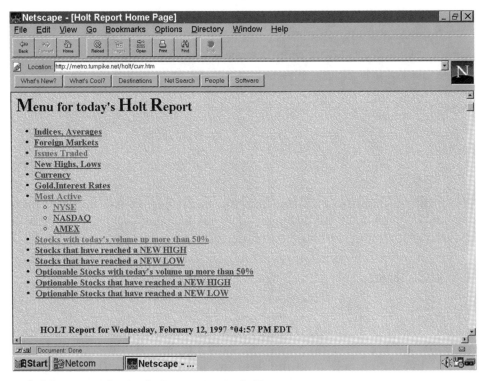

Exhibit 3.2 The Holt Report's stock lists.

planning your portfolio, which we'll get to later, but it also has some good prospecting lists. Among its several "top picks" reports are the top 20 stocks with the highest Master Rating, which is a composite rating by Macro*World based on the ratings of top analysts and brokers; the 20 worst-rated stocks by analysts; and lists of stocks whose forecasts have been recently upgraded or downgraded by Macro*World. (See Exhibit 3.3.) Subscription only.

MarketEdge

http://www.marketedge.com

MarketEdge is one of the half dozen major research sites for investors, the home of Thomson Financial Services and CDA/Investnet, the com-

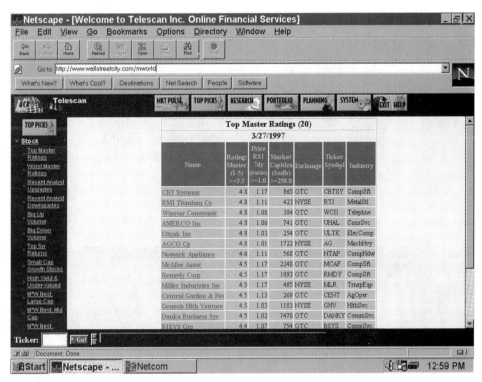

Exhibit 3.3   Top Master Ratings list from Macro*World.

piler of insider trading data. Like most major sites, it offers various
prospecting lists. At the Stock Center page, top performers of the month
are listed in 10 categories for large-cap, mid-cap, and small-cap stocks.
Subscription only.

Market Guide

http://www.marketguide.com

This well-known provider of public company profiles offers a What's
Hot/What's Not page that includes free lists of hottest stocks, biggest
losers, hottest sectors, and hottest industries. The hottest stocks and
biggest losers are divided into two categories: Stocks from $2 to $10 and
stocks $10 and up.

The Motley Fool

http://www.fool.com

The Motley Fool started out on America Online, but now has a home on the Internet. There are free lists of stocks based on the Dow Dividend approach: the Dow 10; the Beating the Dow 5 (from the book of the same name by Michael O'Higgens); and the Motley Fool's Foolish Four. All this is explained in detail at the Motley Fool Web site, with historical performance figures for each approach (see Exhibit 3.4). Free.

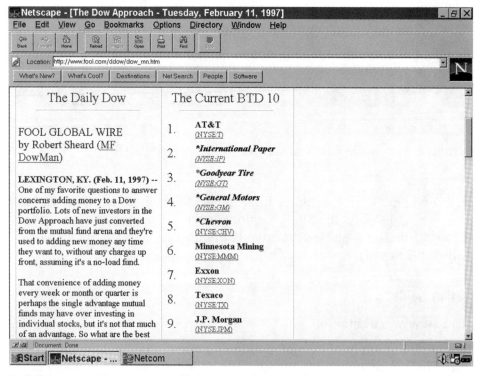

Exhibit 3.4   The Beating the Dow 10 list at The Motley Fool: The Foolish Four are noted with asterisks.

Research:

http://www.researchmag.com

Research:, which is affiliated with the National Association of Investment Clubs, offers a free peek into the portfolios of the experts, including Warren Buffett, Kiplinger's, Money Magazine, S&P, Smart Money, Wired, and several top funds. Buffett's portfolio, by the way, includes American Express, Gillette, Coca-Cola and Wells Fargo.

Stock Smart

http://www.stocksmart.com

Stock Smart is one of the totally free investing Web sites. It seems to specialize in news and statistics, with the latter manifesting in daily lists of percentage winners and losers and volume leaders.

Standard & Poor's

http://www.stockinfo.standardpoor.com

Prospecting lists at Standard & Poor's are all proprietary, but sometimes you'll find one of their STARS-based lists at the Features page. STARS stands for "Stock Appreciation Ranking System," in which S&P rates stocks from 1 to 5 based on its assessment of the stock's potential for price growth. Stocks with 5 STARS are expected to be the best short-term performers in six months to a year.

The subscription-based MarketScope@Home offers several prospecting lists for $12.95 a month. (See Exhibit 3.5.)

FYI Technicians looking for lists of stocks to analyze should check out the two Growth Lists compiled by Geri Crane at http://www.growthlist.com. Some 14 parameters are used to ferret out fundamentally sound stocks poised for growth.

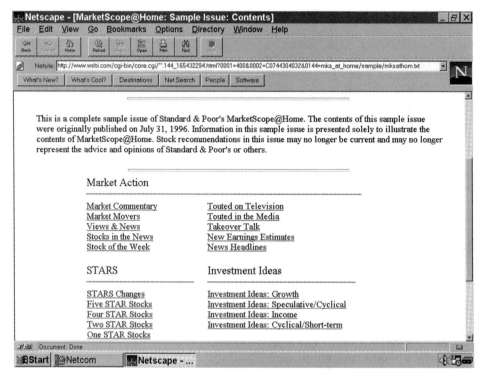

Exhibit 3.5   The contents page from S&P's MarketScope@Home.

StreetNet

http://www.streetnet.com

StreetNet presents its recommended stocks by industry groups. Industry profiles offer an in-depth look at some of the hottest industries. Click on "Recommended Stocks" to jump to a list of hot stocks for the featured industry. Click on a stock symbol in the list and jump to a fairly comprehensive company profile. Free.

Wall Street City

http://www.wallstreetcity.com

You'll find a plethora of prospecting tools at the Wall Street City site, some free, some not. The freebies include an Idea of the Week, which lists stocks from a different ProSearch each week, and a General Best and Worst list, also based on ProSearch. In fact, all of the screening and search tools at this site are derivatives of this powerful PC-based stock search program from Telescan, which we talk about in the next chapter.

Subscription-based lists (starting at $9.95 a month) present the 20 best or worst stocks for each exchange in more than 20 categories, including:

- Analyst Rankings
- Basing Pattern Breakouts
- Chaikin Money Flow
- Earnings Estimates
- Insider Trading
- MACD Breakouts
- Quarterly Earnings
- Telescan Stock Rankings

Each list offers multiple variations. (See Exhibit 3.6.) For example, in the Telescan Ranking list, you can see the best or worst stocks for 11 ranks, including analyst rank, fundamental rank (short- and long-term), growth rank (short- and long-term), insider rank, momentum rank, technical rank (short- and long-term), value rank, and volume rank. In effect, customization creates the potential for more than 160 lists!

There are still other lists of stocks favored by analysts, insiders, and institutions; Standard & Poor's 5-STARS stocks, Fair Value Portfolio, and Platinum Portfolio; technical breakouts, short- and long-term; stocks making new highs and lows over five different periods; and positive and negative basing-pattern breakouts over five periods.

FYI When you click on a stock symbol in a Wall Street City list, a stock graph or report pertinent to that list will be displayed. For example, the Ranking list calls forth a Ranking Snapshot (described in Chapter 7); an Earnings Estimate list presents a Zacks earnings estimate report. Click on the industry group symbol in the list and retrieve an industry group graph.

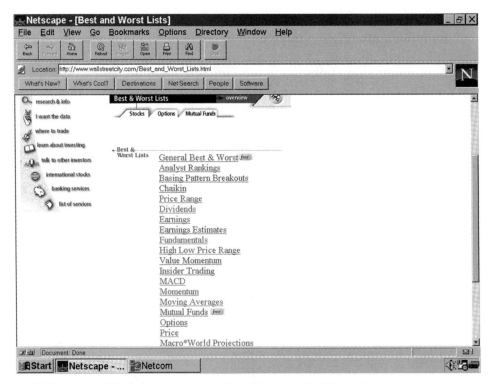

Exhibit 3.6   Wall Street City: The Best and Worst Lists in 20+ categories.

The Web 100

http://www.w100.com

The Web 100 ranks the 100 largest U.S. and international companies with a corporate presence on the World Wide Web. Free.

Zacks Investment Research

http://www.zacks.com

Zacks is the premier provider of earnings estimates. Its Z100 list includes 100 stocks with a #1 ranking based on the Zacks Performance Rank. This ranking system is based on the momentum of analysts' estimate revisions. According to Zacks, stocks with the #1 Zacks Rank have had an average annual return over 15 years (1980–1994) of 36.0 percent, more than twice the return of the S&P 500. Zacks also offers the latest additions and deletions to the Z100 list. The Zacks Web site is subscription-based.

The Best of the Net

If you're going to rely on lists as your major prospecting tool, we'd recommend the Telescan Ranking list at Wall Street City, the Z100 list at Zacks, the S&P 5-STARS or Platinum Portfolio lists, the Macro*World Master Rating list, and, for technicians, any of the technical lists at Equis International.

Newsmakers

Companies that make news because of some newsworthy developments can be a source of prospects. Just keep in mind that by the time the news reaches the mass media, it has probably already been factored into the stock price. There could still be room for growth, however, depending on the type of news. Only a thorough evaluation of the stock will reveal how much potential is left.

Media Sites

Any of the print or broadcast media that has a Web site is a potential source for stocks in the news. Here are some places to start.

Bloomberg Personal (http://www.bloomberg.com) This service offers lists of stocks in the news that, according to its judgment, are poised to rise or fall. Free.

CNN Financial Network (http://www.cnnfn.com) CNNfn has a section called "Hot Stories" which presents news on companies, the economy, and mergers and acquisitions. With each article are hyperlinks to related stories and Web sites. Free.

The Wall Street Journal (http://www.wsj.com) This "Interactive Edition" is a terrific on-line version of the print Journal which we'll be talking about from time to time. It is a good source for stocks in the news, particularly its "Heard on the Street" page. Subscribers only.

Other Newsmaker Sites

All of the major investing sites offer market news. The following offer special pages or categories of news that make for efficient prospecting.

DBC Online (http://www.dbc.com)   The DBC Newsroom at this Data Broadcasting Corp. site has a page called "Movers & Shakers," edited by David B. Wilkerson who takes a look every Friday at "what's hot and what's not." Free.

INVESTools (http://www.investools.com)   INVESTools is one of the major investing sites on the Web. It is a subscription site, but the news is free, and the research alerts reported at the Quotes & News page are a good source of prospects. Look for stocks that have been upgraded from a hold to a buy or have had a recent upward revision of earnings estimates. (See Exhibit 3.7.)

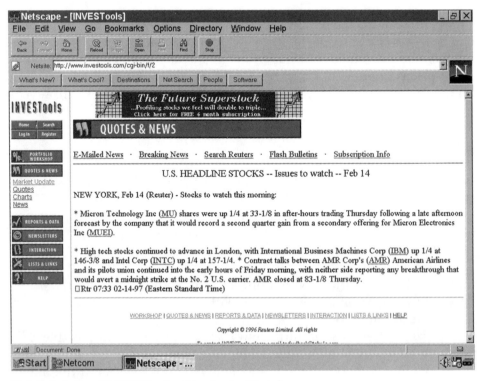

Exhibit 3.7   INVESTools: Stocks to Watch page.

Investing in IPOs

Initial public offerings (IPOs) are problematic investments for amateurs, despite the extraordinary debuts of companies like Netscape Communication, Arbor Software, and Home Shopping Network, with day-one increases of 108, 130, and 136 percent, respectively. It is rare in hot issues like these that the average investor can buy near the offering price. Brokers tend to parcel out shares to favored customers and usually they're oversubscribed.

More important, these IPOs are far from the norm. It is far more likely that an IPO will not increase in value at all and in fact may drop immediately from its opening price.

We suggest that you approach any IPO with caution, unless you have a strong recommendation from a knowledgeable broker. IPOs are exceedingly difficult to evaluate because of the dearth of important information, such as trading history. If you do jump on an IPO bandwagon, be prepared for a bumpy and possibly downhill ride!

Wall Street City

http://www.wallstreetcity.com

Wall Street City (WSC) features IPO lists from Standard & Poor's (at its Find an Investment page), including a new issues calendar and recent performance of new issues. Part of the WSC subscription.

Here are other Web sites that offer information on IPOs.

DBC Online

http://www.dbc.com

Griffin Capital Management Corp.

http://pawws.com/Grif_phtml

Continued

INVESTools

http://www.investools.com

IPO Center

http://nestegg.iddis.com/ipo

IPO Central

http://www.ipocentral.com

IPO Network

http://www.ipo-network.com

IPO Online

http://www.ipo-source.com

The Small Cap Investor

http://www.financialweb.com

Stock Smart

http://www.stocksmart.com

Standard & Poor's (http://www.stockinfo.standardpoor.com)   S&P offers a free list of the top stories of the day and Stocks in the News, both of which might give forth some prospects. The subscriber-based MarketScope@Home offers the stock picks of market gurus that appear in the media and stocks making news because of changes in analyst recommendations.

Stock Smart (http://www.stocksmart.com)   This all-free site has news about corporate mergers and acquisitions that might yield some prospects. Keep in mind that a lot of smart money is involved in mergers and acquisitions, which makes it difficult for an amateur to profit from such ventures. Free.

FYI   There is a clever way to use options to get in the mergers and acquisitions game, which you might want to consider. We'll talk about it in Chapter 22.

TradeAlert (http://tradealert.com)   This is the Web site of several short-term traders who scan the newswires for stories that might affect prices of specific stocks. They give you a synopsis of the news story and the stock that it might affect. It is currently a free site.

Wall Street City (http://www.wallstreetcity.com)   WSC has S&P lists of takeover candidates and takeover talk. Subscription-based.

The Last Word

Lists of stocks are simple prospecting tools. Finding the ones that best match your investing goals and philosophy can be time-consuming, but lists offer a good starting point for those new to the investment game who don't yet have confidence in their investing strategies. Just consider such stocks as *prospects* that must be put through a rigorous evaluation before you place your bet. In the next chapter, we'll show you where to find search tools that will let you design your own prospecting list.

CHAPTER FOUR

THE LITTLE SEARCH
ENGINES THAT COULD

> *If at first you don't succeed, try again. Then quit. There's
> no use being a damn fool about it.*
>
> —W. C. Field

If somebody else's lists do not appeal to you, maybe screens and search
engines that you can control will.

We will begin with the most simple screening programs that filter a
database of stocks through a few successive screens. Then we'll introduce
you to a powerful stock search engine that can sort through nearly 10,000
stocks and identify the ones that *best fit* your investment objectives. (Such
search engines have uncovered some extraordinary stocks in recent years.)
Some of these services are free; some are available on a subscription basis.

Screens and Filters

Filtering stocks through a series of screens is a simple way to generate a
list of prospects. While this is not as effective as a customized search, it
is a way to find stocks that meet some of your objectives. Naturally, any
stock you find on such a list should be evaluated thoroughly.

American Association of Individual Investors

http://www.aaii.org

The AAII has an excellent educational site for members, which we'll
examine further in a later chapter. It offers several stock screens that use

the following strategies: winning stocks, earnings surprises, dividend income, low P/Es, and stocks based on Peter Lynch's ideas. At the moment, this is available only through America Online, but AAII has said they will be expanding their World Wide Web site. $49/year.

INVESTools

http://www.investools.com

INVESTools has a stock-screening tool at its Portfolio Workshop page that lets you manipulate five to six variables in nine preset screens. The screens include:

- Growth and value stocks
- Strong growth stocks
- William O'Neil's winners
- Low price-to-book stocks
- Blue chip stocks
- Small-cap stocks
- Low P/E ratio stocks
- High dividend yield stock
- Insider ownership stocks

For $4.95 a month you can set *all* the variables for this screen. (See Exhibit 4.1.)

MarketEdge

http://www.marketedge.com

MarketEdge offers a screening feature that allows subscribers to customize the screen with a number of variables, including financial performance, size, growth, value, earnings forecasts, and insider trading. For each variable you may select one of five values on a continuum of strong to weak, large to small, high to low, bullish to bearish.

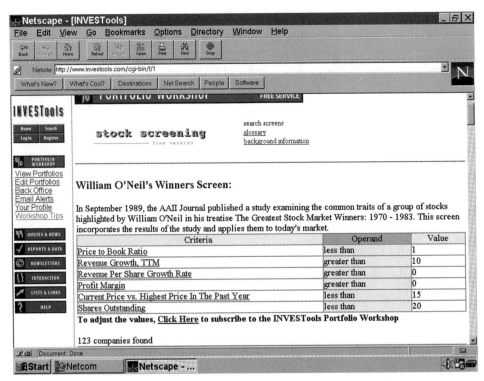

Exhibit 4.1   William O'Neil's Winners from INVESTools.

FYI   If you want to learn more about William O'Neil's investing
strategy, check out *Investor's Business Daily* at http://www.
investors.com. O'Neil is the publisher of IBD, and his C-A-N-S-L-I-M
strategy is one of the topics of IBD's free Investment Education
Course.

Research:

http://www.researchmag.com

Research: is the online site of Research Magazine (which is affiliated
with the National Association of Investment Clubs). It offers a simple
screening mechanism for stocks with seven criteria in the basic search
and an additional 21 criteria in the advanced search. Users are allowed

to enter parameters, but investing criteria are somewhat limited, and the results are listed alphabetically, not in any order of relevancy. A good addition to this site would be help screens. (See Exhibit 4.2.) Free.

Standard & Poor's

http://www.stockinfo.standardpoor.com

S&P offers serious investors a subscription to its stock screens. The 25 screens include increasing institutional ownership, low analytical coverage, high projected growth, consistent earnings and dividend growth, and increasing profit margins. S&P provides a detailed description of the filters and a list of stocks for each screen. $7.95 a month or $79.50 a year gets you six screens a week.

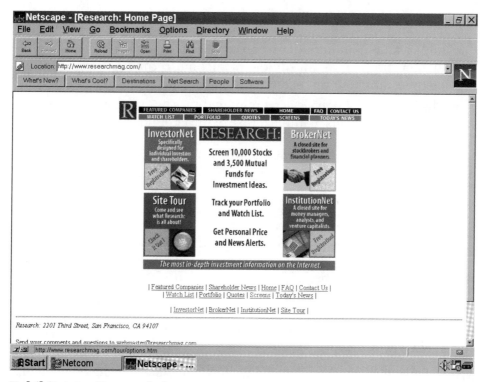

Exhibit 4.2   Research: home page.

Wall Street City

http://www.wallstreetcity.com

Wall Street City offers a simple (free) screening tool called Quick Search which allows you to create a simple search by selecting criteria from a series of successive screens. The first screen defines the universe of the search. The next screen applies one of these filters:

- High Growth
- High Dividend Income
- High Insider Trading Activity
- Technical Analysis

Depending on the filter you select, you'll be presented with a list of secondary screens. For example:

- The High Growth screen offered these secondary screens: undervalued, unheralded, conservative balance sheet, high insider trading, high dividend income, growing dividend income, and high projected earnings.
- The Technical Analysis screen offered these secondary screens: technical breakouts, volume ratios, or turnaround characteristics.

Exhibit 4.3 shows a Quick Search that used a high-growth screen, then an undervalued screen on a search universe of all stocks.

FYI   Wall Street City offers more than 36 backtested search strategies that have produced superior results in past markets. These searches can be run on current data (by subscribers) at the Find an Investment page.

Worth Online

http://www.worth.com

Worth Online is the Web site of the personal finance magazine *Worth*. As a prospecting tool, check out the Stock Screen of the Week which is updated every Tuesday. Screens by Peter Lynch, who writes a column

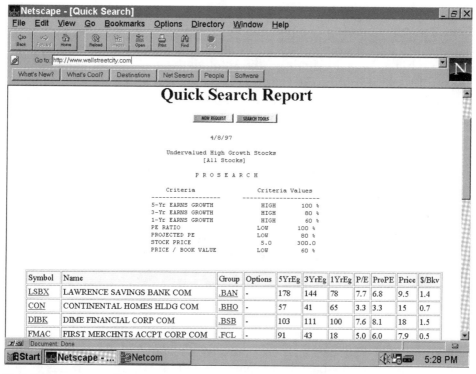

Exhibit 4.3   Wall Street City: A Quick Search Report.

for *Worth,* are sometimes used. Screens are archived and sometimes updated so you can see which stocks had the best performance.

Zacks Investment Research

http://www.zacks.com

Subscribers can screen the Zacks database of more than 5,000 companies using one of 81 screens, most based on earnings and earnings estimates.

The Best of the Net

Of this group of screens and filters INVESTools, Worth Online, and Wall Street City appear to offer the best prospecting tools.

Stock Search Engines

A bona fide stock search engine allows a user to customize a search based on his or her specific investment objectives. You should be able to use multiple criteria in the search and define the variables for each. At this writing, there is only one true search engine that can be used at a Web site—without downloading special PC software—to find stocks that match the investor's objectives. It is Wall Street City.

Wall Street City (http://www.wallstreetcity.com) offers dozens of different searches, all based on Telescan's powerful search engine, ProSearch. ProSearch itself is available at the site, as is ESearch, which uses the ProSearch engine with indicators based on Zacks earnings estimates. In addition, there are *category search engines* that perform minisearches in more than 20 different categories. Here are some details on these search engines, which you'll find at the Find an Investment page.

ProSearch

The Web-based ProSearch offers many of the powerful features of the stand-alone Windows-based ProSearch 5.0. The Web version has some 250 criteria for constructing a search, three different search modes, and two report formats. It searches for the stocks that best fit your criteria, regardless of how many you select (up to 40). This is an important distinction because it lets you score stocks rather than simply eliminate them. Much more powerful! The basic difference between the Web version and the PC version is that you can't save searches or backtest them on the Web. Nevertheless, it far outstrips any search or screening engines that we could find.

ESearch

Also part of Wall Street City's subscription services, ESearch offers almost 300 criteria based on earnings estimates from Zacks Investment Research. These data, which include changes in estimates and earnings surprises, have provided excellent tools in the past for finding big winners.

Category Search Engines

Telescan has unbundled ProSearch, so to speak, and created more than 20 category searches out of the 300+ search criteria. These minisearches use the same ProSearch search engine to offer very focused lists of stocks. They're included with a subscription to Wall Street City.

General Search   To get a taste of the power of Wall Street City's searches, try the free General Search. You can choose any or all of the seven indicators to build a search strategy, including three relative strength indicators and indicators for largest percentage change, largest volume-to-30-day ratio, most active, and P/E ratio.

Ranking Search   This minisearch engine offers 11 ranking criteria—each composed of several regular criteria—for finding highest or lowest ranked stocks in various categories. We strongly recommend this simple, easy-to-use search for anyone not experienced with search engines. Like ProSearch, it ranks the stocks according to best fit. A ranking search report is shown in Exhibit 4.4.

Insider Trading Search   This search offers eight criteria for finding stocks favored by insiders. (*Insider trading* refers to the buying and selling of a company's stock by the officers, directors, and major shareholders of that company.) A number of gurus including Peter Lynch, Mark Arnold, and Marty Zweig have attested to the effectiveness of using insider buying to find stocks that produce large gains.

FYI   The difference between Wall Street City's Best and Worst lists, mentioned in the previous chapter, and the Category Search Engines is this: The Best and Worst lists allow you to use one of several indicators to create the list; the Category Search Engine allows you to construct a search with any or all (up to 40) of the indicators and use the various search modes, just as with ProSearch.

Macro*World Search   This unique search offers a dozen or so indicators based on the Macro*World forecasting indicators. These are advanced tools for the sophisticated investor, made accessible to novices with this search.

The other category searches include Analyst Ranking Search, Cycles Search, Daily Price Range Search, Dividend Search, Earnings Search,

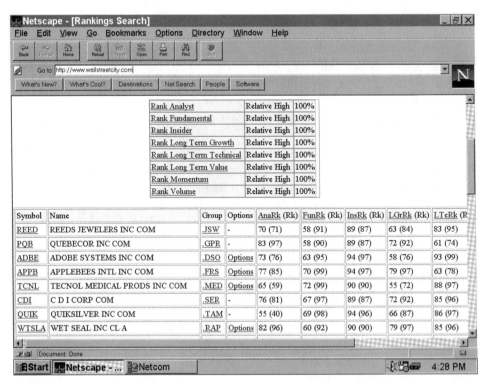

Exhibit 4.4   Wall Street City: The top 10 stocks from a ranking category search.

Fundamental Search, High-Low Price Range Search, Value/Momentum Search, Price Growth Search, Quarterly Earnings Search, Volume Search, and several technical searches based on basing pattern breakouts, the Chaikin indicator, the MACD, moving averages, stochastics, and the Wilder Relative Strength Index. Descriptions of each search can be found at the overview on the Category Search Engine page.

The Best of the Net

Of all the category searches at Wall Street City, the one we recommend most highly—especially for first-time users—is the ranking search. It is easy to use, and it may give you better results than most other category search engines.

The Last Word

We apologize for dwelling at length on the virtues of the ProSearch search engine, but picking stocks without it would be, for us, like trying to find a diamond in a tub full of zircons without the benefit of a jeweler's loupe. But you know where the proof of the pudding is.

In the next chapter we'll talk about another prospecting tool: market gurus. These market experts use a variety of tools to make their stock picks, including, in some cases, ProSearch.

CHAPTER FIVE

FROM THE GURU'S MOUTH TO YOUR EAR

Use newsletters for information, not for decisions.
—Bob Costa, InvestorWEB
Beginner's Guide to Investment Newsletters

What if you're just getting started and can't make any sense out of the investing search engines? What if you don't know which kind of list to put your faith in? Your best bet may be to visit a few Wall Street gurus and see what they're recommending.

The gurus of Wall Street are those audacious souls who are brave enough or foolhardy enough to actually make stock recommendations. Usually they do so in a daily, weekly, or monthly newsletter. Some are free, some charge a fee; but those that charge often offer a free trial. Ideally, you will find one or two that suit your investment objectives and subscribe to them; then you can visit a few of the free sites from time to time to get a ready supply of prospects. The key word here is *prospects*. Be sure to check out any stocks before you buy them—at least until the guru of your choice earns your confidence.

Plug-Ins

There are many free, downloadable software components called *plug-ins* that can extend the visual and audio capabilities of your

Continued

Internet browser or protect the security of the data. In fact, some information cannot be transmitted without certain plug-ins. For example, many newsletters mentioned in this chapter require the use of a plug-in called the Adobe Acrobat Reader. The Reader gives you a WYSIWYG document: What you see is what you get, meaning the headings, typeface, columns, and general look of the newsletter will be reproduced on your screen and on your printer.

Other plug-ins you may encounter include RealAudio or IBM's Cryptolope Containers.

Newsletter Digests

If you don't want to subscribe to a dozen or more newsletters, a newsletter digest might be the answer. These are compilations of the investment news and advice found in other newsletters. Keep in mind that by the time you see a stock pick in a newsletter digest, the original newsletters' subscribers have already seen it. Still, digests may be worth a look.

INVESTools (http://www.investools.com) offers to subscribers of its Web site a newsletter digest that highlights various stock or fund picks from the newsletters published at its Web site. Also at the INVESTools home page is a Most Mentioned section that lists the stocks and funds mentioned most frequently in its publications during the past three months. Free.

Investors Newsletter Digest (http://www.investorsnews.com) by Michael M. Benyacar summarizes publications that cover top-growth stocks, criteria for picking stocks and bonds, mutual funds, foreign banking, technological breakthroughs, and more. (See Exhibit 5.1.) $100 for 12 issues.

The Market Line Letter by Steve Naremore at Wall Street City (http:www.wallstreetcity.com) monitors dozens of market gurus and distills the essence of their stock and option recommendations, market advice, and portfolio strategies. You'll find this at the When to Buy and Sell page under Newsletters. $34.95 a month for daily updates.

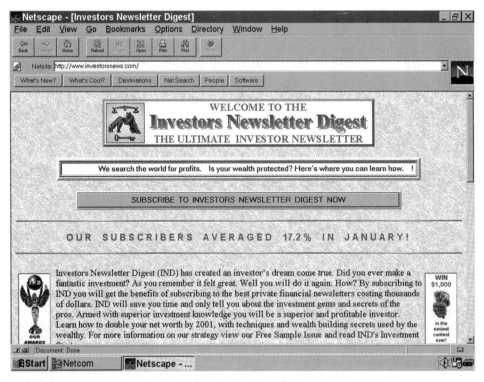

Exhibit 5.1   Investors Newsletter Digest: home page.

Behold! The Gurus

Here are just a few of the hundreds of newsletters and guru sites that appear on the Internet. At least four Web sites offer collections of newsletters: INVESTools, NETworth, the PAWWS Financial Network, and Wall Street City. Others have their own site and URL. In many cases, you can view a sample copy of a newsletter on the Internet but the actual letter is e-mailed, faxed, or (yikes!) sent via U.S. mail. Internet-delivery will no doubt increase as the gurus learn to appreciate the speed and reach of the World Wide Web.

The DBC Newsletter Network

http://www.margin.com

This newsletter network is a joint effort of DBC Online and Newsletter Technologies, Inc., which we discovered shortly before this book went to press. They have many letters not found at other newsletter sites, including two from Martin Pring. Check them out.

INVESTools

http://www.investools.com

INVESTools has a cache of some 23 newsletters at this writing. The following stock letters range in price from $99/year to $242/year.

Argus Research has three stock-picking newsletters: "Director's Choice," with a stock of the month and a list of top 10 stocks; "Portfolio Selector," with Argus's best buys in three categories: income, capital gains, and emerging growth; and "Electric Utility Rankings," which rates 50 utility companies with buy, hold, or sell recommendations.

Decision Point by Carl Swenlin offers technical analysis and commentary, as well as a graphic analysis of a stock or market index in his "Chart of the Week" (Exhibit 5.2). Weekly charts for the past 54 weeks are available for review. In addition, it offers a number of daily stock reports for harvesting prospects. Decision Point is found under Market Update at Quotes & News.

Hussman Econometrics offers three master stock portfolios based on econometric forecasts, which are based on mathematical models of the economy or sectors of the economy.

Individual Investor's Special Situations Report provides "hot picks" from small-cap stocks and emerging companies.

Intelligence Report by Richard C. Young reports on investment bargains and "undiscovered opportunities." Young is a student of Benjamin Graham and Warren Buffett.

Investor's Edge presents "no-nonsense" value-oriented stock picks from J. L. Shaefer.

OTC Growth Stock Watch, written by Geoffrey J. Eiten, is oriented toward high performance Nasdaq stocks with annual growth rates of 15–20 percent. (See Exhibit 5.3.)

The Prudent Speculator's value-oriented portfolio was ranked #1 by The Hulbert Financial Digest.

Strategic Investing by Richard Geist offers small company stock picks. Geist is a value-oriented investor and psychologist.

The Turnaround Letter points out companies that are out of favor and trading at a discount to their true value.

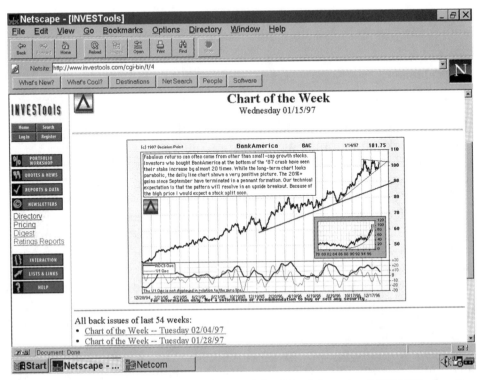

Exhibit 5.2   Decision Point "Chart of the Week" at the INVESTools site.

U.S. Investment Report by Stephen Quickel, offers two model portfolios: the Technology Growth Portfolio and the Conservative Growth Portfolio. Published twice monthly.

The Staton Institute Advisory by Bill Staton offers a monthly "best buys" list.

Wealthbuilder. Adriane G. Berg, the host of WABC's Money Show, offers advice on investing, law, and financial planning.

NETworth

http://www.networth.galt.com

NETworth is the investing Web site of the Quicken Financial Network. It has a section called "Collections of Newsletters" with hyperlinks to other Web sites that feature newsletters, plus links to almost 100 indi-

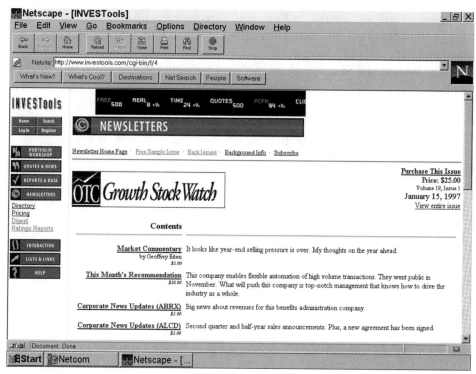

Exhibit 5.3 The *OTC Growth Stock Watch* newsletter at INVESTools.

vidual newsletter sites. To get to this section, click The Insider at the NETworth home page, then click Newsletters.

The PAWWS Financial Network

http://pawws.secapl.com

The PAWWS' newsletter collection is located at the Mutual Fund and Newsletter Info page. Those that deal with stocks are:

The Bowser Report. This newsletter picks stocks priced $3 a share or less, and purports to have returns from 84% in 1988 to 789% in 1994. Published monthly at $48/a year.

Dow Theory Forecasts offers stock recommendations and a review of 30 other market gurus.

Falkner Special Situation Research ferrets out undervalued small-cap stocks not followed by Wall Street firms. Published monthly at an introductory price of $250 a year.

The Low-Priced Stock Survey makes recommendations on low-priced (under $20) small-cap stocks destined to be ground-floor opportunities. Published monthly at an introductory price of $35 for six months.

United & Babson Investment Report gives buy-hold-sell recommendations on stocks and mutual funds, and provides a monthly roundup of other advisory services.

FYI   The PAWWS Financial Network (http://pawws.com) has a free article by Hulbert entitled "On Choosing a Financial Newsletter." It's worth a read if you've never subscribed to a newsletter before.

Wall Street City

http://www.wallstreetcity.com

Wall Street City hosts more than 30 on-line newsletters, as of this writing. Stock newsletters are at the Find an Investment page. Market timing letters, which offer some of the best stock picks, are at the When to Buy and Sell page. Subscription rates for the weekly and monthly letters range from $9 to $35 per month.

Alpha Stock Newsletter by Luiz Alvim and Paul Alvim. This technically oriented, weekly newsletter focuses on the short term with stock recommendations based on the rules of the Alpha Trading System. The Alpha Trading System looks to identify changes in trends by using technical analysis. More specifically, the system focuses on the Alpha MACD, in conjunction with numerous other technical filters to pinpoint trend reversals.

Braddock's $olid Value Report by Tom Braddock recommends fundamentally sound companies whose stocks are underpriced. This is a monthly letter with a medium- and long-term horizon.

Capital Growth Letter by John Bollinger recommends a model portfolio amid a slew of market commentary and information. Bollinger, a regular guest on CNBC, is the world-recognized inventor of Bollinger bands, one of the most popular technical indicators. Updated monthly. Bollinger also ranks industry groups by relative strength each week. [Also available at the INO Web site (http://www.ino.com).]

The Cyber-Investing Newsletter is published weekly by David Brown (coauthor of this book), Mark Draud, and Paul Alvim. They recommend a model portfolio that uses the cyber-investing techniques described in the authors' *Cyber-Investing* book; they illustrate the techniques used to find each stock.

FYI   If you're into shorting stocks, *By The Horns* (http://avidinfo. com/bear) might be of interest. This weekly newsletter bases its short-sell recommendations on charting and technical analysis and is, in its words, "intermediate term in its approach to maximizing market returns." A subscription costs $225 for one year. If you're fuzzy about the concept of short-selling, check out the free "What Is Short-Selling?" section.

Cyrus Barton's 52-Week Review selects technically well-positioned stocks (at their 52-week high) that have good fundamentals. Updated weekly.

The Delta Speculator by Robert Stark uses complex ProSearches to generate lists of industry groups and stocks, whose potential for advance-

---

GoldDigger Alert

If you're interested in gold stocks or other mining stocks, check out these Web sites.

The Alchemist

http://www.investools.com

Continued

Gold Newsletter

http://www.investorweb.com/NEWSLTRS

Info-Mine

http://www.info-mine.com

ment he then assesses using his own proprietary technical analysis (the Parabolic Correlator Forecast). Updated monthly.

Yale Hirsch, the publisher of *Stock Market Almanac,* offers four monthly newsletters aimed at different investors. "Beating the DOW" selects from the DOW's Blue Chip stocks; "Ground Floor" seeks out growth stocks that are "young enough to have most of their growth still ahead of them"; "Higher Returns" recommends stocks that offer "rapid growth or high yield in relation to a low price"; "Smart Money" provides market advice and stock recommendations that "tend toward the overlooked, the undervalued and special situations;" "Turov on Market Timing" offers market-timing advice to traders.

Hi-Tech Watch by Henry Banach recommends science and technology stocks. The newsletter has a long-term horizon and is updated monthly.

Hot Stocks Digest presents 200 hot stocks, based on their formula, along with their percentage change over the past 21 and 50 days.

Hotstocks@StreetLevel combs news releases and the Internet to find stocks that may be headed for a strong price movement. This letter is also available at Market Edge (http://www.marketedge) and Net Capital Communications (http://www.netcapital.com).

Journal of Future Wealth by Mark Smith concentrates on high-growth technology stocks. Updated quarterly.

The Lion's Quest by Robert Valgento recommends a model portfolio with four new selections a month. Stock picks are based on various fundamental and technical qualities. (See Exhibit 5.4.)

The Stock of the Week Report by Harry Plate has a model portfolio of growth stocks with buy/hold/sell recommendations. Near-term and intermediate-term horizon.

THE LION'S QUEST tm

The Essential Guide to High Growth Stocks and Successful Investing
Robert A. Valgento, Editor and Publisher
Jason F. Zenna, Consultant

Volume 2, Number 5   Monday September 2, 1996

Portfolio up 75% after 16 months, up 25% year-to-date

Dear Friends,

Our model portfolio is up 75% in 16 months. Our initial investment of $300,000 has grown to $524,685 since May 5, 1995. The Standard and Poor's Index is up 22% in the same period. As a result our selections are growing about 3 times faster than the SPX.

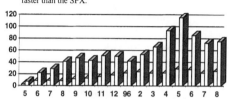

THE LION'S QUEST VS. THE SPX.

Market Conditions

Bearish on the Dow; bullish on computers, semiconductors, and certain drug stocks.

We are still quite bearish on the Dow and the SPX. There is certainly a great deal of concern regarding interest rates and inflationary pressures. There continues to be poor confirmation in advance/decline line and this is clearly a market that lacks leadership. The Federal Reserve did not raise rates in their last meeting and yet the Dow turned down thirty points that day. Perhaps the idea of higher rates is something the market is anticipating and is accepting. September is historically a poor month; the MACD on Dow has turned negative.

Despite these negative factors, we are finding strong companies with favorable charts. Although the small capitalization index, the Russell 2000, is starting to show signs of life compared to the SPX, we are not yet convinced of its safety. Therefore we are pursuing larger companies with with proven financial stability that appear to be in heavy demand. Certain sectors that lead the market down in the last quarter ago are now leading upward. It would appear that the selling has been exhausted in these companies. Among these sectors are computers, semiconductors and drug stocks.

There will be a Jobs Report this week and another meeting of the Federal Reserve later in the month. We should be prepared for further volatility.

News on Holdings

Boeing BA has received more than 30 orders for its hybrid 747 from the Asian market valued at $5 billion. This arrangement may grow to 50 orders when finalized with a value of $9 billion. Boeing will increase production of their 777 by 40% in 1996; employment will increase 13% to 188 thousand people. Technically this stock may dip slightly in coming weeks (consider protective puts?). We consider it a strong long term hold. Methode Electronics METHA reported 23 cents vs 19 cents for the previous year quarter due to increased revenues in their core businesses. Intel INTC was upgraded to outperform from neutral by Smith Barney. Intel has entered important agreements with Computer Associates and Hewlett Packard. The company estimates they will be able to put as many as 1 billion transistors on a single chip by the year 2010. This will confirm their leadership in the field into the next century. JW Charles Securities began coverage of Medical Resources Inc MRII with a buy rating. Their twelve month price target is $14, currently trading at $8.25. We were not stopped out of any positions.

We have been invited to participate in several on-line services including Telescan and their TIPNET and Margin.Com.

Nasdaq is beginning to recover

The hi/lo index had been negative on the Nasdaq and is now starting to recover. We look forward to improved

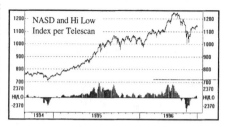

The Lion's Quest is a Trademark and is published monthly by Lion's Quest, L.L.C.
P.O. Box 14486, Scottsdale, Arizona 85267-4486
602-780-3789 or 888-778-5511, e-mail valgento@netzone.com   © 1996 Lion's Quest, L.L.C.

Exhibit 5.4   *The Lion's Quest* newsletter at Wall Street City. Reprinted with permission of Robert Valgento, editor.

Wall Street Research Stock Report by Chris Alster offers leads for trading stocks (and options). Weekly stock recommendations are based on basing pattern breakouts, low-priced stocks, and trend reversals.

The Wall Street SOS by Jerry Gentry recommends stocks based on technical timing. Updated daily.

The Woodward Investment Newsletter is written by Ian Woodward, the popular guru of high-growth stock investing. He doesn't so much recommend stocks as help you find your own stocks using his high-growth stock investing philosophy and Telescan's ProSearch 5.0. He also hosts frequent seminars through Telescan to teach his investing strategy. See http://www.wallstreetcity.com for a schedule.

The Guru's Guru

The Internet has a mind-boggling array of newsletters, many more than are listed in this chapter. The guru who rates the gurus—or at least some of them—is Mark Hulbert, columnist for *Forbes* magazine, a regular on CNBC's Money Club, and publisher of *The Hulbert Financial Digest*.

Hulbert rates more than 160 newsletters and ranks the top-performing newsletters each month, with profiles on four of the best performers. The ratings are purportedly objective, and indeed, Hulbert is considered the quintessential pundit on newsletters.

Critics of Hulbert complain that he selects only a few letters for his analysis. Some complain that his criteria for critiquing the letters are inconsistent. Others say that the charges he allows for brokerage are not reasonable in today's world of deep-discount brokers. These are issues you'll have to decide for yourself if you decide to subscribe to his services.

Hulbert has an introductory price of $59 for 12 monthly issues, which includes his introductory booklet, newsletter directory, and longer-term performance ratings on newsletters back to 1980. You can also order profiles of individual newsletters at $25 each at Hulbert's Web site at www.cybersurfing.com/hfd or from INVESTools at http://www.investools.com.

Other Guru Web Sites

Some market experts have their own Web sites. Here are a few.

Bob Gabele's picks come straight from the horse's mouth, so to speak. He is president and cofounder of CDA/Investnet, one of the processors of SEC forms filed by corporate insiders to disclose their trading activity. His free Tip of the Day at the MarketEdge site (http://www.marketedge.com) is based on insider trading, as is his Stock of the Week, which is available to MarketEdge subscribers. His newsletter, "Insiders' Chronicle," is an additional $20 a month at MarketEdge.

Douglas Gerlach at Invest-o-rama (http://www.investorama.com) picks "on a regular basis" a growth stock that would be of interest to long-term investors and presents a brief analysis. His portfolio of past picks (which boasts an annualized gain of 30.4 percent since 4-11-95) appears at the Web site.

Griffin Capital Management Corp. (http://pawws.com/Grif_phtml) This Web site offers micro-cap "hot stock picks" for free; for a small monthly subscription you can get trade alerts which, according to Griffin analysts, have favorable risk/reward characteristics and superior price appreciation potential. They'll also give you buy/sell signals based on technical-analysis tools.

Investor's Hotline (http://www.investorshotline.com)   Each month, F. Joseph Bradley interviews market experts for their views of new market trends, which often include stock tips. Bradley's incisive, in-depth interviews are highly regarded in investment circles. You can print a summary of the interview or listen to excerpts if you have RealAudio (which you can download on the spot). There are dozens of contributing gurus, including all the big names. Ninety-minute cassettes of the interviews, plus a printed newsletter are $55 a quarter.

Tom Kinakin's StockLine (http://www.stockline.com)   Kinakin reports on undervalued growth stocks by e-mail.

The Market Maven News & Views (at the Financial Center Online, http://www.tfc.com)   This Web site features such luminaries as John Bollinger, Ben Zacks, J. Michael Pinson, Martin Pring, Bob Gabele, Gene Inger, Kirk Kazanjian, Bernard G. Schaeffer, and Jay Taylor. Each week different mavens offer their take on the market and individual stocks. (See Exhibit 5.5.) Free.

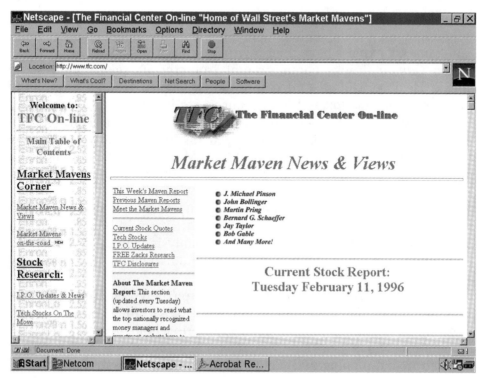

Exhibit 5.5   The Market Maven page at The Financial Center Online.

The Motley Fool (http://www.fool.com)   The Fool offers stock picks in the Lunchtime News section.

Pristine Day Trader (http://www.pristine.com)   Written by professional traders, the Day Trader picks stocks that appear to be poised for a quick, sharp move over the next 2 to 10 days. The editors offer what they consider to be "low-risk trading strategies" to take advantage of this short time frame. At a subscription rate of $125 a month, this is a newsletter for serious traders. A daily hotline with two intraday trading messages can be had for $325 a month. A companion letter to the Day Trader is the *Small Cap Review,* which seeks, in their words, "undiscovered stocks under $10 with explosive upside potentials of 100%+ in 12 months."

Red Chip Review (http://www.redchip.com)   This Portland, Oregon company focuses on about 300 small-cap companies from 28 industries. Subscriptions start at $99/year; company reports can be ordered for $6 each.

The Stock Manager's Investment Report (http://www.lbfinc.com) This report is a monthly on-line newsletter dedicated to the creation of wealth by long-term investment in relatively low-risk stocks. It has a free service that appears to have some worthwhile material, including a stock-of-the-month pick, but recommendations and advice are reserved for subscribers. $25/year.

StreetNet (www.vestnet.com)   This Web site offers free investment ideas from featured Wall Street analysts. The last time we checked in, the featured analysts were from Quick & Reilly, Black & Company, and Van Kasper & Company.

Worden Brothers Online (http://www.worden.com)   The makers of TeleChart 2000 present detailed stock recommendations at their Web site, including short-sell candidates. The site is subscription-based ($89/year).

The Last Word

Much has been said about stock and market prognosticators, some good, some bad. Careful observation, however, reveals that the best of the market letters frequently outperform the market over long periods of time. Our advice is to pick the one or two that appeal to you and use them as prospecting tools. Then do your own analysis of their stock picks. In time, you'll find out if the guru's advice is worth the price.

CHAPTER SIX

ONLY ON THE INTERNET

*Investing in the construction of cyberspace promises to be
one of the most rewarding opportunities of the decade.*
—Alan Chai
*Cyberstocks: An Investor's Guide
to Internet Companies*

The Internet has spawned investment products and resources that are
indigenous to the medium. There are *cyberstocks,* which are companies
involved in building the structure or content of the Internet. There are
direct public offerings or DPOs, which effectively eliminate the investment banker middleman in a company's offering of securities to the
public. There are the *investing newsgroups* where investors can chat
with kindred spirits, pass along stock tips, or seek and offer investment
advice to like-minded cyber-surfers. There are *magazines* that have
never seen paper or ink.

Take a look at what we found.

CyberStocks

Some people are convinced the Internet is the wave of the future. If
you're among them, you might want to invest in companies that are
helping build the World Wide Web, the so-called *cyberstocks.*

Cyberstocks.Com

http://www.cyberstocks.com

Cyberstocks.com gives you the scoop on more than 100 public companies that make the hardware and supply the content of the Internet:

Adobe, Microsoft, Netscape, Reuters, Telescan, and Yahoo! to name a few. You'll find in-depth company profiles, news, quotes, and charts, as well as insights into the industry.

Cyberstocks.com also tells you about the workings of the Internet, its risks and rewards, and even offers a CyberDictionary which sheds some light on the arcane terminology. All this has been published as a book entitled *Cyberstocks: An Investor's Guide to Internet Companies* (Austin, Texas: Hoover's Inc., 1997).

Keeping Up with Cyberstocks

News on cyberstocks is readily available on the Internet.

Electronic Magazines

There are several electronic magazines that can keep you posted on cyberstocks and other Web happenings. We'll discuss these further in Chapter 23.

- *Internet World* (http://www.iw.com)
- *PC Magazine* (http://www.pcmagazine.com)
- *PC Week Online* (http://www.pcweek.com)
- *PC World* (http://www.pcworld.com)

The *New York Times* on the Web

http://www.nytimes.com

The Times' CyberTimes section has enough articles on Internet-related companies and topics to keep you reading for days. There are also columns, archives, forums, and a CyberDictionary to make you fluent in cyberspeak.

Continued

Stock Smart

http://www.stocksmart.com

Stock Smart follows companies that offer products and services related to the Web, the Internet, and intranets in its smartly categorized Market News section.

ISDEX: The Internet Stock Index

http://www.iworld.com

Did you know there is already a market index to track the performance of cyberstocks? It is called the Internet Stock Index or the ISDEX, which claims to be recognized by the investment community. You can check it out at IWorld, the online supplement to *Internet World* magazine. You'll find it at the Internet Stock Report page (Exhibit 6.1). It is also available at Stock Smart.

For a quick look at stocks quotes and links to ISDEX companies, try http://fast.quote.com/groups/isdex.html, which is a joint effort by IWorld.com and Quote.com.

FYI   WWW Internet Fund (http://www.inetfund.com) is the first mutual fund devoted entirely to internet-related companies. It is a no-load fund with a minimum investment of $1,000 (or $250 for an IRA). For an interview with the fund managers, Jim Greene and Lawrence York, visit the InvestorGuide site at http://www.investorguide.com/Inetfund.htm.

Kissin' Cousin to an IPO

One of the most interesting developments on the World Wide Web has been the emergence of *direct public offerings* (DPOs). These are initial public offerings by companies that have chosen to bypass the traditional investment banker and go straight to the public. Their medium of choice: The Internet.

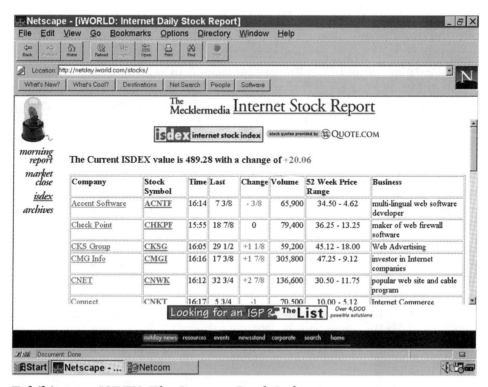

Exhibit 6.1   ISDEX: The Internet Stock Index.

DPOs appeal primarily to companies seeking to raise less than $10 million, especially those seeking less than $5 million. Because investment bankers, in general, are interested in bigger fish, companies like these often find it difficult to wiggle the hook of the investment banking community.

F**YI**   According to a study commissioned by the Small Business Administration, over $30 billion in good quality companies goes unfunded each year by traditional capital sources.

The recognized pioneer for direct public offerings on the Internet is Spring Street Brewery. In 1996, Andrew D. Klein, founder and president, completed the world's first Internet public offering, raising $1.6 million for Spring Street Brewing Company, a three-year-old microbrewery. Dozens of other companies have followed his lead, with about 50 companies using DPOs to raise money on the Internet.

All this has ignited a flurry of activity by state security regulators throughout the country, as well as by the SEC. The upshot is a ruling that says if an *intrastate* DPO posted on the Internet disclaims availability of the offering to other states, the DPO complies with the intrastate exemption. What this means is that relatively small companies, which find it difficult to raise capital through traditional channels, can register in one state and present the offering over the Internet without worrying about whether it meets the rules and regulations of the other 49 states.

The SEC, which apparently wishes to facilitate the raising of capital by small businesses, has engaged in a series of town hall meetings around the country. Last fall, it posted guidelines for publishing a public offering on the Internet.

There is obviously a heightened potential for self-promotion and even fraudulent deals when the traditional due diligence process used by investment bankers is removed. But DPOs do pave the way for undercapitalized companies—sometimes desperately undercapitalized companies—to seek public monies. Which is both good news and bad news. The good news is, many of the smallish service companies that are emerging as the true U.S. industry will be able to raise relatively small amounts of capital ($500,000 to $2 million) without having a lion's share of ownership gobbled up by venture capitalists.

The bad news is that without the due diligence investigations by investment bankers, DPOs present a greater risk to unwary small investors. If you invest in a DPO, *you* will have to perform the research and fact-checking normally performed by the underwriter. You will also have to consider the problem of selling the stock at some future point.

At this writing there is no secondary market for DPOs. The SEC, through a nonaction letter, has given companies permission to operate their own bulletin boards for their stocks. There is also a group called the Small Business Capital Access Association which is working with regulators and industry leaders to establish a secondary market for DPOs.

DPOs on the Web

There are two Web sites you may wish to check out if you're interested in DPOs.

1. The Direct Stock Market at http://www.direct-stock-market.com is involved in the effort to establish a secondary market for DPOs. You can follow their progress at this site.

2. The Emerging Companies Network at http://www.capital-network.com, which is accessible from Wall Street City, will provide an arena for DPOs and other companies traded on pink sheets to disseminate information to potential investors.

DPOs may be the answer to small businesses' dreams. To make them the answer to yours, be wary and do your homework. (See Exhibit 6.2.)

Talk Internet to Me

If you like Talk Radio, you'll love the Usenet newsgroups. These are open forums for people who want to chat about specific topics. (They're also called roundtables, conferences, discussion groups, or bulletin boards.) There are more than 8,000 newsgroups, one for virtually any subject that comes to mind. If you want a list, there are many books on the subject at your favorite bookstore. We're interested in those which have to do with investing.

Netscape offered this comment on investing newsgroups: "Investment tips, economic theories, and consumer advice are among the topics of conversation." Well, we visited a few sites and found precious few economic theories or worthwhile investment tips amid the banter of the newsgroupies. But there was a lot of consumer advice, including a chain letter where "nobody can possibly lose!" and a message from someone named "Opie" soliciting investors for a commercial modular manufacturing factory. (Caveat emptor, for sure!)

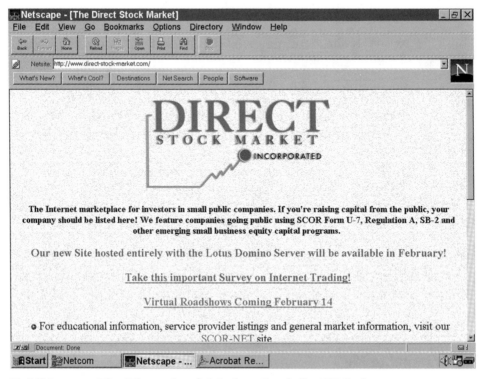

Exhibit 6.2   The Direct Stock Market: Look for DPOs here.

A few good stock tips might be lurking in these groups, but there are other, perhaps more effective, prospecting tools. Still, if you want to chat about investing concepts or ideas or specific stocks, newsgroups may have something to offer.

The Freewheeling Newsgroups

You can access newsgroups by entering the prefix *news:* and then the name of the newsgroup in the URL address window, such as news: misc.invest. Newsgroups are also featured as links on many different sites, including Netscape's home page (under Netscape Destinations, Finance); OnRamp Access (http://www.onr.com), and Wall Street City. (See Exhibit 6.3.)

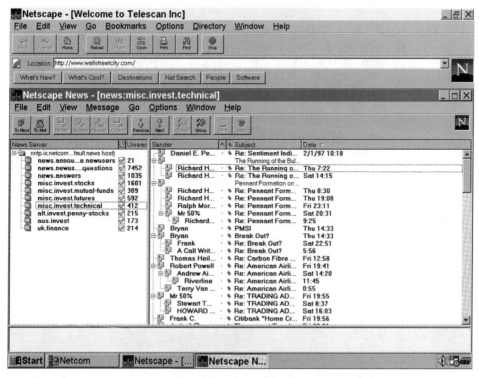

Exhibit 6.3   Netscape News, a newsgroup for investors.

FYI   If you don't want to sift through all the newsgroups to find stock tips, check out "The Wall Street Eavesdropper" at the DBC NewsRoom (http://www.dbc.com). Frank Barnako listens in on Web newsgroups and summarizes what he's "heard on the Net."

Safe Surfing on the Net

The Internet has become something of a cyber-carnival, with electronic barkers selling their wares in Web-site tents. Nowhere is the freewheeling atmosphere more pervasive—and more dangerous for

Continued

investors—than in chat rooms and newsgroups, which are outside the purview of securities regulators. NASD Regulation, Inc., the regulatory arm of the National Association of Securities Dealers, offers the following advice for safe surfing on the Internet.

♦ *Be your own watchdog.* The Internet is vast and resources are limited. Regulators just can't keep an eye on every corner and crevice.

♦ *Question all advice.* If you don't know the source of information or the motives behind the source—as is often the case on the Internet—challenge the validity of the information.

♦ *Measure once and cut twice.* Never make investment decisions solely based on what you read on the Internet. Always consult other resources.

♦ *Do your homework.* Although the Internet opens up access to a variety of new information sources, there is no substitute for your own detailed research.

♦ *Use good judgment.* After all, every investment has its risks. As the saying goes, "If something seems too good to be true, then chances are it probably is." It might be a cliche, but it's right on the mark.

♦ *Call on the experts.* If you suspect something is shady, trust your instincts. Notify the regulators before you act.

Caution Be wary of chatters who hype a particular stock. It is entirely possible they are doing so in the hope that enough of their cohorts will buy the stock to make it go up. By the way, any fraudulent activity can be reported to one of the regulatory agencies mentioned on the next page.

You can file a complaint online at these sources:

NASD Regulation:	http://www.nasdr.com
Securities & Exchange Commission:	http://www.sec.gov
Commodities Futures Trading Commission:	http://www.cftc.gov

Forums and Discussion Groups

If you like a little more structure in your chats with strangers, try one of the forums or discussion groups sponsored by these Web sites. In most cases, the subjects of discussion are categorized so that you can go directly to a topic of your choice. Registration is required by most.

Avid Traders Chat (http://www.avidinfo.com). This is a chat room for technical traders, with special sections for before, during, and after market hours.

INVESTools (http://www.investools.com) sponsors a number of discussion groups at its Interaction section, including ones on stocks, mutual funds, newsletters, and Internet resources.

Mutual Fund Interactive (http://www.fundsinteractive.com) has a monitored newsgroup on mutual funds.

The New York Times on the Web (http://www.nytimes.com) has a number of forums, some of them about investing.

Stock Chat (http://www.stockchat.com) is an offering of DBC Online whose stated goal is to "create an inspired and informed community of [financial] chatters."

Wall Street City (http://www.wallstreetcity.com). In addition to newsgroups, Wall Street City has roundtables and forums at its Talk to Other Investors page. Roundtables are scheduled question-and-answer sessions on a specific subject moderated by a financial expert. Forums are long-term discussion groups sponsored by Telescan.

The Wall Street Journal Interactive Edition (http://www.wsj.com). The Journal has several discussion groups, at least one of which has to do with investing ("Dow 6000, and Beyond"). You can find these under "Join the Discussion" in the Marketplace section. (See Exhibit 6.4.)

Zacks Investment Research (http://www.zacks.com) offers a free Chat Room for the discussion of stocks, trading, and related issues.

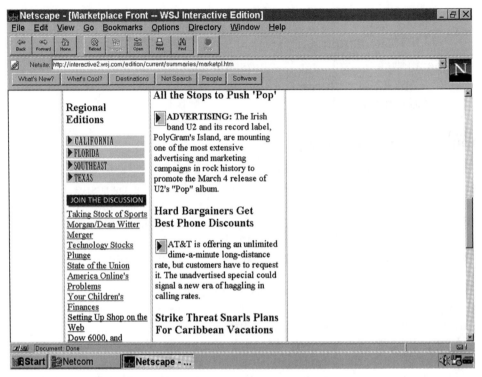

Exhibit 6.4   The *Wall Street Journal*'s Discussion Groups.

The newsgroup phenomenon will likely expand as the Internet continues its astonishing growth. Look for new groups on DPOs, more country groups like UK.fin and misc.invest.Canada, and groups that narrow their focus to a specific aspect of the investing process, a specific technical indicator, for example.

The Last Word

It seems appropriate to end this chapter with a word of caution. First, with regard to direct public offerings, there may well be nuggets among this group, but extraordinary caution will be needed to make up for the lack of due diligence traditionally supplied by investment bankers. Sec-

Web site	Lists		Searches			Stocks in the News	IPOs	Market Gurus	News-groups	Educational Content
	Free	Fee	Screens	Custom	Backtested					
AAII http://www.aaii.org		✔								✔
Bloomberg Personal http://www.bloomberg.com	✔					✔				
CCN Financial Network http://www.ccnfn.com						✔				
CyberInvest.Com http://www.cyberinvest.com	✔									
DBC Online http://www.dbc.com						✔	✔	✔		
Equis International http://www.equis.com	✔									✔
Forbes Online http://www.forbes.com	✔									
The Holt Report http://metro.turnpike.net/holt	✔									
Hoover's Online http://www.hoovers.com	✔									
INVESTools http://www.investools.com			✔			✔	✔	✔	✔	✔
Invest-o-rama http://www.investorama.com								✔		
Macro*World @ Wall Street City http://www.wallstreetcity.com		✔								
MarketEdge http://www.marketedge.com	✔	✔	✔		✔			✔		✔
Market Guide http://www.marketguide.com	✔									✔
The Motley Fool http://www.fool.com	✔							✔		✔
NETworth http://networth.galt.com								✔		
PAWWS Financial Network http://pawws.com								✔		
Research: http://www.researchmag.com	✔		✔							
Standard & Poor's http://www.stockinfo.standardpoor.com	✔	✔	✔			✔				✔
Stock Smart http://www.stocksmart.com	✔					✔	✔			
StreetNet http://www.streetnet.com	✔							✔		
TradeAlerts http://www.tradealert.com						✔				
Wall Street City http://www.wallstreetcity.com	✔	✔	✔	✔	✔	✔	✔	✔	✔	✔
The Wall Street Journal Interactive Edition http://www.wsj.com						✔				✔
The Web 100 http://www.w100.com	✔									
Worth Online http://www.worth.com	✔		✔							✔
Zacks Investment Research http://www.zacks.com		✔	✔							

NOTE: See CyberInvest.Com (http://www.cyberinvest.com) for the latest revisions to this Guide.

Exhibit 6.5   The CyberInvesting Guide for Stock Prospecting.

ond, it will be easy to get caught up in the euphoria about cyberstocks because of the immense potential for this new medium. But the investing public has already discounted much of the future growth of the Internet, and many of the stocks are priced at extraordinary values. So use proper caution in evaluating the underlying value in Internet-related stocks. (See the CyberInvesting Guide for stock prospecting provided in Exhibit 6.5.) That said, it is likely that some of the great companies of the next century will come from Internet companies. The next Microsoft already may have been born.

PART THREE

The Research District

Once you have a list of prospects, the next step—step 2 of the cyber-investing process—is to evaluate them so that you can narrow the list to the best of the best. Before the Internet, this was a formidable task. You had to research the fundamental and technical strengths of a company: its balance sheet, its earnings history, its price growth history, its potential for earnings growth. You had to consider the trading activity of insiders and any news or developments that might affect the stock. Today, the Internet puts all this information at your fingertips.

CHAPTER SEVEN

A Fact-Finding Mission

Facts are simple and facts are strange
Facts are lazy and facts are late
Facts all come with points of view
Facts don't do what I want them to.
 —David Byrne and Brian Eno
 Talking Heads, "Crosseyed and Painless"

The research process begins with evaluating the company. You're looking for anything that will reveal its fundamental health, its potential for
rapidly growing earnings, its chance of being a big winner. For those who
like the research process, this is the fun part of investing. For the rest of
us, it tends to bring back the nightmare of cramming for finals. The Internet, happily, caters to both groups.

For the do-it-yourselfers, the Internet puts research information
within a click of your mouse. In this chapter, we show you where to find
corporate profiles, SEC filings, and corporate Web sites. But first, for the
research-impaired, we look at a bar chart that does it all.

The MRI of Stock Research

For those who'd like to scan a stock and get a graphic image of its essential health, try the Ranking Snapshot at Wall Street City. It reveals in one
concise, color-coded bar chart the fundamental and technical strengths
and weaknesses of a company. This can give you an instantaneous view of
how a company stacks up against all other companies in certain key areas.

Look at the ranking snapshot for Microsoft in Exhibit 7.1. The bars on the right show areas in which Microsoft has positive rankings; the bars on the left show areas in which it's not doing so hot, compared with other stocks. Specifically, this snapshot reveals how the stock ranks—compared with all other stocks—in certain key areas: short-term and long-term growth, value, and technical patterns; analysts' opinion of the company; insider activity; fundamental strength; momentum; and volume, which is basically a money flow indicator.

Each of the rankings is a composite of several different indicators. Value rank, for example, is made up of ratios that measure company growth compared to its P/E, relative P/E, relative price-to-book, and current stock price relative to its short-term or long-term price pattern. Fundamental rank is composed of balance sheet items such as debt/equity ratio and current ratio. Technical rank combines indicators based on

Exhibit 7.1   Wall Street City's Ranking Snapshot shows how Microsoft ranks in various fundamental and technical categories in early April 1997.

moving averages, volume, relative performance, and the moving average convergence/divergence (MACD) indicator. Analyst rank shows the consensus of analysts' opinion about the stock. Each indicator has been backtested to determine the suitability of its composites.

The bars on the ranking chart are expressed in percentiles. If a company is in the highest or 99th percentile in one of the ranking categories, that bar will extend all the way to the right. Conversely, if the company is ranked in the lowest or 1st percentile, the bar will extend all the way to the left. Thus, you can see at a glance where a company stands in each area.

It is important to note that there is nothing subjective about these ranks. Each is based on a carefully developed algorithm that combines a number of facts about the company's position and computes a score that has been shown through careful backtesting to be representative of that particular rank.

A ranking snapshot is a great first look at a company and a quick way to determine which companies to discard based on poor rank and where to concentrate your attention and research. If nothing else, it may shorten the evaluation process by allowing you to eliminate prospects that have poor rankings in important categories.

Essentially Yours: The Company Profile

For those who wish to do their own research, the Internet offers a variety of reports on public companies.

Some reports summarize a company's essential facts, such as the Market Guide Snapshot in Exhibit 7.3. Others go into considerable detail. The longer reports—called company profiles or stock reports—include some or all of the following:

- ◆ Description of the company's business
- ◆ Brief commentary on the current state of the company, and perhaps the outlook for the company
- ◆ Summary financials
- ◆ Earnings history summary
- ◆ Consensus earnings estimates from analysts
- ◆ Summary of buy/hold/sell recommendations of analysts
- ◆ A rating by the service preparing the report

We pay particular attention to ratings, if available; earnings estimates for the current and next fiscal year; the projected five-year growth rate; and any commentary regarding the stock's potential, value, and risk. We also compare the current P/E with the P/E range to determine whether the P/E is high or low relative to its own history.

Some investors may wish to delve into the lengthy and expensive research reports (described in the next chapter), but we have found that a company profile along with the ranking snapshot described earlier are sufficient for this stage of the research.

Here are Web sites that offer stock reports or company profiles.

Barron's Online

http:/www.barrons.com

Barron's Dossiers provide an overview of a company's performance. (See Exhibit 7.2.) They include annual and quarterly fundamental figures, trading performance, and a comparison of the company with its industry. Handy links to related Barron's articles lets you check the latest news on the company at the same time.

Hoovers Online

http://www.hoovers.com

Hoovers' "company capsules" offer quick takes on more than 10,000 companies and in-depth profiles on more than 2,500. The free capsules provide the basic facts about a company, much like Market Guide's snapshot. The company profile is much more extensive, with the corporate history, roster of current officers, descriptions of products and services, and current financials. Company profiles are available by subscription or from a number of Internet sites including:

- Bloomberg Personal (http://www.bloomberg.com
- CNN Financial Network (http://www.cnnfn.com)
- PAWWS Financial Network (http://pawws.com)

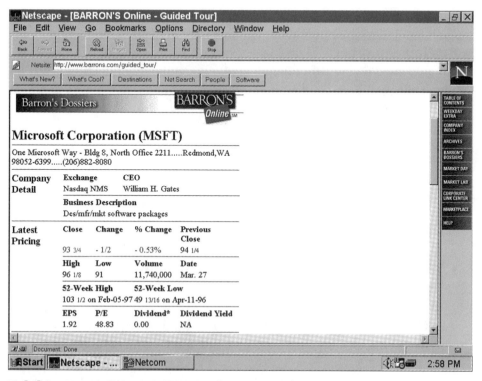

Exhibit 7.2   A Barron's Dossier for Microsoft.

INVESTools

http://www.investools.com

INVESTools offers the S&P stock report and all the Market Guide reports on a per-report basis. (The Market Guide Snapshot is free.) When you register at this site, you'll receive a $5 credit for purchasing reports.

Macro*World @ Wall Street City

http://www.wallstreetcity.com

Macro*World offers a fundamental analysis that compares key financial ratios (such as P/E, price/book value, dividend yield, five-year EPS growth, growth consistency, return on equity, and price volatility) with the stock's industry group and the S&P 500. It also gives a Master Rating to each stock which shows what the industry analysts think of the company's future prospects. The Master Rating is an average of the ratings by all analysts who follow the company. A comparison is shown for the industry group and market index.

Market Guide

http://www.marketguide.com

Market Guide packages its information on more than 8,300 companies in several different reports.

- ◆ A Market Guide Snapshot (Exhibit 7.3) describes the company briefly and provides information on the industry, stock price, earnings, and key financial ratios.
- ◆ A Quick Facts Report has all that, plus operating results, institutional and insider ownership, and quarterly revenues and earnings data.
- ◆ A Company Profile has all the foregoing, plus selected items from the quarterly and annual income statements, balance sheet, and cash flow statements, capital structure (including a breakdown of institutional ownership) and comparisons to industry, sector, and market. All this is in a clear, easy-to-read tabular form.
- ◆ The most comprehensive report is the ProVestor Report which includes, among other things, historical quarterly and annual financial statements, a ratio and comparison report, institutional ownership, insider trading data, price performance, and short-interest information.

Other reports provide ratio comparisons, earnings estimates, and detailed financial statements. Market Guide reports are offered by INVESTools and Wall Street City, plus several brokerage firms described in Chapter 12.

Microsoft Corp.

One Microsoft Way
Redmond, WA 98052
(206) 882-8080

Ticker: MSFT
Exchange: NASD
Sector: Technology
Industry: Software & Programming

Complete Financials: Sep 1996	Earnings Announcement: Dec 1996

Business Summary

Microsoft Corp. develops, manufactures, licenses, sells, and supports software products and operating systems. MSFT also offers online services, sells computer books and input devices, and researches and develops technology software products. For the three months ended 9/30/96, revenues rose 14% to $2.30B. Net income rose 23% to $614M. Results benefitted from an increase in sales for both Windows NT Workstation and Windows NT Server.

*Earnings Announcement : For the quarter ended DEC 1996, revenues were 2,680,000; after tax earnings were 741,000. (Thousands)

RATIOS AND STATISTICS AT A GLANCE
(As of 02/14/97)

Price $	100.13	EPS (TTM) $	1.92*
52 Week High $	103.50	P/E Ratio (TTM)	52.18*
52 Week Low $	47.31	Book Value (MRQ) $	6.10
3 Month Avg Daily Vol (Mil)	9.22	Price/Book (MRQ)	16.43
Beta	1.14	Sales Per Share (TTM) $	7.32*
Market Cap (Mil) $	119,668.20	Return on Assets (TTM) %	25.06*
Shares Outstanding (Mil)	1,195.19	Return on Equity (TTM) %	36.74*
Float (Mil)	729.00	Cash Per Share (MRQ) $	5.95
Indicated Annual Dividend $	0.00	Current Ratio (MRQ)	3.09
Dividend Yield %	0.00	Total Debt/Equity (MRQ)	0.00

Note:
Mil = Millions
MRQ = Most Recent Quarter
TTM = Trailing Twelve Months

Additional Reports Available on this Company		
Quick Facts	Company Profile	Ratio Comparison
Earnings Estimates	Detailed Financials	ProVestor

Exhibit 7.3 A company snapshot of Microsoft Corporation as of 2/14/97. Copyright 1997 Market Guide Inc., 2001 Marcus Avenue Suite S200, Lake Success, NY 11042. All rights reserved. (http://www.marketguide.com)

MarketEdge

http://www.marketedge.com

MarketEdge, which is owned by Thomson Financial Services, offers its own reports on more than 7,000 companies. These reports include income statements and balance sheets for four years, interim results, performance ratios, growth rates, share price performance, insider holdings and trades, institutional holdings, broker forecasts, and summary investment reports from major brokerage firms.

The Red Chip Review

http://www.redchip.com

The Red Chip Review covers about 300 small-cap companies and 28 industries, with reports on a unit ($6 each) or subscription basis ($99 to $1,249/year.

Reuters Money Network

http://www.moneynet.com

Reuters Money Network has S&P reports at its Premium Research page. You will need a First Virtual account to pay for the reports from Reuters. See "How to Pay for Stuff On-line."

FYI   Value Line is not yet on the Internet, although Value Line reports are available through CompuServe.

Standard & Poor's

http://www.stockinfo.standardpoor.com

The S&P stock report, shown in Exhibit 7.4, is the industry standard for company profiles. It includes an analysis of a stock's outlook; Wall Street consensus opinions about the earnings potential; an industry analysis; news related to the stock; S&P's buy, hold, sell recommendations; and an S&P STARS rating, if the stock is rated. (STARS ratings are discussed in Chapter 3).

STANDARD &POOR'S

STOCK REPORTS

Sun Microsystems

5343M

Nasdaq Symbol **SUNW**

In S&P 500

09-FEB-97

Industry: Data Processing

Summary: Sun makes high-performance workstations for engineering, scientific and technical markets and also sells servers and operating system software.

S&P Opinion: Accumulate (★★★★)	Recent Price • 34	Yield • Nil
	52 Wk Range • 35⅛-20⅜	12-Mo. P/E • 23.6

Quantitative Evaluations

Outlook
(1 Lowest—5 Highest)
• **2+**

Fair Value
• **30⅝**

Risk
• **High**

Earn./Div. Rank
• **B**

Technical Eval.
• **Bullish** since 1/97

Rel. Strength Rank
(1 Lowest—99 Highest)
• **87**

Insider Activity
• **Neutral**

Earnings vs. Previous Year
△=Up ▽=Down ▷=No Change

10 Week Mov. Avg. - - -
30 Week Mov. Avg. ·····
Relative Strength ——

2-for-1

VOL. MIL.

OPTIONS: P

Overview - 20-JAN-97

Revenues are forecast to grow 20% in FY 97, benefiting from a new and more powerful product line-up, growing contributions from Internet-related products, and Sun's continued success in penetrating new commercial markets with client-server solutions. Sun is in the early stages of new workstation and high-end server product cycles based on its UltraSPARC processor technology, and is seeing strong demand for these products. Gross margins have been in a strong uptrend, benefiting from strong sales of more richly configured servers, but are likely to remain flat to down as SUNW takes aggressive pricing actions in certain key markets. Expense growth should remain brisk, owing to continued efforts to build up Sun's commercial enterprise infrastructure and enhanced R&D initiatives. EPS comparisons should remain favorable, helped by additional share buybacks. Sun's goal is to achieve compound earnings growth of 15% over any three-year period.

Valuation - 20-JAN-97

The shares remain attractive as Sun is well positioned to capitalize on strong growth opportunities in commercial client-server and Internet/intranet markets. It has aggressively launched new products that target these markets, as exhibited by the recent introduction of the Ultra Enterprise servers and JAVA line of microprocessors. These efforts should prove to be additive to both revenues and gross margins and should fuel EPS growth of some 15%-20% over the next several years. Against this favorable backdrop and based on the current valuation, the shares should be accumulated for their above average appreciation potential.

Key Stock Statistics

S&P EPS Est. 1997	1.82	Tang. Bk. Value/Share	6.06
P/E on S&P Est. 1997	17.4	Beta	0.92
S&P EPS Est. 1998	2.15	Shareholders	3,800
Dividend Rate/Share	Nil	Market cap. (B)	$ 12.5
Shs. outstg. (M)	367.3	Inst. holdings	61%
Avg. daily vol. (M)	6.503		

Value of $10,000 invested 5 years ago: $ 47,929

Fiscal Year Ending Jun. 30

	1997	1996	1995	1994	1993	1992
Revenues (Million $)						
1Q	1,859	1,485	1,273	960.5	856.0	755.0
2Q	2,082	1,751	1,475	1,131	1,051	909.0
3Q	—	1,840	1,505	1,196	1,141	952.0
4Q	—	2,018	1,648	1,403	1,261	973.0
Yr.	—	7,095	5,902	4,690	4,309	3,589
Earnings Per Share ($)						
1Q	0.32	0.21	0.10	0.04	0.01	0.07
2Q	0.46	0.32	0.21	0.11	0.06	0.12
3Q	E0.50	0.36	0.27	0.15	0.12	0.15
4Q	E0.55	0.31	0.32	0.21	0.18	0.09
Yr.	E1.82	1.21	0.90	0.51	0.37	0.43

Next earnings report expected: mid April

Dividend Data

Amount ($)	Date Decl.	Ex-Div. Date	Stock of Record	Payment Date
2-for-1	Aug. 08	Dec. 11	Nov. 18	Dec. 10 '96

 A Division of The McGraw·Hill Companies

Exhibit 7.4 A Standard & Poor's stock report for Sun Microsystems on February 9, 1997.

How to Pay for Stuff On-line

There is no universal way to pay for the reports or merchandise ordered over the Internet. Each company chooses the method it wishes to offer. Here are a few we ran across:

◆ *Credit card.* Many sites will take your credit card information over the Web. However, many feel uncomfortable sending this information into cyberspace, despite assurance by experts that the new scrambling and encryption techniques make Internet transactions as safe as those in the real world. Sites that offer payment by credit card usually give the option of faxing or calling in the information.

◆ *Debit account.* Several sites allow you to purchase prepaid *units.* Your account is then debited each time you purchase a report. Payment is still by credit card, but only when you purchase the units. In some cases, reports are heavily discounted with a debit account.

◆ *CyberCash Wallet (http:///www.cybercash.com).* CyberCash offers downloadable software that is password-protected. Credit card information is entered just once when you set up the account and is just between you and the approving merchant bank. CyberCash claims its encryption technology is created by the same people that the FBI uses. There is also a CyberCoin Wallet that accommodates very small purchases. Visit the CyberCash site for more information.

◆ *First Virtual account (http://www.fv.com).* A First Virtual account is similar to a debit account, except it is your credit card that is debited each time you make a purchase. You provide your credit card information by telephone and receive a VirtualPIN number via e-mail. When

Continued

you purchase an item, it is charged against your credit card but only after you receive an e-mail confirmation from First Virtual. If you reply "Yes" to the e-mail, the transaction will take place; otherwise, it won't. An annual fee of $2.00 is charged when you set up the account. For more information, visit the First Virtual site.

The S&P report is sold on a per-unit basis (from $1.50 to $3.00 each, depending on the purchase plan you choose). Prepayment by credit card is required, with the cost of the report deducted from your balance. You can get a selection of free reports just for registering at the S&P Web site, if you have the Adobe Acrobat Reader. S&P reports are also available from INVESTools, Quote.com, Research, Reuters Money Network, and Wall Street City.

Wall Street City

http://www.wallstreetcity.com

At the Wall Street City site, you can research a stock six ways from Sunday. Go to the Research & Info page and take a look at the long list of company reports. Some are shown in Exhibit 7.5. The company snapshot is free; the rest of the reports are part of Wall Street City's subscription services, which start at $9.95 a month.

Westergaard Online

http://www.westergaard.com

Westergaard Online purports to be the leading Internet provider of investment research on micro-cap companies (which Westergaard defines as companies with less than 300 million market capitalization). This site includes over 400 pages of investment research on dozens of companies organized into environmental, medical, oil and gas, and security and crime-control industry groups. Free.

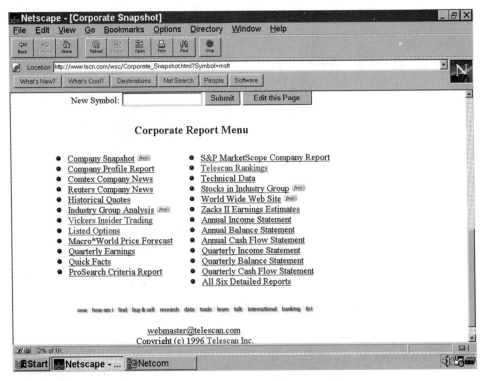

Exhibit 7.5   Wall Street City: Corporate Reports Menu.

The Best of the Net

Any of the company profiles will tell you what you need to know about a company. It just depends on how deep you want to drill. Market Guide has the widest variety of reports and they're easy to read; S&P has its value-added STARS ratings. Wall Street City and INVESTools have them both, plus a whole lot more.

The EDGAR Files

The most diligent investors will insist on reading a company's 10K or 10Q before buying a stock. If you're one of these, the SEC has made it easy to get official filings by opening a Web site for its EDGAR database.

EDGAR, which stands for Electronic Data Gathering Analysis and Retrieval, is the government's database of SEC filings by public companies, mutual funds, and others. The EDGAR files go back to January 1, 1994, although not all companies will have files that far back, even if they were public at the time. The SEC had a phase-in period for companies to begin filing electronically, but, as of May 1996, all public companies were required to file electronically. The EDGAR filings are now posted to the SEC Web site 24 hours after they are filed.

The Securities & Exchange Commission

http://www.sec.gov

The EDGAR database at the SEC Web site contains an enormous amount of raw data with filings back to January 1, 1994. The site is completely free, and if all you want to do is download a 10K or 10Q on a company whose name you know, you can do it as well here as at any other site.

Several companies have developed tools to organize the EDGAR data in a more user-friendly fashion and much of it is now available on the Internet at the following sites.

Disclosure

http://www.disclosure.com

Disclosure is the most prominent and largest of the EDGAR processors, with some 100,000 SEC filings each year from more than 11,000 U.S. public companies. These filings are organized into several user-friendly databases which are available at the Disclosure Web site and through other vendors described below.

Disclosure has a search retrieval tool called *EDGAR Access.* For a small subscription charge, you can access up to 25 company reports and set up personalized alerts for notification by e-mail of filings by specific companies. Reports are also available by fax or overnight mail.

EDGAR reports are also available through Primark, the parent company of Disclosure (http://www.pirc.com) on a per-report basis. A number of commercial online vendors, such as America Online and CompuServe, also offer access to one or more of Disclosure's EDGAR databases.

EDGAR Online

http://www.edgar-online.com

EDGAR Online is a product of Cybernet Data Systems, Inc., whose database goes back to January 1994 and covers only corporate SEC filings, not mutual fund filings. EDGAR Online has structured its subscriptions into three levels, allowing for notification of x number of filings per month for selected companies or specific form types.

NYU

http://edgar.stern.nyu.edu

NYU's Stern School of Business Information Systems was one of the first to develop search tools for the EDGAR database. You'll find a list of tools at the Get Corporate SEC Filings page. You can search by stock symbol or partial company name, or by a specific industry or sector, using Zacks industry and sector codes. The latter is a joint effort with Zacks Investment Research.

Smart EDGAR @ DBC Online

http://dbc.smart-edgar.com

Smart EDGAR at the DBC Online Web site is a product of Data Broadcasting Corporation and Internet Financial network. It offers real-time receipt and transmittal of EDGAR documents, intelligent search capability, and user-defined watch lists.

Wall Street City

http://www.wallstreetcity.com

Wall Street City offers SEC Online as part of its subscription services.

The Best of the Net

The EDGAR filings seem to be a case of free versus ease of use. The SEC site is free, though somewhat daunting, but it'll get the job done if all you want is an occasional 10K or 10Q.

Corporate Headquarters

You can tell a lot about a company by visiting its headquarters. But unless it is located in your city, that isn't practical. The next best thing is to visit the company's home page on the Internet. Most Web sites of public companies offer a Webmaster e-mail address where visitors can ask questions or request annual reports. The most important thing to look for is the message from the chairman, if available, and perhaps a mission statement.

The following sites offer links to home pages of public companies.

The American Stock Exchange

http://www.amex.com

This exchange has links to companies listed on its exchange.

CNN Financial Network

http://www.cnnfn.com

CNN offers links to corporate Web sites for companies that appear in CNN stories.

Companies.online

http://www.companiesonline.com

This is an offering of Lycos (http://www.lycos.com), one of the major indexers of the Web. Enter a company name and you'll get its address, telephone number, trade names, industry, Web address (URL), ticker symbol, links to a Dun & Bradstreet report (which you can purchase), and stock quotes.

InvestorsEdge

http://www.irnet.com

Companies use this site to disseminate investor relations information, along with links to their Web sites.

InvestorWEB

http://www.investorweb.com

Company links appear in alphabetized lists at this site.

InvestQuest

http://invest.quest.columbus.oh.us

InvestQuest publishes company presentations for about 30 companies, with basic information on some 10,000. There are links to Web sites where available.

Nasdaq

http://www.nasdaq.com

For companies listed on Nasdaq, a link to the home page comes with stock quotes and graphs.

NETworth

http://networth.galt.com

At NETworth's Investors Relation page, you can search for companies by name or select from lists of stocks in the Dow 30, S&P 500, S&P Small-Cap 60, S&P Midcap 400, Nasdaq 100, or the Fortune 500.

Reuters

http://www.moneynet.com

Inc.Link at the Reuters site is an investors-relation page where public companies may communicate with investors and shareholders, with links to their Web pages, if available.

The Wall Street Journal Interactive Edition

http://www.wsj.com

The Journal offers links to companies that appear in its news articles.

FYI   About 3,200 public companies distribute their annual reports through The Public Register's Annual Report Service (PRARS). You can order reports without charge at the PRARS Web site (http://www.prars.com). Requests are processed within 24 hours. At this time, PRARS does not have links to corporate Web sites.

The Last Word

Only you can determine the level of comfort you need in gathering enough facts about a company to make an investment decision. We find that the ranking snapshot and a company profile from S&P or Market Guide satisfies our comfort level (along with the earnings estimates and insider trading report that we'll talk about in the next chapter). Fortunately, the Internet provides a number of choices. Experiment with the various sites until you can develop a process that meets your time requirement and monetary budget.

CHAPTER EIGHT

THE INSIDERS

There's no better tip-off to the probable success of a stock than that people in the company are putting their own money into it.

—Peter Lynch
One Up On Wall Street

Facts go only so far. When you're trying to judge the direction of stock prices, you have to make a leap of faith into the future. You have to put your money on a stock that you think has the best potential for future growth. Usually, that means putting your faith in someone else's predictions about that company's future. When it comes to predicting a company's future, the best prognosticators we know are the corporate insiders and the research analysts who make a career out of studying the company.

You can find the crystal balls of both groups on the World Wide Web.

Corporate Insiders: Those in the Know

Heavy buying by insiders is one of the two best indicators of future stock growth. (The other is an upward revision in earnings estimates by analysts, which we'll talk about later in this chapter.) The profitability of following the insiders' lead has been proven in several studies. Norman G. Fosback described the classic study on insider activity in his article, "How to Use Insider Signals for Maximum Profit."[1]

---

[1] Norman G. Fosback, Editor, "How to use Insider Signals for Maximum Profit" (Ft. Lauderdale, Florida: The Institute for Econometric Research, 1994).

This study, conducted at Portland State University by Shannon Pratt and Charles DeVere, analyzed 2,000 insider transactions in 800 stocks between 1960 and 1966. Fosback reported that "stocks with heavy insider buying significantly outperformed stocks with heavy insider selling."

FYI   Insiders are defined by the SEC as the officers, directors, and major shareholders (those who own more than 10 percent of the company's shares). Insiders are required by the SEC to file reports on all trades made in their company's stock within the first 10 days of the month following the trade.

The results of this study have been confirmed by others. Market wizard Marty Zweig, author of *Winning on Wall Street,* did a study in 1974–76 on stocks with insider buying and found that stocks with heavy insider buying outperformed the S&P 500 by almost 200 percent.[2] (He documents four other academic studies that confirm his findings.)

Mark W. Arnold, former vice president of a major Wall Street brokerage firm and author of *Trading on Tomorrow's Headlines,* says that no one has shown him an approach that generates consistently better results than following the insiders' lead. His portfolio of stocks based on insider buying outperformed the S&P 500 three years running:[3]

| | *Percent Return* | |
Year Ended	S&P 500	Insiders' Portfolio
March 1994	0.7	68.2
March 1995	8.5	19.8
March 1996	31.3	87.4

Research conducted by author David Brown and Mark Draud supports the wisdom of following the insiders. They backtested the insider trading indicator from Telescan's ProSearch over several historical peri-

---

[2] Martin Zweig, *Winning on Wall Street* (New York: Warner Books, 1986).

[3] Mark W. Arnold, *Trading on Tomorrow's Headlines* (Houston: Telescan, Inc., 1995).

ods, searching for stocks with high insider buying. Over a 12-month period (4/1/92 through 3/31/93), the insider buying search had a higher return (40.4 percent) than all other searches tested during that period.[4] Similar results were achieved for other time periods. In addition, in a recent study by Paul Alvim of Telescan, an insider trading search beat the market 8 out of 8 times.[5]

Insider buying does not occur in a vacuum, however. There are other factors to consider when researching a stock. Those who pick stocks based on high insider buying usually consider such things as earnings estimates and the size and fundamental strength of the company. They may also consider the number of insiders buying, whether they're simply exercising options, and how much insider selling is going on.[6] Nevertheless, if the people in the know—the officers and directors of the company—are shelling out hard cash for their company's stock, it is very likely they know of some event or business trend that should have a positive effect on the stock price.

As Mark Arnold says, "There's only one reason [for insiders] to buy [company stock]. They think it's going up."[7]

Finding the Insiders on the World Wide Web

Insider trading data is based on forms filed by insiders with the SEC. The two major compilers of this data are Vickers and CDA/Investnet. Vickers has no Web site of its own at this time; CDA/Investnet is located at the MarketEdge site. Both provide insider data to other Web sites, some of which are mentioned here. It is not always clear who is providing the data to the Web site, but that is of no great importance since it is all based on SEC filings. Following are some of the companies offering insider trading reports.

[4] David Brown and Mark Draud, *ProSearch Strategy Handbook* (Houston: Telescan, 1993).

[5] Paul A. Alvim, ProSearch 5.0 Strategy Handbook (Houston: Telescan, 1997).

[6] Insider selling should be interpreted carefully, because sometimes insiders are simply cashing in options that are part of their compensation package. Furthermore, thorough backtesting of insider selling has shown no correlation to stock performance, except in the most egregious cases.

[7] Mark W. Arnold, as quoted in the Minneapolis–St. Paul Star Tribune, May 21, 1995.

Dow Jones

http://bis.dowjones.com

Dow Jones has a Corporate Ownership Watch with insider transactions on more than 8,000 companies.

Insider Trader

http://www.insidertrader.com

This is the Web site of Jonathan Moreland, assistant director of research and columnist at *Individual Investor* magazine (he writes their "Insider's Edge" and "Insiders Out" columns). He provides weekly and monthly summaries of SEC filings on insider trading (free). For $4.95 a month, he'll tell you how to profit legally from insider trading with stock selections based on insider trades, follow-up analysis on recommended stocks, and special screens that combine insider trading and fundamental data.

MarketEdge

http://www.marketedge.com

MarketEdge is the home of CDA/Investnet, a Thomson Financial Services company that compiles data on insider trading. The Thomson company reports, which come with a MarketEdge subscription, include data on insider trading activity. Bob Gabele, president of CDA/Investnet, writes a column at MarketEdge called "Insider's Trading Watch," which is part of the MarketEdge subscription. Another source of his insider expertise is the *Insiders' Chronicle* newsletter, available by separate subscription to MarketEdge subscribers. (See Exhibit 8.1.)

Quote.com

http://www.quote.com

Quote.com offers Vickers insider trading reports as part of its second level subscription at $24.95 per month.

CDA Investnet ®

INSIDERS' CHRONICLE™

BOB GABELE, EDITOR

March 31, 1997 VOL. 22, NO. 12

Buy Side Activity

■ HUNTCO INC. - HCO

Huntco's Q3 results were negatively affected by the purchase of Coil-Tec and higher prices for domestically purchased steel. These circumstances have impacted the shares, driving them down more than 25% from their November price at the $16 level. However, the impact of these factors should abate in coming quarters, as the positive aspects of the acquisition are realized, and the company is able to purchase cheaper foreign steel. Further, executives at the firm have indicated that they find value in the shares at these price levels through their recent, unprecedented accumulation. From February 20 to February 28, three executives acquired 116,140 Class A shares at $11.50-$12.75 each. Director James Gavin purchased 40,000 Class A shares in his largest open-market acquisition since initially filing in '93. Officer & Director B. Hunter, a filer since '93, completed his first buy in the open market, adding 37,000 Class A shares. This transaction represents Hunter's largest open-market purchase across all of his 7 affiliations. Finally, Officer & Director Robert Marischen acquired 39,140 Class A shares in his largest open-market buy since becoming a filer in '93. This round of accumulation surpasses each annual insider buy total since the company's IPO in '93. Huntco is an intermediate steel processor, specializing in flat rolled carbon steel.

Continued on page 3

CONTENTS

The Picture... *Any Change?*

Our interpretation of insider activity at this time continues to be one that urges investors to exercise caution. This is primarily because of the pickup in insider selling that has more than outweighed any recent increase in insider accumulation. We are monitoring an expansion of insider distribution in a growing number of large cap companies, to an extent that we have not traditionally been accustomed to. Take **Owens Illinois (OI)** for instance, where insiders sold a combined 1.4 million shares at prices around $23 - $24 in January and February. These sales far surpass the previous highest *annual* total for shares sold by Owens Illinois insiders, which stood at just 112,000 shares ('95). **Ingersoll-Rand (IR)** is another case in point. In February, six executives disposed of 139,000 shares at prices between $46-$49. This number surpasses the previous highest *annual* total shares sold by company executives, which stood at 48,550 shares ('93). In addition to these issues, we are monitoring high levels of insider selling in the likes of **Chrysler (C), International Paper (IP) and Clorox (CLX).**

In times such as these, with so many stock charts showing breakdowns, be sure to not assume that one insider's action contains the whole puzzle. All insider activity needs to be put into perspective before making conclusions. A recent case in point here is **Oakely Inc. (OO)**, where a February buy of approximately 1 million shares by Chairman & President Jim Jannard was accompanied by a glowing company press release. On the surface, this $9 million aquisition would seem to be a bullish event, worthy of serious investor attention. What the press release failed to mention, however, was the fact that Jannard's purchase paled in comparison to the approximately $214 million he raised by selling 9 million shares (split-adjusted) back in June of '96 at much higher prices. It is not out of the realm of possibility that promotional value may have weighed heavily in Jannard's decision to reinvest about 4.5% of what he had sold in June.

Though it could be said that insider buys have gotten a bit more interesting in recent weeks, in the interest of perspective, we must stress that some pickup should be expected given the heavy hits levied on so many issues recently. It should be expected that executives will, in knee-jerk fashion, pick up some shares at the first appearance of low prices. Persistent accumulation over time, however, is what makes a trend, or in the case of the insider picture, a trend reversal. At this time, it is too early to determine whether insider sentiment has changed. Based on past experience, our hunch is that it hasn't.

Sell Side Activity

■ CITICORP - CCI

Citicorp's much-praised global strategy ("global uniqueness", "global franchise") has gone a long way in segregating Wall Street opinion of the company from its peers. This, combined with enthusiasm generated by corporate repurchases and the recent disclosure that Saudi Prince Alwaleed has accumulated an 8.85% position (through the conversion of preferred shares) have helped fuel the revaluation fires further to the upside in recent months. Some interested parties, citing the company's emerging market strategies, are suggesting that Citicorp shares should be valued more as a global consumer products company than as a money center bank. With all this uniqueness, one would figure that insiders may be acting differently than those of other major banks where company executives have been unloading shares as the tide continues to rise. In a sense, they are...they've been selling a lot more shares than their peers have. Take a look at the buildup in annual sales by insiders at the company since the '90 banking debacle: 1991 = 135,280 shares, 1992 = 39,858 shares, 1993 = 349,743 shares, 1994 = 582,039 shares, 1995 = 1,166,919 shares 1996 = 1,512,883 shares. The most recent sales occurred in January and February, when seven insiders dropped a total of 271,817 shares at prices in the $109 to $119 range. Although high Wall Street expectations are the norm for many of the large banking issues, executives in the industry are hardly holding onto their shares and options. The continuing divergence of insider sentiment regarding their potential stock movements from Wall Street's enthusiasm causes us increasing concern over the risks of potential negative surprises in the quarters ahead.

Continued on page 16

SUBSCRIPTION INFO 1-800-243-2324 • **OUR WEB SITE http://www.cda.com/investnet**

Exhibit 8.1 Bob Gabele's *Insiders' Chronicle* at MarketEdge. Reprinted with the permission of Bob Gabele.

Standard & Poor's

http://www.stockinfo.standardpoor.com

Standard & Poor's offers Vickers insider trading reports on a per-report basis.

Wall Street City

http://www.wallstreetcity.com

Wall Street City offers insider trading data in several formats. One is a proprietary search tool that allows you to quickly locate stocks that have heavy insider buying or list the amount of insider buying or selling on any search report. You can also search for changes in insider buying or selling. This search tool is available in ProSearch, one of the category search engines, or a best/worst list.

The insider trading report at the Research & Info page plots insider trading on a stock graph, which allows you to see how it has tracked the rise and fall of the stock price in the past (Exhibit 8.2). The report also lists the names, holdings, and trading information of insiders. The Ranking Snapshot, described earlier, also provides a percentile ranking that summarizes insider activity.

The Analysts: Insiders on the Outside

Analysts are employed by various brokerage houses or investment firms to study a company in depth and write research reports on its current condition and future growth potential. A General Motors or a Microsoft may have as many as 50 analysts following their every move, whereas some new or small companies are not followed by anyone. Most companies fall in the middle of these two extremes.

The *analysts,* who are referred to as industry analysts, research analysts, or Wall Street analysts (whether or not they reside on Wall Street), draw upon SEC filings and trade publications for information. They consult market studies and industry reports. They usually visit the company and talk with corporate officials. In short, they become experts on the company and the industry.

As experts, they give their objective opinions about the current state of the company and its potential for growth. They make forecasts about

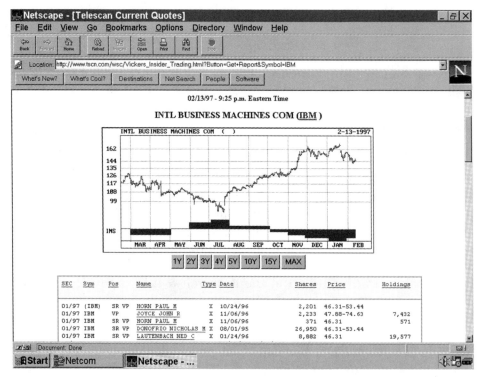

Exhibit 8.2   Wall Street City: Insider trading graph for IBM. Actual trades are listed below the graph.

a company's earnings for the current and next quarter, and the current and next fiscal year. Sometimes, they will project a growth rate five years into the future because of their intimate knowledge of the company—and also, in the course of their research, they may be privy to inside information about the company.

Where to Find Research Reports

The research reports from which earnings estimates are compiled are aimed at the professional investment community. They are very

Continued

expensive for an individual investor and, for the most part, not absolutely necessary to the evaluation process because information such as earnings estimates and analysts' recommendations is available in an S&P or Zacks report. Nevertheless, if you're interested, the Internet has made research reports accessible through such sites as Multex Systems (http://www.multexnet.com) and M.A.I.D./Profound (http://www.maid-plc.com). Investext, another well-known publisher of research reports, has a Web site that caters just to professionals.

More useful to individuals are the abstracts and listings at the Zacks site (http://www.zacks.com) and at Barron's Online (http://www.barrons.com). At Zacks, you can enter the name or symbol of a company to retrieve a list of all recent reports and the analyst's recommendation, with a link to an abstract of the report, if available. Barron's publishes summaries of recent reports, along with the analysts' recommendations.

Such research may take months, and the publication of the research report is an event eagerly anticipated—or in some cases, dreaded—by corporate officials. What everyone is anticipating or dreading are the earnings estimates and the buy/hold/sell recommendations that are incorporated in the report.

Because of the importance of these numbers, several companies (such as First Call, I/B/E/S, and Zacks Investment Research) make a business of extracting the earnings estimates and buy/hold/sell recommendations from research reports and putting them into various tables, reports and other usable formats. Companies such as Standard & Poor's and Market Guide also incorporate analysts' earnings estimates in their stock reports or company profiles. In this way, the numbers buried in a research report accessible mainly by professionals (from a practical standpoint) become available to the individual investor. Now, these numbers are disseminated on the World Wide Web.

When considering earnings estimates, there are four groups of numbers to consider:

1. The actual estimates for the upcoming quarter and fiscal year
2. Revisions of either of these numbers
3. The five-year projected growth rate
4. Earnings surprises (An *earnings surprise* occurs when a company exceeds or falls short of the analysts' estimates.)

The most important of these numbers is perhaps the revisions. When an event occurs in the industry, in the economy, or within the company itself, to change an analyst's mind about the future of the company (as published in the original report), the analyst will issue a revised earnings estimate. Some experts believe that an *increase* in a company's earnings estimates—an upward revision—is the best harbinger of future stock price growth, especially a consensus revision. (Backtests have consistently confirmed this!) Upward revisions, of course, are what we want to see when we research a stock. A consensus decrease or downward revision would be considered a red flag.

Finding Earnings Estimates on the World Wide Web

The three major providers of earnings estimate summaries—First Call, I/B/E/S, and Zacks—have their own Web sites, but their summaries are also available at other sites.

First Call

http://www1.firstcall.com

First Call originally served the institutional investment community, but the Internet apparently has prompted them to reach out to the individual investor. Their Web-based Estimates on Demand service offers reports on individual companies on a per-unit basis ($1.50 to $3.00). Other subscription-based reports are delivered by fax: a monthly Consensus Estimate Guide at $25.00/month; a daily Earnings Surprise report at $75/month; a weekly Estimate Watch (summary of revisions) at $35/month.

I/B/E/S Financial Network

http://www.ibes.com

I/B/E/S Financial Network offers worldwide earnings estimate summaries from more than 7,000 financial analysts for some 16,000 public companies in 42 countries. Subscriptions to consensus earnings reports and earnings surprise reports start at $9.95/month. I/B/E/S reports are also available through its parent company, Primark (http://www.pirc.com).

Standard & Poor's

http://www.stockinfo.standardpoor.com

Analysts' earnings estimates are part of the S&P Stock Report (see Exhibit 8.3).

Zacks Investment Research

http://www.zacks.com

Zacks Investment Research summarizes earnings estimates on more than 5,000 public companies. (See Exhibit 8.4.) The Analyst Watch on the Internet is a subscription-based service that includes, among other things, detailed earnings estimates reports on more than 5,000 public companies, portfolio alerts, and screening of the Zacks database ($150/year). For an additional $75/year, you can get the Z-100 list which are stocks with the highest Zacks ranking and Ben Zack's weekly market commentary.

Wall Street City offers the Zacks reports as part of its subscription, plus a search tool called ESearch, which is based on the Zacks reports. Other Web sites, such as INVESTools, NETworth, and Quote.com, offer the Zacks reports on a per-report basis or as part of their subscription.

Sun Microsystems

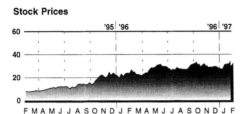

SELL [BUY UY]

AQO = 1.24

WALL STREET CONSENSUS

07-FEB-97

Analysts' Recommendations

Stock Prices

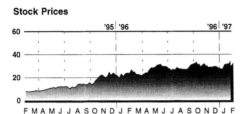

Analysts' Opinion

	No. of Ratings	% of Total	1 Mo. Prior	3 Mo. Prior	Nat'l	Reg'l	Non-broker
Buy	15	52	15	12	5	7	3
Buy/Hold	5	17	5	6	2	2	1
Hold	6	21	6	6	3	3	0
Weak Hold	0	0	0	0	0	0	0
Sell	1	3	1	1	1	0	0
No Opinion	2	7	2	2	0	1	1
Total	29	100	29	27	11	13	5

Analysts' Opinions

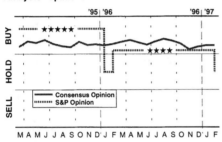

Stock Evaluation Measures

Average Qualitative Opinion (AQO)   1.24 = Buy

Buy	> 1.00	≤ 2.00	The Average Qualitative Opinion
Buy/Hold	> .75	≤ 1.00	(AQO) summarizes the current
Hold	> .35	≤ .75	investment opinions of the Wall
Weak Hold	> 0	≤ .35	Street analysts who follow the
Sell	≥ -2.00	≤ 0	company.

AQO gives you an average of buy/hold/sell opinions. A buy is greater than one. A sell is less than or equal to zero.

Standard & Poor's STARS   ★★★★
(Stock Appreciation Ranking System)

★★★★★	Buy
★★★★	Accumulate
★★★	Hold
★★	Avoid
★	Sell

Standard & Poor's STARS ranking is our own analyst's evaluation of the short-term (six to 12 month) appreciation potential of a stock. Five-Star stocks are expected to appreciate in price and outperform the market.

Number of Analysts Following Stock

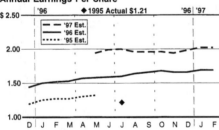

Analysts' Earnings Estimate

Annual Earnings Per Share

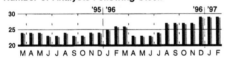

◆ 1995 Actual $1.21

- '97 Est.
- '96 Est.
- '95 Est.

Current Analysts' Consensus Estimates

Fiscal years	Avg.	High	Low	S&P Est.	No. of Est.	Estimated P-E Ratio	Estimated S&P 500 P-E Ratio
1997	1.69	1.83	1.32	1.82	28	20.1	17.6
1998	2.02	2.24	1.72	2.15	10	16.8	—
3Q'97	0.42	0.48	0.21		13		
3Q'96	0.36 Actual						

A company's earnings outlook plays a major part in any investment decision. S&P organizes the earnings estimates of over 2,300 Wall Street analysts, and provides you with their consensus of earnings over the next two years. The graph to the left shows you how these estimates have trended over the past 15 months.

Exhibit 8.3   Standard & Poor's: The Wall Street Consensus is part of the S&P Stock Report.

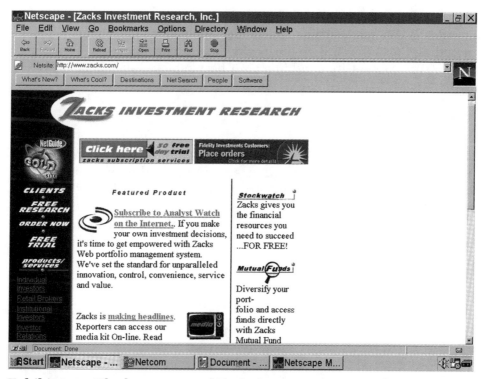

Exhibit 8.4   The home page of Zacks Investment Research.

F**YI**   If you want to see how a company stacks up against all other companies on insider trading and earnings estimates, check out Wall Street City's Ranking Snapshot, described earlier. It summarizes a company's insider data and earnings estimates and expresses each as a percentile ranking. If your stock ranks in the top 80 or 90 percent, you can comfortably dispense with any in-depth research on these two items.

The Best of the Net

Earnings estimate summaries are compiled from many of the same sources, so as far as quality of data, there is little difference. If you use these reports infrequently, buying them individually from I/B/E/S or First Call might be your best bet. But if you depend on them regularly, as we do, you might want a subscription to Zacks Analyst Watch on the Internet. If you need earnings estimates along with other investing tools, including those that utilize the Zacks data in various ways, a subscription to Wall Street City would be your best bet.

The Last Word

History has shown that the two best predictors of a company's future performance are buying by insiders and an upward revision in consensus earnings estimates by Wall Street analysts. Regardless of the other merits of a stock, it is probably unwise to go against both of these indicators. On the other hand, if insiders are buying the stock *and* analysts are upping their estimates—well, that seems to us like two thumbs up from those in the know.

CHAPTER NINE

THE NEWS ROOM

Buy on the rumor; sell on the news.

—Wall Street saying

The Internet is a virtual newsroom, where late-breaking stories reach your computer as quickly as they reach the newswires in actual news-rooms across the country. Unfortunately, this isn't as important as it sounds. It's a common fallacy among beginning investors to buy a stock based on a big news story. For example, they might buy a stock that has just received FDA approval for an important new drug, and then they're disappointed when the stock price fails to move. Had they researched the stock more closely, they would have seen that it had already moved up sharply in the past few weeks or months. Why? Because the rumor of imminent FDA approval had been floating around for weeks and was already reflected in the stock price.

In evaluating stocks, it is important to look at the latest news, just to see if it explains the recent market behavior of the stock. You will find that it normally does.

Business News

Financial and worldwide news are widely available on the Internet, but when evaluating stocks, we need *business news* that can be searched by company name or ticker symbol. The following sites have searchable news databases, which are free unless stated otherwise.

American City Business Journals

http://www.amcity.com

American City Business Journals is the parent company of 35 regional business newspapers with information on local public companies (see Exhibit 9.1). You can search the entire database by topic or keyword. (Seeing how a public company fares locally can be very valuable.)

Barron's Online

http://www.barrons.com

You can search Barron's Online by company name or symbol and get a company snapshot, *plus* links to related current and past news articles that have appeared in Barron's.

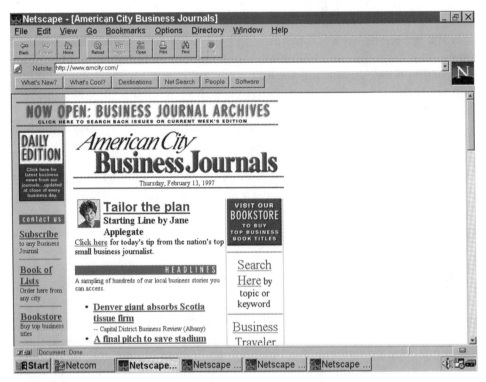

Exhibit 9.1   *American City Business Journals:* home page.

Bloomberg Personal

http://www.bloomberg.com

Bloomberg is a supplier of business news and information to brokerage firms and institutional investors. It now offers a new magazine called *Bloomberg Personal,* which includes enhanced access to the Bloomberg Web site for analysts' earnings estimates, historical data, proprietary Bloomberg data, and more. $22.95/year.

Business Wire

http://www.businesswire.com

Business Wire distributes news releases for public companies and offers a search engine for finding news on specific companies. The news is free, because the companies pay for the distribution. They also have company profiles written by the companies themselves.

CNN Financial Network

http://www.cnnfn.com

CNN has a search feature to find news on a specific company, with hyperlinks to related stories and to the home pages of companies mentioned in the story. CNNfn is also a good source of general news, with a home page of continuously changing headlines linked to the full story. News pages include "hot stories," "markets," "your money," and "digital jam" (high technology).

Dow Jones

http://bis.dowjones.com

Dow Jones now offers its DowVision on the Internet. DowVision is a searchable news database that contains a 90-day archive of *The Wall Street Journal, The New York Times,* and other newswires, but it is aimed primarily at corporate users.

FYI   *Investor's Business Daily* (http://www.investors.com) has a searchable database under construction.

Forbes

http://www.forbes.com

Forbes has a searchable database that extends back to August 1996.

Fox News

http://www.foxnews.com

In its business section, Fox News has a simple searchable database which you can seach by company name for stories over the past 14 days.

IBM InfoMarket

http://www.infomarket.ibm.com

IBM InfoMarket offers a megadatabase of more than 75 newswires, 300 newspapers, 819 newsletters, journals, and 11 million companies! You can search the database for free and buy the information on a per-document basis (beginning at $0.75 each). There's one catch: You have to download a piece of IBM software called Cryptolope Containers to purchase the documents.

INC. Online

http://www.inc.com

Inc. Online focuses on growing companies with a searchable database of 5,000 articles from various Inc. publications dating back to 1988. Searches can be made by company name, author name, or keyword. Many companies followed by Inc. are not publicly held.

M.A.I.D./Profound

http://www.maid-plc.com

M.A.I.D./Profound has a news database containing more than 4,700 newspapers, magazines, and trade journals from over 190 countries (translated from 17 languages). Its WorldSearch feature allows you to search the database by company name, industry, or news event. You can also search just the newswires or individual newswires by industry or by free text. A list of all the sources that feed the M.A.I.D. news database is available at the site. Subscription required.

The New York Times on the Web

http://www.nytimes.com

The Business Section of the Times has a database that can be searched by company name to find all or just the most recent articles about the company (see Exhibit 9.2). Every article has links to related articles and Web sites. News alerts are delivered daily by e-mail if you have Netscape 3.0 or higher. Registration required.

Exhibit 9.2 *The New York Times* on the Web: home page.

Newspage

http://www.newspage.com

Newspage offers a searchable database of various newswires. You can search by company name or by industry. You may also customize this page for news alerts.

PR Newswire

http://www.prnewswire.com

PR Newswire distributes news releases for public companies. It has a Company News On-Call section containing current full-text stories and archived releases for one year. The database is searchable by company name, or you may click on the name in an alphabetized list of companies.

Quote.com

http://www.quote.com

At the Quote.com site you can search S&P news by company name or symbol. Subscription-based.

Rating Your Prospects

All this research can be overwhelming, especially if you're reviewing a number of stocks. What you need is a systematic process for rating your prospects for each report. We use a sort of report card system and give each stock a letter grade for each item of research:

A = Excellent
B = Good
C = Average
D = Below Average
F = Unacceptable

Then we average the grades or eliminate those with the lowest grades. Another way is to rate each stock from 1 to 10 for each

Continued

report (10 being high), then average the scores to determine the best overall stock.

It doesn't really matter what kind of system you use, as long as you use one. Without a systematic way to rank your prospects, you'll be at the mercy of hunches and emotions.

Reuters

http://www.moneynet.com

Search the Reuters news database by company name or symbol and retrieve a list of headlines that link to the full story. (See Exhibit 9.3.) Free. You can also search the Reuters news database from the INVESTools Web site.

Exhibit 9.3   Reuters' Web site is called MoneyNet.com.

Standard & Poor's

http://www.stockinfo.standardpoor.com

Standard & Poor's offers a news service on more than 6,500 public companies. The searchable news database includes earnings and dividends, stock buybacks, new product announcements, capital restructuring, and other developments. It is filtered so as to emphasize events that might impact the value of a company's stock.

Wall Street City

http://www.wallstreetcity.com

Wall Street City has two comprehensive news databases searchable by company name or ticker symbol. You'll get a list of the most recent headlines with hyperlinks to the full story. News alerts are available.

The Wall Street Journal Interactive Edition

http://www.wsj.com

The electronic Journal has everything the print version has, plus a searchable news database with hyperlinks to background information on companies mentioned in its articles. (See Exhibit 9.4.) For example, if an article mentions America Online, click on the company name and see a Company Snapshot that displays current trading information for America Online. Then click on that screen to go to a Briefing Book which gives a comprehensive portrait of the company, plus a list of all the Journal's recent coverage. You must be a subscriber to search the database.

The Wall Street Journal recently announced a new searchable database of 3,600 top newspapers, and trade and industry publications. Subscribers to the WSJ Interactive can search free and retrieve full-text articles for $2.95 each. As an introductory offer, the first 10 articles are free.

Worth Online

http://www.worth.com

Worth Online allows you to search for articles by company name or other keyword, topic, or date.

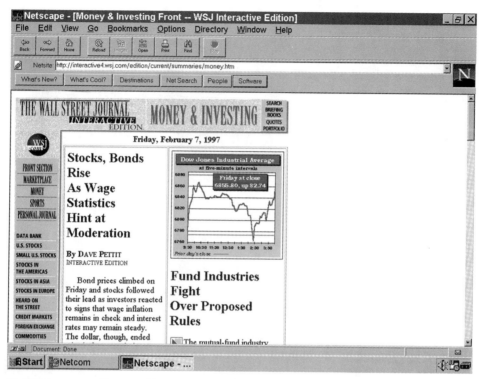

Exhibit 9.4 *The Wall Street Journal* Interactive Edition: The Money & Investing page.

The Best of the Net

For the convenience of hyperlinks to company-related sites and data, we'd go for *Barron's, The New York Times,* and *The Wall Street Journal.*

The Last Word

While news has frequently been discounted by the market, it is probably unwise to ignore it when evaluating a stock. (See the CyberInvesting Guide for stock research, Exhibit 9.5.) With the Internet, the cyber-investor no longer has to wait for the six o'clock news or the morning paper to deliver the latest headlines. Just remember, the stories that make tomorrow's headlines have typically been in the Wall Street rumor mill for days or weeks.

Web site	Ranking/ Rating	Company		Small Cap	SEC Filings	News: Searchable	Insider Report	Earnings		Research Reports
		Shapshot	Profile					Estimates	Surprises	
Barron's Online http://www.barrons.com			✔			✔				
DBC Online http://www.dbc.com					✔					
Disclosure http://www.disclosure.com					✔					
EDGAR-Online http://www.edgar-online.com					✔					
First Call http://www.firstcall.com								✔	✔	
Forbes http://www.forbes.com						✔				
Hoovers Online http://www.hoovers.com		✔	✔							
I/B/E/S http://www.ibes.com								✔	✔	
IBM Infomarket http://www.infomarket.ibm.com						✔				
INVESTools http://www.investools.com		✔	✔					✔	✔	
M.A.I.D./Profound http://www.maid-plc.com			✔		✔	✔				✔
Macro*World @ Wall Street City http://www.wallstreetcity.com	✔									
Market Guide http://www.marketguide.com		✔	✔							
MarketEdge http://www.marketedge.com			✔				✔	✔	✔	
Multex http://www.multex.com										✔
NETworth http://www.networth.galt.com			✔		✔			✔	✔	
NYU http://edgar.stern.nyu.edu					✔					
Quote.com http://www.quote.com		✔	✔			✔	✔	✔	✔	
Red Chip Review http://www.redchip.com				✔						
Reuters Money Network http://www.moneynet.com			✔			✔				
SEC http://www.sec.gov					✔					
Standard & Poor's http://www.stockinfo.standardpoor.com	✔		✔			✔	✔	✔	✔	
Wall Street City http://www.wallstreetcity.com	✔	✔	✔			✔	✔	✔	✔	
Westergaard http://www.westergaard.com				✔						
Zacks Investment Research http://www.zacks.com	✔							✔	✔	

NOTE: See CyberInvest.Com (http://www.cyberinvest.com) for the latest revisions to this Guide.

Exhibit 9.5   The CyberInvesting Guide for Stock Research.

PART FOUR

Purchasing a Stock

When you've found a stock that meets your objectives, you're almost ready to buy it. *Almost.* There is an optimum time to purchase any stock in order to minimize risk and maximize return, and astute investors attempt to find this point with technical timing tools. Generally, these tools, which have been developed by some of the best technicians in the market, indicate the direction of the stock's current trend and help pinpoint reversals in that trend. In this section we'll show you where to find technical tools on the World Wide Web. Then we'll tell you about the brokers that offer Web-based trading.

CHAPTER TEN

TECHNICAL TIMING TOOLS ON THE NET

If you can understand what is happening to a stock price, you increase your chances of taking the right actions at the right time.

—Clifford Pistolese
Using Technical Analysis

Technical analysis is the study of historical price and volume patterns of individual stocks, industry groups, and market indexes in order to predict future trends. That's why we include technical timing as part of the purchase decision. We want to get into a stock somewhere near the beginning of an uptrend, or at least when the trend is strengthening and not weakening.

Trends are often difficult to predict. What looks like a smooth upward or downward trend on a historical graph is an illusion of 20-20 hindsight. In actuality, stocks don't advance steadily from one price level to another, not even if earnings are better than expected and momentum is great and the industry group is performing well and the market is roaring toward the next century mark. Instead, on its climb from, say, $10 to $20, a stock will go through fits and starts, making higher highs and higher lows. A downtrend mirrors the uptrend, with the stock making lower highs and lower lows as it declines.

Technical analysis tools (dozens of them) have been developed to help identify the beginning of a new uptrend and the point at which an uptrend is over and a downtrend is beginning. To put it another way, technical tools attempt to measure the upward or downward momentum in a stock to determine when the momentum runs out. At that point, a change in direction will most likely become a reversal of the trend. The reason we bother with technical analysis (even those of us who are fundamentalists at heart) is that we want to know *in advance* whether a slight pullback is the likely beginning of a trend reversal.

Some investors think of charting and technical analysis as voodoo investing, but our research indicates otherwise. Using technical tools to time the entry and exit points in a stock (steps 3 and 5 of the cyber-investing process) can add as much as 3 percent to your annual returns. Some experts would say more. More important, these tools can keep you out of stock meltdowns.

Minilessons in Technical Analysis

There are many different technical tools you can use to time your entry and exit points in a stock. Almost any of them will do just fine. We have not found much value in using a great number of indicators, nor do we look for multiple signals in those we use. We use just three basic indicators for our technical analysis, all based on market psychology. They are the moving average convergence/divergence indicator (the MACD), the stochastics index, and trading bands. The MACD gives us our basic signal, and we simply require that the trading bands and the stochastics index be positive, rather than negative, when we enter the stock.

These and other indicators are adequately defined at several Web sites, but you don't have to know the theory behind the indicator in order to use it. You just have to know how to interpret the signals. Before we tell you where to find technical analysis tools on the Web, we want to give you a few minilessons in interpreting some of the signals.

The MACD

The *MACD* was developed and popularized by Gerald Appel. We use the daily MACD for our basic buy signal, but rely on the weekly signal for most of our sells. Exhibit 10.1 shows a daily 8/17/9 MACD histogram for Microsoft. (The 8/17/9 refers to the length of the three moving aver-

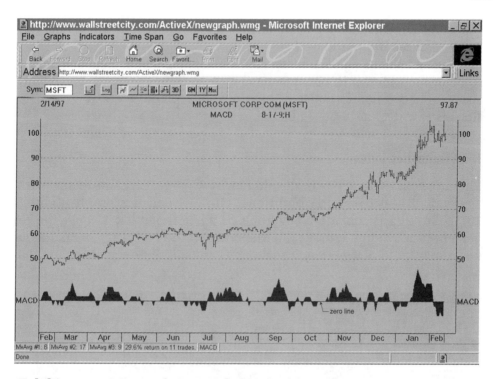

Exhibit 10.1 Microsoft Corp.'s daily 8/17/9 MACD is negative on 2/14/97 (Wall Street City's ActiveX graphs).

ages on which the MACD is based.) We plot the MACD as a histogram, rather than a graph, because it is easier to read. The horizontal line labeled *zero line* is an equilibrium line.

When the histogram is above the zero line, it is in positive territory; when it is below the zero line, it is in negative territory. The stock has a positive breakout—which can be interpreted as a buy signal—when the histogram crosses the zero line from negative to positive. Crossing from positive to negative is a negative breakout and can be used as a sell signal.

The daily MACD is designed to generate early signals (which are preferred by many momentum investors), but it produces a lot of whipsaws as it jumps back and forth across the zero line. To eliminate false signals, we require that the weekly MACD be positive before we act on the daily MACD signal. A weekly 8/17/9 MACD uses an 8-week, a 17-week, and a

9-week moving average. The weekly MACD smooths out the histogram, as you can see in Exhibit 10.2.

We may give up a point or two by waiting, but we prefer to sacrifice some of the uptrend in order to have a more reliable signal. We would also feel more comfortable if the stock has positive readings on its stochastic index and trading bands.

The Stochastics Index

The *stochastics index* was developed by George C. Lane to measure overbought and oversold conditions. On a stochastics graph (Exhibit 10.3), the stock is considered overbought when the index is above the 75 percent line; when it crosses the line downward (a negative breakout), a new downtrend is signaled. The stock is considered oversold when the

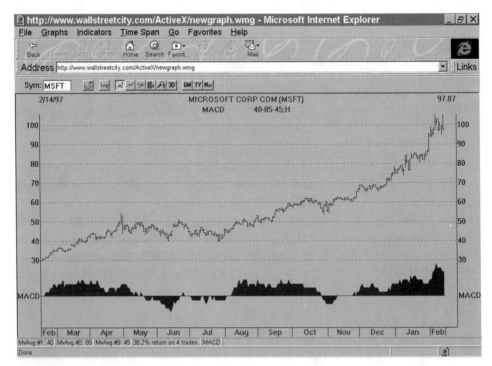

Exhibit 10.2   The weekly 8/17/9 MACD for Microsoft Corp. is positive on 2/14/97 (Wall Street City's ActiveX graphs).

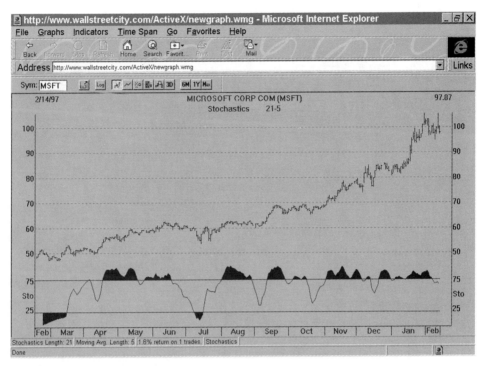

Exhibit 10.3   The 21/5 Stochastics for Microsoft Corp. recently gave a sell signal (Wall Street City's ActiveX graphs).

index is below the 25 percent line; when it crosses that line upward (a positive breakout), a new uptrend is anticipated.

The daily 9/3 stochastic gives a very early signal (9/3 refers to the length of the moving averages on which the stochastics is based). We use a longer stochastic, a 14/5 or a 21/5 to confirm an oversold condition.

Trading Bands

Trading bands are an envelope drawn around a moving average so as to enclose *x* percent of the price action of the stock. We use a 30-day moving average and a 75 or 80 percent envelope, as shown in Exhibit 10.4. Some investors prefer Bollinger bands, developed by John Bollinger, which use a formula based on standard deviations to plot the bands.

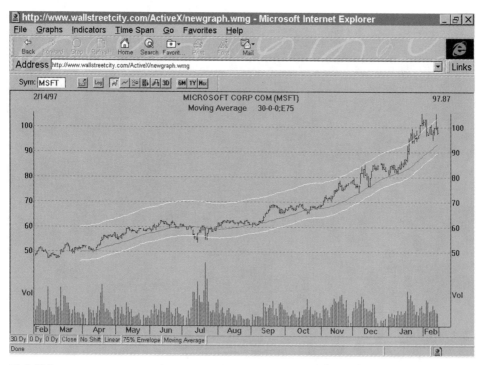

Exhibit 10.4   Microsoft penetrated the top trading band on 2/14, but closed below it several days in a row (Wall Street City's ActiveX graphs).

Interpreting trading band signals is a little less straightforward than reading MACD signals. We look for signs of strength. One sign of strength is *significant* penetration of the top band. Another is when the stock bounces off the moving average, after penetrating the top band. In addition, if the stock reverses direction at the bottom without touching the band, that is considered a positive sign. A sign of weakness is when the stock fails to reach the top band and reverses direction.

> **F**^{YI}   We have not found any value in using a lot of different technical indicators or trying to get multiple buy signals. Our suggestion is to find an indicator you like and trust, use it for your basic signal, and use just one or two indicators for confirmation.

Basing Period Breakouts

An alternative signal that we sometimes use for a buy signal is a basing period breakout, shown in Exhibit 10.5. When a stock trades within a fairly narrow range for a long period of time, it is said to be *basing*. When it breaks out of that pattern upward, as Home Port Bancorp did in mid-February, it is a strong indication of a new uptrend, especially if the breakout is accompanied by high volume.

Learning More about Technical Analysis

Learning about technical analysis can be a lifetime project. There are literally dozens of technical tools and each has its legions of advocates.

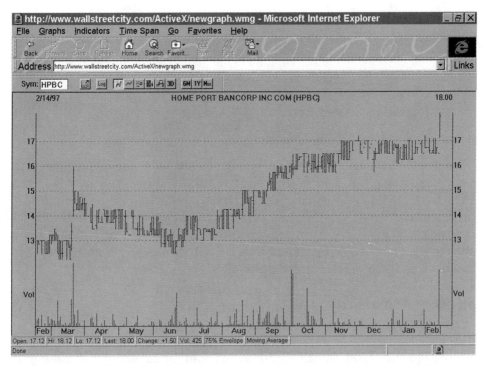

Exhibit 10.5   Home Port Bancorp had a significant basing period breakout on high volume on 2/14/97 (Wall Street City's ActiveX graphs).

The minilessons in this section will get you started. If you want to pursue the subject further, check out the following sources for educational material on technical analysis, or refer to our *Cyber-Investing* book.

Bridge News

http://news.bridge.com

Bridge News has a free section called "Tech Tips" which features articles on a number of technical theories written by Michael Kahn. Some of the topics include sentiment indicators, Gann analysis, relative strength, money flow analysis, and cycle analysis.

Equity Analytics

http://www.e-analytics.com

Equity Analytics has fee-based trading recommendations for options and T-bonds, but it also has a large free zone that includes descriptions of more than 20 technical indicators and a glossary of technical analysis terms.

Market Technicians Association

http://www.teleport.com/~lensmith

Market Technicians Association is a professional organization for market technicians. You can learn about seminars sponsored by MTA, the New York Society of Security Analysts, and the International Federation of Technical Analysts. John Bollinger's weekly *Capital Growth Topics* newsletter is available to members here. You can also download demo software for dozens of technical analysis programs and a variety of pre-defined technical charts and graphs.

Stocks & Commodities Magazine

http://www.traders.com

Both beginning and seasoned investors can learn about old and new technical trading methods and techniques at the Web site of *Technical Analysis of Stocks & Commodities* magazine (see Exhibit 10.6).

Technical Bookstores

The Equis Online Bookstore (http://www.equis.com) has an excellent selection of books on technical analysis. So does Traders Library (http://www.traderslibrary.com). A good book to start with is Martin Pring's *Technical Analysis Explained.*[1] For a general reference, try *The Encyclopedia of Technical Market Indicators* by Robert W. Colby and Thomas A. Meyers.[2]

Trading Techniques, Inc.

http://www.tradingtech.com

This is the Web site for Elliott wave aficionados. Here you can learn about the Elliott wave theory, download a demo of Advanced GET software which incorporates Elliott wave analysis, and find out where and when free seminars will be held on Elliott techniques.

Wall Street City

http://www.wallstreetcity.com

Wall Street City has a number of free articles on technical indicators at the Learning About Investments section. Topics include the MACD, relative strength, stochastics, trading bands, and the Wilder relative strength index.

Technical Analysis on the World Wide Web

True technical analysis tools on the World Wide Web are in the embryonic stage. There are several sites that offer charts of stocks or market indexes on which technical signals are already plotted; a few let you change the time horizon of the graph or select from predefined parame-

---

[1] Martin W. Pring, *Technical Analysis Explained* (New York: McGraw-Hill, 1991).

[2] Robert W. Colby and Thomas A. Meyers, *The Encyclopedia of Technical Market Indicators* (Homewood, Ill.: Business One Irwin, 1988).

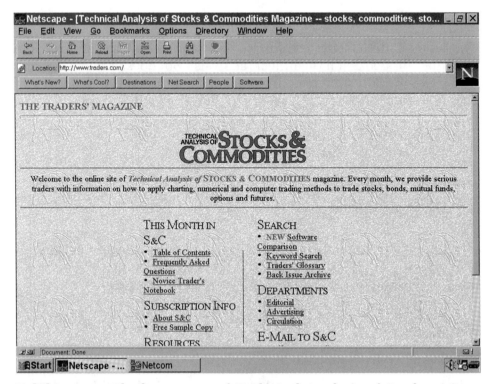

Exhibit 10.6   The home page of *Technical Analysis of Stocks & Commodities* magazine.

iers. Only one to our knowledge—Wall Street City—allows full technical analysis with a wide range of indicators and user-defined parameters.

Alphachart

http://www.techcharts.com

Alphachart lets you plot 14 technical indicators, including MACD, stochastics, Bollinger bands, Chaiken oscillator, Wilder RSI, candlesticks, and others. The time span is fixed for a six-month period, although you can zoom in to focus on a shorter period. Parameters can be changed, but when we tried to get a new graph with different parameters, it defaulted to the original parameters. The tutorial, by the way, connects to the Equity Analytics site for definitions of various technical indicators. This is a free site.

Ask Research

http://www.askresearch.com

There is a free charting and technical analysis at Ask Research where you can plot several indicators, including the MACD, moving averages, stochastics, Wilder RSI, and on-balance volume. Six time periods are available, along with three different kinds of charts (bar, line, or candle) and minimal user input. This is also available at the INVESTools site. (See Exhibit 10.7.)

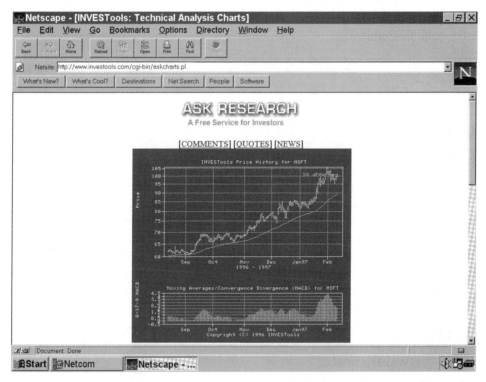

Exhibit 10.7   A MACD chart for Microsoft from Ask Research at the INVESTools site.

Avid Trading Company

http://avidinfo.com

The Avid Trading Company's mission is "to be the premier on-line source of technical market opinion." Current market opinion is found at the Heads-Up page. Discounts are offered on combination packages of four technically oriented market letters:

1. *InsightInformation* offers very short-term, chart-based stock trades, plus personal analyses of stock situations.
2. *By the Horns* focuses on chart-based trades.
3. *OTC Surfer* offers mechanical buy/sell signals on the NASD composite.
4. *Mutual Momentum* offers weekly commentary on sector momentum.

Regular subscription rates for these letters range from $225 to $775 per year.

Interactive Quote

http://www.iqc.com

Interactive Quote offers daily, weekly, and monthly charts of nearly 9,000 U.S. stocks and indexes. Interactive analysis uses eight technical indicators with user-adjustable parameters. Indicators include moving averages, stochastics, relative strength index, momentum, MACD, directional movement index (DMI), ultimate oscillator, and volume. You can choose bar, line, or Japanese candlesticks charts. They offer a tutorial of the analysis methods used.

Wall Street City

http://www.wallstreetcity.com

Wall Street City is the only Web site we found which has true technical analysis where you can actually generate the technical timing signals that are so important to the purchase decision.

- *ActiveX graphs.* The technical indicators shown in Exhibit 10.8 have completely user-defined parameters with time spans back to 1973. Charts can be plotted as linear or logarithmic, high/low/close, point and figure, candlestick, equivolume, or 3-D. Trendlines are not yet available, but are expected to be added soon. Microsoft Internet Explorer supports ActiveX graphs. With Netscape 3.0, you must have the Ncompass plug-in, which you can download at the Netscape home page (http://home.netscape.com).

- *Technical break-out searches.* Another way to check technical timing signals is with the technical breakout searches at the Find an Investment page. Run the search daily; when your stock appears on the search, you've got your signal. Wall Street City

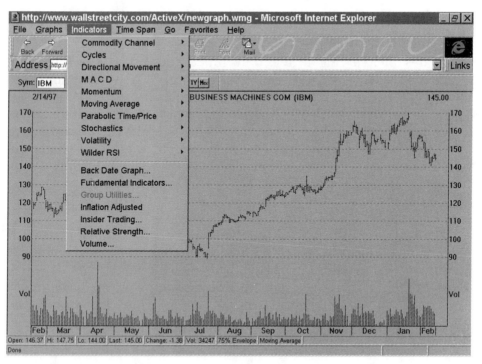

Exhibit 10.8 Wall Street City offers technical and fundamental indicators with user-defined parameters on its ActiveX graphs.

has several searches to choose from: short-term, intermediate-term, and long-term technical breakouts; basing-pattern breakouts; or MACD, stochastics, or Wilder RSI breakouts. With ProSearch, you can use all the breakouts in one search with the "Absolute OR" search mode to find stocks that have had technical breakouts from any of several indicators.

♦ *Ranking percentile.*   Want the benefit of technical analysis without the burden? Use the ranking indicators in ProSearch or the ranking category search, both at the Find an Investment page. The short-term and long-term technical rank indicator is a composite of short- or long-term MACD, volume, relative performance, and moving average criteria. If your stock is ranked in the top 30 percent of all stocks for either of these indicators, you can be pretty sure it is in good technical condition.

Other Technical Charts

These sites offer varying degrees of technical charting.

Charts by CPCUG InvestSIG (http://cpcug.org)   This site, which is an offering of the Investment Special Interest Group of the Capital PC User Group, has a smorgasbord of free charts, mostly for market indexes. There are a variety of charts (including candlestick charts) for intraday, daily, weekly, and long-term stock indexes. There are also charts on individual stocks, options, bonds, T-bills, futures, mutual funds, gold prices, oil prices, commodities, economic indicators, interest rates, price indexes and inflation, and more. Check out the links to the dozen or so Web sites that also offer charts. $35/year.

Silicon Investor (http://www.techstocks.com)   This site offers charts on technology stocks in five categories: computers, software, communications, semiconductors, and miscellaneous. Each chart compares the stock with the Nasdaq composite index. Free, but registration required.

Shopping the Tech Shops

Until the speed of the Internet improves, avid technicians may want to stick with PC software for in-depth technical analysis. As the Internet continues to evolve, some software producers will no doubt offer Web versions of their products. Meanwhile, it is much easier to shop the Internet than to visit a computer store. The Web sites listed below have descriptions, reviews, and/or demos of their software which you can order on-line or by phone, fax, or e-mail. In some cases you can download the software itself at the Web site.

AIQ MarketExpert

http://www.aiq.com

AIQ MarketExpert is a free PC-based program that can be downloaded at the Web site, along with enough data from Dial/Data to get you started. There's a chart of the day at the site, along with a good demo. AIQ's more advanced TradingExpert for Windows is $695.

MetaStock

http://www.equis.com

For intermediate-to-advanced technical analysis, visit the Web site of the publisher of MetaStock, Equis International (now a division of Reuters) and learn about the latest version 6.0 for Windows 95 and Windows NT. *Barron's* calls it the "Rolls Royce" of the technical analysis packages. At $394, it is also the most expensive. You cannot, at this point, order the program on-line, but you can download a demo.

SuperCharts

http://www.omegaresearch.com

Omega Research, publisher of SuperCharts, offers a modicum of fundamental analysis, along with its traditional technical analysis system. SuperCharts 4 users can download the beta update. For beginning investors, Omega offers Wall Street Analyst SE, a special version of which you can download free at the Omega Web site. Those wary of downloading can order the program at the Web site or through a toll-free 800 number listed at the site. The cost is $199.

Telescan, Inc.

http://www.telescan.com

Telescan has a powerful, Windows-based PC software package called Telescan Investor's Platform (TIP). Its charting and technical analysis is easy to use, yet sophisticated enough for intermediate to advanced technicians. There are more than 80 technical and fundamental indicators, with an historical database that goes back to 1973. TIP also includes equity screening, market reports, analysts' reports, portfolio management, Internet access data downloading, and an optimizer program. The cost is $199.

Window on Wall Street

http://www.wallstreet.net

Window on Wall Street's latest version (Pro 5.0) blends fundamental analysis with its traditional technical analysis techniques into something called Super Indicators. Data is supplied by CD-ROM or from third-party data suppliers. You can download a free evaluation copy. The cost is $295.

Other Tech Shops on the Web

Anderson Investor's Software, Inc. (http://www.invest-soft.com) has a large selection of investment software for the PC and MAC, plus financial and investment books. You can order by phone, fax, mail-in order, or the Internet.

Delphi Software (http://www.delphi-software.com) offers a product called Market Forecast that allows the user to backtest technical strategies on historical data.

Ezy Group (http://www.ezygroup.net.au) has a group of "Ezy" products for the novice technician.

Falkor Technologies (http://www.falkor.com) has two programs called BB Stock Tool and BB Stock Pro, both of which feature, among other things, charting and technical analysis.

FlexSoft (http://www.flexsoft.com) offers a Technical Analysis Scanner for analyzing price/volume historical data. It features a profit tester to test historical data with various trading strategies.

Robert-Slade, Inc (http://www.itsnet.com/~rsi) Learn about the trading features of FirstAlert software.

Stock Blocks (http://www.stockblocks.com) You can download a demo of Insider TA, which performs "innovative technical analysis on your data and . . . provides real-time feedback."

Technical Tools (http://www.techtool.com) This is the home of TT Chartbook 95.

The Total Investor (http://ourworld.compuserve.com) is a portfolio management and technical analysis program that works with Lotus 1-2-3.

Web site	Charts				Variable Time Span		Indicators				Parameters			Educational Features
	Bar or Line	Candle.	Index	Other	Yes	No	MACD	Stoch.	Trend-lines	Other	User-Defined	Ltd.	None	
AlfaChart http://www.techcharts.com	✔				✔		✔	✔		14		✔		
Ask Research http://www.askresearch.com	✔	✔			✔		✔	✔		✔		✔		
Avid Trading Co. http://avidinfo.com														✔
Bridge News http://www.krf.com/KRF														✔
Charts by CPUG InvestSIG http://cpcug.org	✔	✔	✔		✔									
Equity Analytics http://www.e-analytics.com														✔
Interactive Quote http://www.iqc.com	✔	✔			✔		✔	✔		✔				✔
Market Technicians Assn. http://www.teleport.com/ ~lensmith														✔
Silicon Investor http://www.techstocks.com	✔	✔				✔							✔	
Stocks & Commodities Magazine http://www.traders.com														✔
Traders Library http://www.traderslibrary.com														✔
Trading Techniques, Inc. http://www.tradingtech.com														✔
Wall Street City http://www.wallstreetcity.com	✔	✔	✔	✔	✔		✔	✔	Soon	40	✔			✔

NOTE: See CyberInvest.Com *(http://www.cyberinvest.com)* for the latest revisions to this Guide.

Exhibit 10.9 The CyberInvesting Guide for Technical Analysis on the Web.

Winterra Software Group, Inc. (http://www.winterra.com) offers a free 30-day evaluation copy (downloadable) of Stable Technical Graphs, along with "tips and tricks" for using it.

The Last Word

Technical timing tools can improve your results by helping you select entry and exit points that have an improved risk/reward relationship. Our considerable research in this area leads us to believe that, at minimum, technical analysis helps keep you out of waterfall declines. Whether you ever become a market technician, at least take advantage of these tools.

CHAPTER ELEVEN

TRICKS OF THE TRADE

The point is to get so much money that money's not the point anymore.

—William Hamilton cartoon
The New Yorker, December 7, 1992

On-line trading is experiencing phenomenal growth. Two years ago, it was predicted that on-line brokerage accounts would reach 800,000 in 1996. In fact, because of investors' increasing comfort level with computers and the rapid expansion of the Internet, on-line brokerage accounts had shot to 1.5 million accounts by the end of 1996. By 2001, that figure is expected to reach 10 million.[1]

On-line trading began in the 1980s when brokerage firms such as Charles Schwab and Fidelity introduced PC-based trades through their proprietary on-line databases. The benefits of on-line trading that accrued to individual investors included reduced commissions, more control over their accounts, and 24-hour-a-day trades (although trades are executed only during business hours). As discount brokers (and others) scramble to jump on the Internet bandwagon, Web-based trading promises to increase these benefits dramatically.

Before Web-based trading, discount brokers reduced commissions because they offered no in-house research, no investment advice, no personal broker whom you could chat with about your account. They were there simply to execute the trade. On the Web, however, competitors are just a mouse-click away, which has had a leveling effect on commissions

[1] The Forrester Report, "Money & Technology: Brokers and the Web" (Cambridge, Mass.: Forrester Research, Inc., September, 1996).

and investment services. Even deep-discount brokers are beginning to offer a variety of research and other services on a pay-as-you-go basis or through links to other Web sites. In fact, as we were writing this book, several brokers that we reviewed slashed their commissions and beefed up their on-line research. The picture can only get brighter for the individual investor.

Comparing Web-based Trades

If you do your own research and use a broker just to place a trade, you're a prime candidate for on-line trading. In the next chapter, we review 19 brokers on specific features. In this section are several areas that you should consider in selecting a Web broker.

There are certain standard features that most discount brokers offer, including:

- 24-hour trades and access to your account, although trades can be executed only during market hours
- A variety of order types: market, limit, stop, good-till-canceled, all-or-none, do-not-reduce
- Real-time quotes for placing a trade
- Instantaneous confirmation of an order before and after it is placed; confirmation of executed orders via e-mail or regular mail
- Portfolio tracker that updates your portfolio and tracks your account balance, outstanding orders, and historical transactions

You will get what you pay for. The deeper the discount, the fewer the frills. If you want dirt-cheap commissions, you'll sacrifice free research and other perks. At the end of the next chapter is a feature-by-feature comparison of the current Internet trading sites. Here are some specific areas you might want to check out before signing on with a broker.

Total Cost Per Trade

At present, commissions from discount brokers on the Internet start from $10 to about $35 per trade, with various conditions. The actual cost of the trade may be higher. A charge of *x* cents per share may be made in addition to the base fee. The advertised fee may apply only to listed stocks, not for Nasdaq stocks, or vice versa. (*Listed stocks* refer only to those traded over the New York Stock Exchange or the American Stock Exchange.) In one case, a highly touted low commission was only for orders of 5,000 shares or more.

Types of Orders

Most on-line brokers offer the types of orders mentioned earlier, but a few do not accept stop-limit orders. Make sure the broker you choose can execute the type of order you wish to place. (See the order entry screen in Exhibit 11.1.)

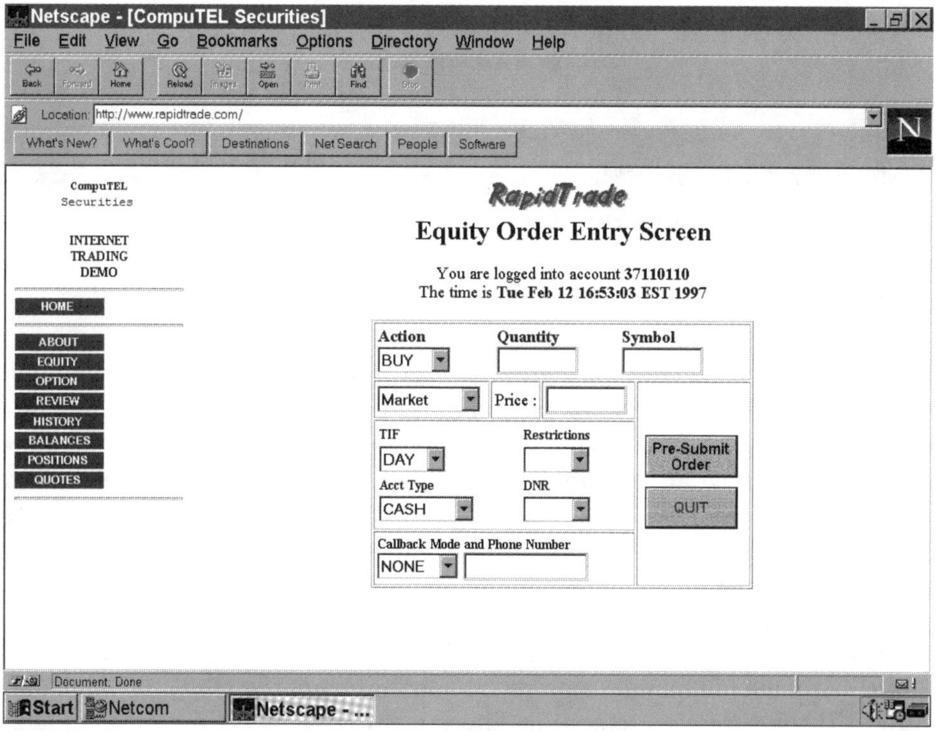

Exhibit 11.1   Order entry screen for stocks at CompuTEL Securities.

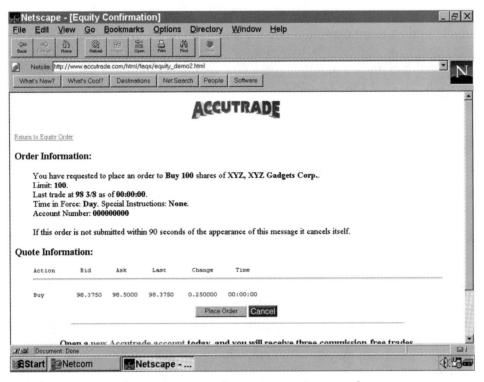

Exhibit 11.2   Order request confirmation at Accutrade.

Speed of Execution

How quickly is the trade executed in the broker's office? In theory, all trades are handled automatically by computers, but some firms require that a live broker review all trades before they are executed, which can slow down the process. Others require only a live review of trades that are deemed unusual (by the computer) in some respect. Review by an actual broker will obviously take more time, but if you are a new investor and uncertain of your order skills, you may *want* someone to review your order.

On the other hand, if you're a sophisticated investor who's comfortable with a computer, you'll want the quickest execution possible to avoid slippage (a change in price that occurs from the time you place an order till the time you execute). The only way to find this out is to ask. (*Hint:* Send your question via e-mail.)

Method of Confirmation

All the brokers we reviewed confirmed the trade instantaneously, first with a screen that reiterated the details of the order, and then, when we indicated our wish to continue, a confirmation that the order had been received by the broker. A confirmation of the execution of the order is usually sent by mail or e-mail. Be sure you understand your broker's confirmation procedure. (See the confirmation screen in Exhibit 11.2.)

Trading Terms of Endearment

Many brokers have definitions of trading terms at their Web sites. Here are a few to get you started.

All-or-None (AON) Order: An instruction to execute an order in its entirety or not at all.

Day Order or Good-for-Day Order: An order that automatically expires at the end of the trading day if it cannot be executed according to customer instructions.

Do-Not-Reduce (DNR) Order: A DNR order prohibits the exchange from reducing the order price on the ex–dividend date. (The price of a stock is usually reduced by the amount of the dividend.)

Good-Till-Canceled (GTC) Order: A GTC order remains in effect until it is executed or canceled by the customer. Some brokers limit the duration of a GTC order.

Limit Order: An order to buy or sell a security at a specific price (the *limit* price) or better.

Market Order: An order to buy or sell a security as soon as possible at the best obtainable price.

Open Order: Same as good-till-canceled order.

Partial Fill Order: An instruction to fill an order in increments, either during one day or over several days.

Stop Order: A stop sell order is an order to sell a stock if it falls to a certain price, usually used to protect unrealized profits or to

Continued

---

limit loss on a holding. A stop buy order is used on a short-sell to buy a stock if it reaches a particular price in order to limit loss or to protect unrealized profits.

Stop-Limit Order: A combination of a stop order and a limit order, with both a stop price and a limit price specified.

Source: Adapted from American Association of Individual Investors; *Dictionary of Investing*; and other glossaries.

Types of Securities Traded

What kinds of securities are traded? Listed stocks? Nasdaq stocks? Penny stocks? Global stocks? Mutual funds? Options? Futures? Bonds? Certificates of deposits? Most Web trading, at this time, is limited to stocks, options, and mutual funds, although not all brokers trade all three. Other types of securities can sometimes be handled in broker-assisted trades. The CyberInvesting Guide at the end of Chapter 12 provides a rundown on this feature.

Mutual Funds

If mutual funds are traded, can you buy any fund or must you select from an approved list? What kinds of fees or sales charges are attached to buying and selling mutual funds? Is there a fee for trading no-load funds? (A *no-load fund* means that the fund itself does not charge a fee, but some brokers add their own fee.) If fees are charged, consider purchasing shares directly from the fund's Web site (some funds allow this).

Backup Communications

Consider the broker's capacity to handle your trades in the event of a computer shutdown. Many discount brokers also have Touch-Tone telephone trading, which carries a higher commission but could be used in an emergency. This is not something you can really test, but be sure you understand how orders would be handled in such an event.

> **F**YI   The American Association of Individual Investors (http://www.aaii.org) has several articles related to brokers and trading stocks, including one entitled "Placing Stock Market Orders: Strategies for the Individual Investor."

Portfolio Trackers

How and when will your portfolio be updated? Immediately? End of day? End of the day is fine for most investors, but if you're an intraday trader, you'll want a broker who will update your portfolio after each trade.

What kind of reports are available for keeping track of your portfolio? The deeper the discount, the simpler the report, generally speaking. Nevertheless, even the deepest discounter usually provides a history of all transactions and list of unfilled orders. (See, for example, Exhibit 11.3.) Extras would be a portfolio summary report, an asset allocation report, dividends and interest report, price alert report, security transaction list, and a tax summary report for filing with the IRS.

Rates Paid on Idle Funds

What is the interest rate on idle cash in your account? Does the firm offer an automatic sweep of idle funds into a money market account, which normally pays a higher interest rate? This is an important point, as interest rates affect your total return.

Margin Accounts

Does the firm offer margin accounts? A *margin account* currently allows you to borrow up to 50 percent of the current value of your marginable securities. In general, stocks priced above $5 are marginable. Options are not marginable. The interest rate charged for borrowed funds varies. Find out what it is.

Reinvestment of Dividends

Many investors want cash dividends reinvested in the same stock. If you do, be sure your broker offers this service.

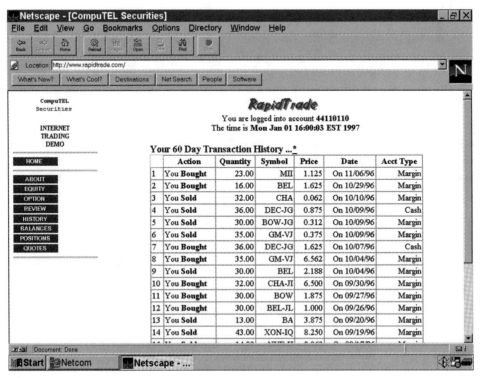

Exhibit 11.3   60-day transaction history at CompuTEL Securities.

Customer Support

What kind of support is provided by the broker? Is there a help section at the site? How will you get answers to questions about a particular trade? These are the kinds of questions you'll need to ask a potential broker.

Investment Tools

What kind of research or prospecting tools are available? Search or screening services? Company profiles? Earnings estimates? Industry group analysis? In some cases, these services are free to customers; in other cases, the broker has affiliated with a third party who offers its services on a per-item basis or reduced monthly charge. Some merely provide links to sites that offer investment tools.

Opening an Account

Many on-line brokers let you fill out the application on-line, although some Web sites require the use of the Adobe Acrobat Reader. All give you the option of requesting forms by mail or fax and returning them the same way. The initial funds to open the account must be wired, transferred, or sent by mail. To open an options account, you must usually complete an agreement stating that you understand the risks involved and most brokers require a larger initial deposit. Margin accounts also require a separate agreement and a larger initial deposit.

How Secure Are Your Trades?

Security is one of the biggest concerns of on-line investors. Andrew Lih, director of technology for Columbia University's Center for New Media, says that sites that offer security are secure enough to protect your transactions. Nevertheless, you may want to look at some of the security measures they take.

First of all, brokerage sites use secure encryptions for account information and transactions, which requires the use of secure browsers, such as Netscape Navigator 2.0 or higher and Microsoft Internet Explorer 2.0 or higher. How can you tell if you're in a secure site? Usually, the Web site displays a message window advising that you're entering a secure site, but there are other ways to tell.

- ◆ With a Netscape browser, the *broken key icon* in the lower left corner of the status bar *becomes whole* when you are sending or receiving encrypted information.
- ◆ With Microsoft Internet Explorer, a *lock* will appear in the lower right corner of the status bar.
- ◆ The URL is usually a giveaway. In a secure site or secure section of a site, the URL will change from *http://* to *https://*.

There are other security measures, such as firewalls, which are electronic communication barriers between linked networks, and "cookies," which are strings of data that help you navigate securely within a secure site. If you want to read more about these, see the FAQ at PC Financial Network (http://www.pcfn.com). Also, an article entitled "This Cookie Monster is as Harmless as Sesame Street" by Rob Gebeloff may shed some light on cookies. (Gebeloff writes "The Missing Link" column for Money Talks at http://www.talks.com.)

Still another layer of security is achieved with account numbers and passwords or personal identification numbers (PINs) which are assigned to each user. You must enter the account number and the password or PIN to access member services and your account. To help protect your account and individual trades:

◆ Guard your account number and password or PIN with the same intensity you guard your ATM card and secret code.

◆ If you make trades at an office, don't leave your computer unattended when logged on to a Web site. It is possible that someone could use the Back feature of your browser and find out your account number and password, although the sites we checked do not show the actual password when it is entered.

With regard to protecting your funds in a brokerage account, check to see what the broker has to say about security and insurance at the Web site. If the broker is a member of Securities Investor Protection Corporation (SIPC), it usually will be noted on the home page. SIPC is to broker-dealers what the Federal Deposit Insurance Corporation (FDIC) is to bank accounts. SIPC protects accounts up to $100,000 in cash and $400,000 in securities. Most brokers offer additional insurance for accounts up to $50,000,000.

Also, make sure your broker is registered with the National Association of Security Dealers (NASD) and registered in your state. NASD's regulation division has a toll-free hotline (1-800-289-9999) you can call to find out any disciplinary actions taken against a brokerage firm or securities representative.

The Last Word

The key to selecting an on-line broker is to take a hard look at what you really want from your brokerage account. Certainly, the brokerage fee is

Tips for Placing Online Trades

Placing live trades on-line can be scary (and expensive) if you aren't very careful. Here are some cautionary tips.

- ◆ Understand the kind of order you are placing. Review the "Terms of Endearment" in this chapter.
- ◆ Double-check your order-entry screen carefully, paying special attention to the security symbol and share quantity. Many stock symbols are *very* similar.
- ◆ If you're placing more than one order at a time, be sure to clear the screen before entering the next order.
- ◆ Don't click a Process or Submit Order button more than once. On-line brokers have a caveat somewhere in their instructions that they will not be responsible for duplicate orders.
- ◆ If you're in doubt about whether an order was executed, check your confirmations or order-execution screen. To avoid duplicate orders, you might wish to check by telephone before re-placing the order.
- ◆ Many brokers add a postage, handling, and/or insurance fee for mailing a confirmation. This can add $3 or $4 to every trade. To avoid this, ask for e-mail–only confirmation, if available.

important, but it's not the only consideration. If your typical trade is $10,000, the difference between a $15 commission and a $35 commission may be insignificant when you consider the total value offered by the brokerage firm. For example, if your broker executes the order inefficiently and has to pay an extra ⅛ of a point, that could consume the $20 savings in commission. The quality of the execution, the amount of support provided, and other factors discussed in this chapter may well be worth the relatively small difference in commissions.

CHAPTER TWELVE

THE CYBERBROKERS

The more you know about brokers, the easier it will be to choose among brokers and maintain good relationships with them.

—The American Association
of Individual Investors

Selecting an on-line broker can be a challenge, with nearly 20 discount brokers vying for your business on the Web—and others rapidly entering the arena. Firms like Charles Schwab, Fidelity, and newcomer American Express offer a variety of investment tools and perks for commissions that hover in the high $20s and low $30s. Deep discount brokers such as Ceres and Datek offer no frills for commissions as low as $10, although many offer links to research tools at other Web sites.

In this chapter, we give you a quick tour of 19 brokers that currently offer Web trading. Keep in mind that we're reviewing *only* those Web-based features and services, not the entire brokerage firm. Remember, too, things change, and on the Internet they change rapidly. By the time you read this, competition among the brokers could expand the services offered by all. The CyberInvesting Guide at the end of this chapter gives a line-by-line comparison of broker features. As the picture changes, we'll keep you posted at CyberInvest.Com (http://www. cyberinvest.com).

The Accutrade Tour (http://www.accutrade.com)

Accutrade has a large collection of financial research, with commissions that start at $28 + 2 cents per share. Here's what they offer.

Quotes and charts   Accutrade has real-time quotes for placing trades and unlimited access to 15-minute delayed quotes, 10 at a time. Real-time quotes are available on a subscription basis. Two-year price and volume charts are available.

Securities traded on the Internet   Stocks, options, and mutual funds.

Accounts   Margin accounts.

Extras   Accutrade customers get free tips from insider trading guru Bob Gabele, cofounder of CDA Investnet and editor of Insider's Chronicle.

Portfolio alerts   Pager or e-mail alerts for stocks and mutual funds:

- Stock alerts include price changes of more than 3 percent, earnings announcements, earnings surprises, and dividend reports for stocks.

- Fund alerts include the fund's one-month return and changes in asset composition, and fee structure.

Market news   Real-time analysis of financial news:

- Updates on market indexes
- News on mergers and acquisitions, debt markets, and technology stocks
- News and analysis from municipal markets, plus regional review of bond activity
- Weekly economic calendar

Prospecting tools   Accutrade offers: ranking tables that give performance ratios for large-, middle-, and small-cap stocks and ranking tables for top-performing mutual funds. It also has a screening mechanism that offers 18 different variables for stocks and 12 variables for mutual funds.

Research tools   Thomson company reports on 7,000+ companies and 5,000+ mutual funds, plus qualitative and quantitative analysis of industry sectors.

Emergency backup   Fax and Touch-Tone telephone.

Games   Yes. See "Games Investors Play" on pages 170–171.

Commissions   Stocks: $28 + 2 cents per share, regardless of the price of the stock. You get three commission-free trades when you open an Accutrade account. Options: $35 minimum.

Accutrade, Inc.
4211 South 102nd Street
Omaha, NE 68127
1-800-494-8939
E-mail: info@accutrade.com

The American Express Tour
(http://www.americanexpress.com/direct)

American Express Financial Direct offers two levels of accounts: The basic account (Invest/Direct) starts at $26.95 per trade; the higher-level account (InvestDirect/pt) comes with the "power tools" described below (for $34.95/month) and commissions at $34.95 per trade, with discounts for frequent traders.

Quotes and charts   American Express has real-time quotes for placing trades and unlimited access to 15-minute delayed quotes for stocks, options, funds, bonds, and indexes. Price and volume graphs are available for one day to 10 years. (See Exhibit 12.1.)

Securities traded on the Internet   Stocks and mutual funds.

Accounts   Margin accounts. Money market accounts with nightly automatic sweep of idle cash with an InvestDirect/pt account. Interest paid on idle funds with an InvestDirect account.

Portfolio alerts   Price and news alerts via e-mail throughout the day.

Extras   InvestDirect/pt customers get a free American Express Gold Card, unlimited free check writing, ATM access, dividend reinvestment service, and a line of credit to qualified customers.

Market news   A market snapshot captures real-time market updates on the Dow Jones averages and major market indexes.

Power tools   The InvestDirect/pt account comes with an assortment of prospecting and research tools, which American Express calls *power tools*. A limited version of the tools is free with the InvestDirect/pt account; an enhanced version can be purchased for $34.95/month. The power tools include some or all of the following:

◆ Four "minisearch" engines based on Macro*World forecasting indicators, industry group performance, insider trading, and ranking indicators

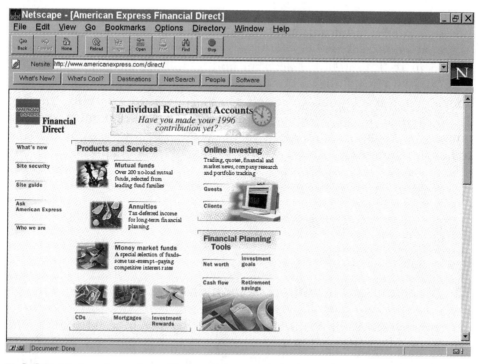

Exhibit 12.1 American Express Financial Direct: home page.

- ProSearch, the powerful stock search engine by Telescan
- ESearch, which uses the ProSearch engine to search for stocks based on earnings estimates
- Market Guide fact sheets and company profiles
- Macro*World price forecasts
- Zacks earnings estimates
- Valuation data reports
- SEC-searchable database
- Two keyword-searchable news databases

Mutual funds Customers have access to American Express proprietary funds, plus 200 nonproprietary mutual funds and money market funds.

Options   This is one of the two places on the Net you can use a bona fide search engine for options. (The other is Wall Street City.)

Commissions   American Express's commission schedule begins at $26.95 in its Invest/Direct account and $34.95 in the Invest/Direct/pt account (which includes a limited version of the power tools described above). Each has an additional charge of $0.005 per share for the first 1,000 shares. The Invest/Direct/pt account offers a frequent trader discount after 10 equity trades in a year that reduces the base commission to $29.95. Commissions vary with the price of the stock.

American Express Financial Direct
P.O. Box 59196
Minneapolis, MN 55459-0196
1-800-658-4677

The K. Aufhauser Tour (http://www.aufhauser.com)

K. Aufhauser's WealthWEB claims to be the first Internet trading site with trades that start at $22.49.

Quotes and charts   WealthWEB has real-time quotes for placing trades, with free (delayed) quotes, 10 at a time, and 12-month price charts. You can subscribe to unlimited real-time quotes for $30/month.

Securities traded on the Internet   Stocks, options, and mutual funds.

Accounts   Margin accounts. Cash management plan includes money market account with automatic sweep of idle funds, debit card, and free check writing with a $25,000 balance.

Market news   Latest figures for the DOW, S&P 500, and Nasdaq are on the home page.

Prospecting tools   Download the free, Windows-based StockQuest to screen more than 8,300 stocks with 50+ predefined variables. Data updated weekly.

Research tools   Market Guide quick facts and company reports. Earnings estimates from First Call.

Emergency backup   Touch-Tone telephone.

Commissions   Web stock trades are $22.49 for 1–399 shares; $30.60 for 400–1700 shares. Add 2 cents per share for trades of more than 1700 shares. *Power Traders:* 20 equity trades a month for 12 months costs a flat fee of $800. After that, any equity trades above 20 a month are $8 per trade.

K. Aufhauser and Company, Inc.
140 Broadway, 40th Floor
New York, NY 10005
1-800-368-3668
Email: info@aufhauser.com

The Ceres Online Tour (http://www.ceres.com)

Ceres Securities Online is a deep-discount brokerage firm for the independent investor, with a standard commission of $18, regardless of the number of shares traded.

Quotes and charts   Ceres has real-time quotes for placing trades, with free (delayed) quotes, 10 at a time. You can subscribe to unlimited real-time quotes for $30/month.

Securities traded on the Internet   Stocks, options, and mutual funds.

Accounts   Margin accounts.

Extras   Daily commentary from Andrew Tobias. A helpful Internet Tutorial gives you tips on using multiple screens, among other things.

Market news   Ceres' home page shows the latest figures for the Dow, S&P 500, Nasdaq, NYSE, and Amex.

Emergency backup   Touch-Tone telephone, Sharp Zaurus PDA, and broker-assisted.

Commissions   Stocks: $18, regardless of number of shares *and* regardless of how placed. Options: $35. Hard-copy confirmations at no charge.

Ceres Securities
P.O. Box 2209
Omaha, NE 68103-2209
1-800-669-3900
E-mail: info@ceres.com

The CompuTEL Tour (http://www.rapidtrade.com)

CompuTEL Securities, a division of Thomas F. White & Co., Inc., is a deep-discount broker for experienced traders. In fact, for commissions as low as $9.00 for 1,000-share trades or more per trade, they *require* that customers have two or more years of experience and know how to use their Internet accounts.

Quotes and charts CompuTEL has real-time quotes for placing trades, and free delayed quotes. There are several ways to get more real-time quotes. Customers accumulate 100 real-time quotes with every trade; with four trades a month, they can receive unlimited real-time quotes (from Data Broadcasting) for $5.00 per month. Charts are provided through DBC Online.

Securities traded on the Internet Stocks, options, and mutual funds.

Accounts Margin accounts; money market accounts with automatic sweep of idle funds and free check-writing privileges.

Portfolio alerts Earnings alerts from MarketEdge.

Market news Free market news from DBC Online.

Research tools CompuTEL offers no frills with its low commissions, but has arranged for free trials and discounted services from other Internet providers with hyperlinks via the Investor's Internet Toolbox:

- ◆ 20 free S&P company reports when you open an account with CompuTEL.
- ◆ With one trade a month 50 free stock and mutual fund reports each month from Thomson's MarketEdge, as well as industry reports, intraday charts, and news.
- ◆ Free one-month subscription to Zacks Investment Research.
- ◆ Access to Wall Street by Internet which offers more than 200,000 research reports on a unit basis (as low as $1.50 each) from Standard & Poor's, First Call, Vickers, Argus, and Business Wire.
- ◆ A $35 credit toward stock and mutual fund reports at the INVESTools Web site.

Emergency backup Touch-Tone telephone trading and broker-assisted trades.

Commissions   Stocks: $9 per trade for market orders of 1,000 shares or more. Otherwise, $14 per trade for market orders; $19 for limit orders. There is also a charge of 2 percent of principal on foreign stocks and stocks under $2. Options: $24/trade, plus $1/contract. Frequent trader discounts available.

CompuTEL Securities
Thomas F. White & Co., Inc.
1 Second Street, 5th Floor
San Francisco, CA 94105
1-800-432-0327
E-mail: support@compu-tel.com

The Datek Tour (http://www.datek.com)

Datek Online is a deep-deep-discount broker without the barest hint of a frill—no graphs, no alerts, no research, no telephone trades—which is perhaps why it can cut its commissions to $9.99 per trade up to 5,000 shares. (See Exhibit 12.2.)

Quotes and charts   Datek lets you check a real-time quote (for free) on the stock you wish to trade. Period. Confirmation is yours in five seconds.

Securities traded on the Internet   NYSE and Nasdaq stocks only, at this writing. Options are planned for 1997.

Accounts   Margin accounts. Interest paid on idle funds.

Extras   Datek posts customer orders on Nasdaq's SelectNet system, the insider market used by Nasdaq market makers. The system allows Datek to match buyers and sellers on a more narrow spread than the bid/ask prices.

Research tools   Datek offers no other research services, but it is generous with its hyperlinks, offering jumps to a couple dozen interesting investing spots, including its competitors.

Emergency backup   Broker-assisted or dial-up PPP connection (this is a special telephone number for use with your browser).

Commissions $9.99/per trade up to 5,000 shares. Period.

Datek Securities
50 Broad Street, Sixth Floor
New York, NY 10004
(212) 514-7531

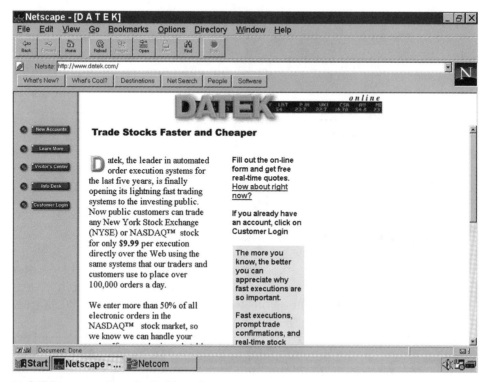

Exhibit 12.2   Datek Online: home page.

The eBroker Tour (http://www.ebroker.com)

eBroker is the Internet-only trading arm of All American Brokers. This deep-discount broker offers $12 trades.

Quotes and charts   Real-time quotes available at time of trade. Free (delayed) quotes, 10 at a time; unlimited real-time quotes available for $30/month. No charts.

Securities traded on the Internet   Stocks and options.

Accounts   Margin accounts.

Emergency backup   A toll-free telephone number is provided when you open an account.

Commissions   Stocks: $12 flat fee. Options: minimum, $35.

eBroker
All American Brokers
P.O. Box 2226
Omaha, NE 68103-2226
E-mail: info@ebroker.com

The E*Trade Tour (http://www.etrade.com)

E*Trade is a deep-discount broker offering online trading of listed stocks for as low as $14.95 a trade and Nasdaq stocks for $19.95.

Quotes and charts   E*Trade has real-time quotes for placing trades with unlimited real-time quotes for $30/month. Free delayed quotes may be requested, one security at a time. Charts are available.

Securities traded on the Internet   Stocks and options.

Accounts   Margin accounts. Interest paid on idle funds. Money market accounts with automatic sweep of idle funds. Free checking.

Portfolio alerts   News alerts, alerts for earnings releases, and analysts' estimates.

Extras   Extras include:

◆ E*Trade Canada offers E*Trade's Web-trading to Canadian investors.

◆ Options leverage analysis and options price analysis.

◆ Technical charting with almost a dozen indicators.

Market news   Customized Personal Market Page with links to Reuters news and free, unlimited access to Briefing.com for market news and analysis.

Research tools   Links to the SEC EDGAR database and Hoover's Online for company reports. Links to Baseline Financial Services for historical prices, earnings estimates, and fundamental data.

Emergency backup   Touch-Tone telephone.

Games   Yes. See "Games Investors Play" on pages 170–171.

Commissions   NYSE and Amex stocks: $14.95 for up to 5,000 shares; add 1 cent per share for orders over 5,000 shares. Nasdaq stocks: $19.95

for trades of any size at any price. Options: $20/trade plus $1.75/contract with a $29 minimum.

E*Trade Securities, Inc.
Four Embarcadero Place
2400 Geng Road
Palo Alto, CA 94303
1-800-786-2575
E-mail: service@etrade.com

The Fidelity Tour (http://personal.fidelity.com)

Fidelity Investments has long offered on-line trading through its own proprietary software, but it just recently entered the Internet on-line trading scene. Stock trades on the Web start at $39.00, but rates are scheduled to change soon.

Quotes and charts   Real-time quotes and news can be earned as credits for certain activities: 100 news and quote credits for establishing your account; 100 for each Web trade; 100 for each $50,000 of assets in a Fidelity account. The latter credits expire at the end of each month and are refigured for the next month.

Securities traded on the Internet   Stocks, ADRS, and mutual funds.

Accounts   Margin accounts.

Extras   Scrolling color-coded ticker of global and domestic market indexes.

Market news   Market commentary; intraday market graphs (at The Hub page); market news headlines and stories from Thomson Market-Edge and Reuters; clever Econoday Calendar that defines the various government reports.

Mutual funds   Fidelity's FundsNetwork offers access to 3,300+ Fidelity and non-Fidelity funds from more than 300 fund companies.

Emergency backup   Touch-Tone phone.

Commissions   Stocks: Commissions start at $39.00 for trades of less than 1,000 shares; $0.02/share for trades in excess of 1,000 shares.

Fidelity Investments, Inc.
82 Devonshire Street
Boston, MA 02109
617-570-7000

The InvestEXpress Online Tour (http://www.investexpress.com)

InvestEXpress Online is the Web trading arm of Investex Securities Group, Inc., a deep-discount broker. Commissions are $13.95 for a minimum $500-share market order.

Quotes and charts InvestEXpress has real-time quotes for placing trades and delayed quotes, five securities at a time. You can subscribe to real-time quotes for $29.95/month.

Securities traded on the Internet Stocks, mutual funds, options, bonds, and CDs.

Accounts Margin accounts. Money market accounts with automatic cash sweeps at end of day.

Extras InvestEXpress aggregates orders for figuring commissions (i.e., you can buy *x* number shares of a stock in the morning and *y* number of shares of the same stock in the afternoon and incur only one commission and one service fee).

Market news Business and market summary from USA Today Moneyline; custom news headlines from Yahoo!.

Research tools Links to Hoover's and MarketEdge for company reports and to Reuters for a searchable news database.

Emergency backup Toll-free telephone.

Commissions Stocks: The $13.95 commission requires a minimum trade of 500 shares for a stock of $3.00 a share or more; limit orders are $17.95. For 1 to 500 shares, $30/trade. Options: $20 per trade, plus $1.75/contract with a 10 contract minimum.

Investex Securities Group, Inc.
50 Broad Street
New York, NY 10004
1-800-392-7192

The Lombard Tour (http://www.lombard.com)

Lombard Brokerage is a deep-discount broker (recently acquired by Dean Witter) that offers Web-based trades for as low as $14.95.

Quotes and charts Lombard offers a "quote-basket" feature that allows you to monitor up to 10 securities at a time, with the screen updated every two minutes. (You may define up to five different baskets.) Intraday graphs and market index graphs available.

Securities traded on the Internet   Stocks, options, and mutual funds.

Market news   Lombard's market summary is updated every hour, and includes major market indexes.

Accounts   Margin accounts. Money market accounts with automatic money market sweep and check-writing privileges.

Extras   Asset-allocation breakdown of your portfolio; good help screens and glossary of trading terms.

Prospecting tools   Lombard has lists of most active and gainers/losers on the NYSE, AMEX, and NASDAQ.

Research tools   Lombard customers get free company reports from Thomson Financial Services (7,300 stocks and 6,800 mutual funds). Lombard's "Wall Street by Fax" service offers a number of reports on a per-unit basis (as low as $1.50/report):

- ◆ First Call earnings estimates
- ◆ S&P stock reports, news stories, and industry reports
- ◆ Argus company reports
- ◆ Vickers insider trading reports
- ◆ Business Wire press releases
- ◆ Historical price charts

Emergency backup   Touch-Tone telephone.

Commissions   Stocks: Market orders (up to 5,000 shares) are $14.95; limit orders are $19.95. Trades over 5,000 shares of *listed* stocks are charged at the rate of 1 cent per share. OTC Stocks under $1.00 are charged $25.00 per trade, plus 2.75 percent of principal amount. Options: Minimum commission is $27.50.

Lombard Brokerage, Inc.
595 Market Street, Suite 780
San Francisco, CA 94105
1-800-566-2273
E-mail: support@lombard.com

The NDB Online Tour (http://www.ndb.com)

NDB Online is a service of National Discount Brokers, Inc. and one of the three discount brokers affiliated with the PAWWS Financial Network. Commissions start at $14.75 a trade.

Quotes and charts   Real-time quotes for placing trades; free delayed quotes otherwise. Stock graphs available.

Securities traded on the Internet   Stocks, options, and mutual funds.

Accounts   Margin accounts; money market funds with automatic cash sweep of idle funds; free check-writing and MasterCard debit card with a balance of $10,000; link to PAWWS for portfolio accounting.

Extras   NDB Online has a *price-improvement system* that mimics Nasdaq's SelectNet system, which matches buyers to sellers on a more narrow spread than bid/ask prices.

Prospecting tools   Link to PAWWS Financial Network.

Research tools   Link to PAWWS Financial Network, plus company reports by fax on a per-report basis:

- First Call earnings estimates
- Standard & Poor's company reports
- Morningstar company reports
- Vickers insider trading reports

Emergency backup   Telephone backup.

Commissions   Stocks: $14.75/trade for market orders; $19.75/trade for limit orders. One cent per share is added to over-5,000-share trades. Options: $29 for up to 5 contracts; add $2.50 per contract for trades in excess of 5 contracts.

National Discount Brokers
7 Hanover Square, 4th Floor
New York, NY 10004
1-800-888-3999
E-mail: help@ndb.com

The Net Investor Tour (http://pawws.secapl.com/invest.html)

The NET Investor is a division of Howe Barnes Investments, Inc., one of the three discount brokers affiliated with the PAWWS Financial Network. Trades start at $29.00.

Quotes and charts   Real-time quotes for active accounts, free for frequent traders. Delayed quotes for all accounts. Historical and intraday price and volume graphs.

Securities traded on the Internet   Stocks, options, mutual funds, bonds, and CDs.

Accounts   Margin accounts. Money market account with daily sweep of idle funds. Unlimited checking and free VISA debit card. Automatic dividend re-investment. Link to PAWWS for portfolio accounting tools.

Portfolio alerts   A PawTracks "hot list" will track up to 150 securities.

Extras   The "True Price Advantage" system mimics Nasdaq's Select-Net system, attempting to match buyers and sellers on a more narrow spread than the bid/ask prices.

Market news   Link to PAWWS Financial Network.

Prospecting tools   Link to PAWWS Financial Network.

Research tools   Research tools include:

- Research reports from Howe Barnes analysts and third parties
- Proprietary reports on price forecasting and earnings momentum analysis
- Link to PAWWS Financial Network

Mutual funds   Mutual Funds InfoLine is a request line for information on more than 3,000 mutual funds. One-page Morningstar reports on 1,500 mutual funds delivered by fax or U.S. mail.

Bonds and CDs   Inquiries and searches on bonds and CDs.

Emergency backup   Touch-Tone telephone.

Commissions   Stocks: $29.00/trade plus 1.5 cents a share. Stocks trading for less than $1.00/share, add one cent per share. Stop orders for listed stocks, add one cent per share. Postage and handling fee of $2.75 a trade. Options: $35 plus $2.50/contract.

The Net Investor
Howe Barnes Investments, Inc.
135 S. LaSalle St., Suite 1500
1-800-638-4250
E-mail: invest@pawws.com

The JB Oxford Tour (http://www.jboxford.com)

JB Oxford has commission-free trading if you have an account equity of $250,000 and make 1,000-share trades. Otherwise, commissions are $15.00 a trade.

Quotes and charts   Real-time quotes: 100 free when you open an account and 100 free with every trade. Unlimited delayed quotes. Unlimited free access to charts.

Securities traded   Stocks, options, bonds, and mutual funds.

Accounts   Margin accounts. Interest paid on idle funds. Money market accounts with free sweep of idle funds and check writing.

Research tools   These research tools are available on a per-unit basis ($1.50 or more per unit):

- S&P stock reports, industry reports, and news reports
- First Call earnings estimates
- Argus company report
- Historical price charts
- Business Wire press releases
- Vickers insider trading reports
- IPO reports from Renaissance Capital
- Lipper mutual fund reports

Emergency backup   Touch-Tone telephone.

Commissions   Stocks: $15 per trade for any Nasdaq security or any listed security up to 3,000 shares, if securities are priced $1 or higher. For trades of listed securities in excess of 3,000 shares, a flat fee of $0.01/share. For securities priced less than $1, $0.03 per share or 5 percent of principal. Options: $25 plus $2.50/contract. Postage and handling fee: $3.00/trade.

J. B. Oxford & Company
9665 Wilshire Boulevard, Third Floor
Beverly Hills, CA 90212
1-310-777-8888
E-mail: sales@jboc.com

Games Investors Play

Some broker sites and other investing sites offer contests and games to allow you to test your skill at stock-picking without risking any money. Here are some that we thought particularly interesting:

Accutrade (http://www.accutrade.com) Free Trade Zone is an ongoing game with a grand prize of one commission-free trade per day for the life of your Accutrade account.

EBN Interactive (http://www.ebn.co.uk), the Web site of Europe's 24-hour business news channel, has a global portfolio management game designed by The Bankers Network, which challenges you to "experience the perils and rewards of a genuine stock broker on the world's leading *bourses*" (i.e., exchanges). It is partnered by Dow Jones Broadcasting Europe, Inc & Flextech Television, Ltd.

*E*Trade* (http://www.etrade.com) Trade stocks and options with $100,000 in game money in E*Trade's stock market game. The game features real market prices with portfolio and transaction records updated automatically. Top 10 players are posted daily. There's a new game every month.

Sandbox Entertainment and various sponsors present several *Final Bell* games at http://www.finalbell.com. The main event is "Play the Market" where you start with a virtual account of $100,000 and make stock picks from the NYSE, AMEX, or Nasdaq.

Continued

The grand champion wins $5,000 cash; others win prizes and "Sand Dollars" or "Market Bucks" that can be exchanged for merchandise or services.

INVESTools (http://www.investools.com) has a Hot Stock Contest in which you may try to pick the biggest gainer of the month in penny stocks and non-penny stocks.

Invest-o-rama and *MarketPlayer* cosponsor regular stock picking competitions at the MarketPlayer Web site (http://www.marketplayer.com/sponsor/investorama). The purpose seems to be to promote MarketPlayer investment tools, but you can test your skills and maybe win a cash prize.

Mutual Funds Interactive (http://www.brill.com) sponsors a portfolio contest at the newsgroup at its Web site.

Worth Magazine (http://www.worth.com) has a Stock Challenge Contest with cash prizes. Entrants start with $100,000 in fantasy funds and pick 10 out of 100 preselected stocks.

The Pacific Brokerage Tour (http://www.tradepbs.com)

Pacific Brokerage Services is another deep-discount broker, offering Web-based trades as low as $15.

Quotes and charts   Real-time quotes are available at the time of trade. You can get 10 free (delayed) quotes at a time. Stock charts are available.

Securities traded on the Internet   Stocks and options.

Market news   PBS offers a real-time market watch, updated automatically every 1 to 2 minutes, for the DOW, NYSE, Nasdaq, and a dozen indexes.

Accounts   Margin accounts; interest paid on idle funds.

Prospecting tools   PBS has daily lists of gainers and losers in various categories.

Research tools   Market Guide reports for more than 8,200 companies are available on a per-unit basis or by monthly or annual subscriptions.

Emergency backup   Telephone backup procedures.

Commissions   Stocks: Flat fee of $15 for Web-based trades. Options: $1.75/contract ($15 minimum).

Pacific Brokerage Services, Inc.
Internet Service Center
401 North Maple Drive
Beverly Hills, CA 90210
1-800-416-7113
E-mail: tradepbs@interramp.com

The PC Financial Network Tour (http://www.pcfn.com)

PC Financial Network, a service of Donaldson, Lufkin & Jenrette Securities Corporation, offers on-line trading for $39.95 per trade. Frequent traders can bring that down to $29.95/trade.

Quotes and charts PC Financial Network (PCFN) has real-time quotes for placing trades and credit for 100 free real-time quotes (stock and option) when you open your account and 100 free real-time quotes with each trade. Unlimited delayed quotes. (See Exhibit 12.3.)

Securities traded on the Internet Stocks, mutual funds, options, and bonds.

Accounts Margin accounts; money market accounts with automatic sweep of idle funds. Free unlimited check-writing and no-fee Master-Card debit card.

Extras PCFN has three plug-ins and ActiveX controls to simplify and improve its services (Plug-ins are for Netscape Navigator; ActiveX controls are for Microsoft Explorer). EZ Chart speeds up the downloading of charts and creates charts. EZ Info Menu facilitates the access to news, quotes, charts, and research within the PC Financial Network. Navigational Ticker allows the creation of a custom scrolling ticker to monitor up to 10 stocks, plus the 10 most active stocks and eight market indexes.

Portfolio alerts Free portfolio alerts inform you of events that affect your holdings. PCFN's "Smart Portfolios" keep track of the last 20 or most frequent 20 securities for which you retrieved quotes the previous day.

Market news PC Financial Network has a snapshot on its home page of the Dow, the Nasdaq index, and the S&P 500. Market headlines are well-categorized, and include IPO highlights and offerings, U.S. treasuries, economic indicators, and mergers and acquisitions.

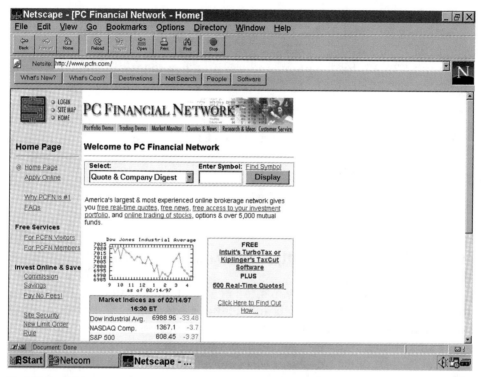

Exhibit 12.3 PC Financial Network: home page.

Research tools

- Searchable news database from Reuters and S&P Marketscope@Home
- Earnings estimates from Zacks
- Company digests from PCFN's own research department are available for the companies in which PCFN makes a market

Mutual funds PCFN's FundCenter has Lipper profiles on over 5,000 mutual funds. FundScan lets you screen this database with your own criteria.

Emergency backup Toll-free telephone.

Commissions Stocks: For trades less than 1,000 shares, $39.95. Over 1,000-share trades, add $0.03/share. Frequent traders (those generating

$1,000 or more in commissions during the 12-month period prior to the trade) pay $29.95/trade for less than 1,000 shares; add $0.02/share for over 1,000-share trades. Stocks priced less than $1.00: 4% of principal, minimum $39.95; for frequent traders, it is 3 percent of principal, with minimum of $29.95. Options: $35 plus $1.75/contract, minimum.

PC Financial Network
Donaldson, Lufkin, Jenrette Securities Corporation
One Pershing Plaza
Jersey City, NJ 07399
E-mail: info@pcfn.com
1-800-237-PCFN

The Quick & Reilly Tour (http://www.quick-reilly.com)

Quick & Reilly's brokerage Web site is called QuickWay Net. They have an aim-to-please attitude, with an excellent site demo, a thorough FAQ section, and an invitation to clients to e-mail suggestions about changes to the site. If they like your suggestion and implement the change, you'll get a free T-shirt or a commission-free trade! Commissions start at $26.75.

Quotes & charts   Unlimited real-time quotes: $29.95/month. Free delayed quotes.

Securities traded on the Internet   Stocks, options, and mutual funds.

Accounts   Margin accounts. Money market accounts with automatic sweep of idle funds. Free check writing.

Portfolio alerts   Daily e-mail price alerts for stocks in your portfolios (you can have up to 10 portfolios and 30 securities in each).

Market news   Quick & Reilly has a customizable Market Snapshot which allows you to select which sections, indices, stats, and graphs to include. Sections include index numbers, market statistics, intraday index graphs, news headlines, market commentaries, and economic reports.

Research tools   Links to Morningstar and Standard & Poor's reports.

Emergency backup   Touch-Tone telephone.

Commissions   Stocks: $26.75/trade for the first 1,000 shares; $0.02 a share for trades over 1,000 shares. Options: Minimum $37.50 plus $1.75/contract.

Quick & Reilly, Inc.
26 Broadway
New York, NY 10004
1-800-837-7220
E-mail: donato@Quick-Reilly.com

The Schwab Tour (http://www.eschwab.com)

If you have a Schwab account, you can save 20 percent on commissions by using their Web-based trading system, SchwabNOW. (See Exhibit 12.4.) The discount, however, doesn't apply to eSchwab accounts, which is Schwab's proprietary on-line trading system and portfolio management software. Schwab offers a lot of research and commissions that start at $29.95 for up to 1,000 shares.

Quotes and charts   Real-time quotes are available for placing trades; delayed quotes otherwise. You will receive 50 free real-time quotes when you open an account, with a credit for 50 more with every trade. Intraday, daily, and weekly charts available.

Securities traded on the Internet   Stocks, treasuries, mutual funds, and options (except straddles and spreads).

Accounts   Margin accounts. Interest paid on idle funds. Money market accounts with automatic sweep of idle funds and check writing.

Extras   Free e.Schwab software for portfolio management. Customer service via e-mail.

Market News   Schwab customers can get market news at http://www.schwab.com without charge, or they can subscribe to S&P MarketScope for an additional cost.

Prospecting tools   Schwab's Research on Request service offers a list of S&P's 5-STAR stocks and a free monthly screening package of investing ideas from S&P.

Research tools   Research On Request also offers reports for as low as $1.50 each. Delivery is via the Internet or fax. Reports include:

◆ Standard & Poor's news headlines, stock reports, and industry outlook reports

◆ Insider trading reports from Vickers

◆ Morningstar international stock reports

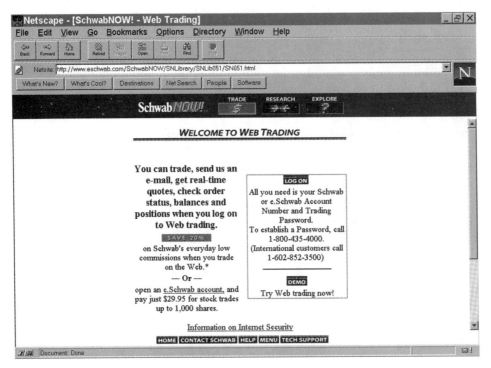

Exhibit 12.4   SchwabNOW: home page.

- ◆ First Call's earnings estimates, earnings surprises, and earnings estimate revisions
- ◆ Business Wire earnings announcements and press releases
- ◆ Historical price charts
- ◆ Argus Action Facts
- u Schwab company research reports

Mutual Funds   Mutual fund research includes:

- u Performance data on 1,100 funds
- ◆ Morningstar mutual fund reports
- ◆ SchwabFunds family, with prospectuses

◆ Mutual Fund OneSource Funds: More than 575 no-load, no-transaction fee funds from over 70 fund companies.

Emergency backup   Toll-free telephone.

Games   Yes. See "Games Investors Play," on pages 170–171.

Commissions   Stocks: $29.95 price for trades of up to $1,000 shares; $0.03 per share after that. Options: $39 minimum.

The Charles Schwab Corporation
101 Montgomery Street
San Francisco, CA 94104
415-627-7000
1-800-435-4000

The Jack White Tour (http://www.jackwhiteco.com)

Jack White & Company is one of the three discount brokers located on the PAWWS Financial Network. Its Internet trading arm is called PATH On-Line (see Exhibit 12.5). Commissions start at $25/trade.

Quotes and charts   Real-time quotes for placing trades; free delayed quotes otherwise. You can subscribe to real-time quotes, intraday charts.

Securities traded on the Internet   Stocks and mutual funds.

Accounts   Margin accounts. Money market accounts with automatic sweep of idle funds and check writing. Link to PAWWS Financial Network for portfolio accounting.

Market news   Links to PAWWS, DTN Wall Street, and Nasdaq.

Prospecting tools   Link to PAWWS Financial Network.

Research   Links to SEC's EDGAR database for company reports. Research tools at the PAWWS Financial Network are available to Jack White customers.

Emergency backup   Automated Touch-Tone telephone; PC software; toll-free, broker-assisted trades.

Commissions   Stocks: A flat commission of $25 per trade for up to 1,250 shares; trades over 1,250 shares are 2 cents per share with a minimum of $25 per trade. Options: $33.00 plus $3/option.

Jack White & Company
9191 Towne Centre Drive, Second Floor
San Diego, CA 92122
1-800-753-1700
E-mail: jwc@pawws.com

FYI   For an up-to-date comparison of brokers on the Web, check out the CyberInvesting Guide at CyberInvest.Com (http://www. cyberinvest.com). Invest-o-rama (http://www.investorama.com) provides customer comments about brokers at the Directory of Investing Resources page.

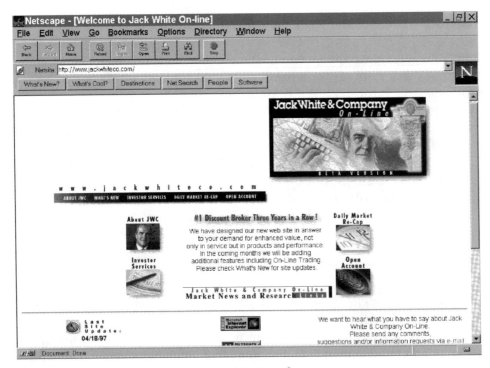

Exhibit 12.5   Jack White PATH On-Line: home page.

The PAWWS Financial Network Hosts Three Brokers

Three discount brokers reside at the PAWWS Financial Network (http://pawws.com): Howe Barnes' Net Investor, Jack White & Company's PATH On-line, and NDB Online. Customers of these firms have access to the following services at PAWWS:

Portfolio accounting   Basic portfolio accounting, including PawTracks, is free. PawTracks allows you to track up to 150 securities. Integrated Tax-Lot Accounting is available for $8.95 a month, or $95 a year.

Market news   Link to DTN Wall Street.

Prospecting tools   Griffin Financial Services offers trade alerts and new issue alerts, each $9.00 a month. Stock Market Index, Inc. provides a *market screen with a weekly market report at $7.95 a month.*

Research tools   Ford Investor Services provides fundamental data starting at $10 a month. Hoover company profiles are $5 a month for 30 reports.

Full-Service Brokers

A number of full-service brokers have established Web sites. They don't offer on-line trading as yet, but some allow customers to access their accounts on-line, and many of them offer educational material for beginning investors. Here are the ones that are open for business at this writing.

A.G. Edwards & Sons	http://www.agedwards.com
Cutter & Co., Inc.	http://www.stocktrader.com
J.P. Morgan	http://www.jpmorgan.com
Merrill Lynch	http://www.ml.com
Oppenheimer & Co.	http://www.oppenheimer.com
PaineWebber	http://www.painewebber.com
Prudential Securities	http://www.prusec.com
Smith Barney	http://www.smithbarney.com

Web site	Minimum to Open	Min. Comm./Stocks 100@$20	Min. Comm./Stocks 500@$10	Trans. Fee	Other Web Trades	Margin Acct.	Money Market Account Avail.	Money Market Account Auto Sweep	Money Market Account Checks	Portfolio Tracker	Portfolio Alerts	Investment Tools
Accutrade http://www.accutrade.com	$5,000	$30.00	$38.00	-0-	Funds Options	✓	—	—	—	✓	✓	LINKS
American Express Financial Direct http://www.americanexpress.com/direct	$5,000	$27.45	$29.45	-0-	Funds	✓	✓	✓	✓	✓	✓	YES
K.Aufhauser http://www.aufhauser.com	-0-	$22.49	$30.60	-0-	Funds Options	✓	✓	✓	✓	✓	—	YES
Ceres http://www.ceres.com	$5,000	$18.00	$18.00	-0-	Funds Options	✓	—	—	—	✓	—	—
CompuTEL http://www.rapidtrade.com	$5,000	$14.00/$19.00	$14.00/$19.00	$2.50	Funds Options	✓	✓	✓	✓	✓	✓	LINKS
Datek http://www.datek.com	$2,000	$9.99	$9.99	-0-	Options	✓	—	—	—	✓	—	LINKS
eBroker http://www.ebroker.com	$10,000	$12.00	$12.00	-0-	Options	✓	—	—	—	✓	—	—
E*Trade http://www.etrade.com	$1,000	$14.95/$19.95	$14.95/$19.95	-0-	Options	✓	✓	✓	✓	✓	—	LINKS
Fidelity Investments http://personal.fidelity.com	$5,000	$40.50	$67.70	-0-	Funds	✓	✓	✓	✓	✓	—	YES
InvestEXpress http://www.investexpress.com	-0-	$30.00	$13.95	-0-	Funds Options	✓	✓	✓	✓	✓	—	LINKS
Lombard http://www.lombard.com	$1,500	$14.95/$19.95	$14.95/$19.95	-0-	Funds Options	✓	✓	✓	✓	✓	—	YES
NBD Online http://www.ndb.com	$2,000	$14.75	$14.75	-0-	—	✓	✓	✓	✓	✓	—	LINKS
The Net Investor http://www.netinvestor.com	$5,000	$30.00	$36.50	$2.75	Funds, Bonds Options, CDs	✓	✓	✓	✓	✓	—	LINKS
J.B. Oxford & Co. http://www.jboxford.com	$5,000	$15.00	$15.00	$3.00	Funds, Bonds Options	✓	✓	✓	✓	✓	—	YES
Pacific Brokerage http://www.tradepbs.com	$1,000	$15.00	$15.00	-0-	Options	✓	—	—	—	✓	—	YES
PC Financial Network http://www.pcfn.com	-0-	$39.95	$39.95	-0-	Funds, Bonds Options	✓	✓	✓	✓	✓	✓	YES
Quick & Reilly http://www.quick-reilly.com	-0-	$26.75	$26.75	-0-	Funds Options	✓	✓	✓	✓	✓	—	LINKS
SchwabNOW http://www.eschwab.com	$5,000	$29.95	$29.95	-0-	Funds, Options Treasuries	✓	✓	✓	✓	✓	—	YES
Jack White & Co. http://www.jackwhiteco.com	$5,000	$25.00	$25.00	-0-	Funds	✓	✓	✓	✓	✓	—	LINKS

NOTE: See CyberInvest.Com at (http://www.cyberinvest.com) for the latest revisions to this Guide.

Exhibit 12.6   CyberInvesting Guide for Web Brokers.

The Last Word

Choosing among these brokers may seem daunting, but your decision is not written in stone. If you become dissatisfied, you can switch your account with only minor inconvenience. Better to make a decision and get started than to agonize over the details of who has the best deal.

PART FIVE

Portfolio Management

Finding and evaluating stocks may be more fun than managing a portfolio, but portfolio management is as crucial to investment success as watering and weeding is to a healthy garden. In this section we will deal with the essential components of effective portfolio management:

- Monitoring your investments
- Evaluating market conditions
- Assessing industry group performance
- Planning the sell

CHAPTER THIRTEEN

Monitoring Your Portfolio

The first rule is not to lose. The second rule is not to forget the first rule.

—Warren Buffett

A garden must be tended carefully to ensure a healthy crop. It must be watered and fertilized regularly. Leaves must be checked for insects that could damage the budding fruit. Weeds must be eliminated so as not to choke the healthy growing plants. In a similar manner, stocks must be monitored regularly as they grow toward their targets. You need to stay aware of any external factors that could stop a stock in its tracks and send it reeling. Should an event occur that could affect the stock, you will need to reassess the situation and decide whether to sell your shares, hold on to them, or increase your position. You also need to be aware of the optimum time to sell the stocks that meet your investment goals.

If you're a long-term investor who basically buys and holds stocks, monitoring your portfolio may only require only a few minutes a month. If you're a more active investor who uses an evaluation process and technical timing tools like those described in this book, you'll need to set aside a few minutes every day to review your positions. The Internet has greatly facilitated the monitoring process.

Portfolio Trackers and Alerts

Portfolio trackers are almost as ubiquitous as stock quotes on the Web. All online brokers have free portfolio tracking of some kind for their customers. So do many of the major investing Web sites. Most perform the basic functions of portfolio tracking: updating stock prices and volume change and calculating the gain/loss and total current value of each position and of the total portfolio. The differences lie in these areas:

- Number of portfolios allowed
- Number of securities allowed in each portfolio
- Types of securities tracked
- Timeliness of the updates
- Richness of the reports that can be compiled from the portfolio data, such as reports for the IRS
- Availability of price and news alerts

Alerts are extremely helpful in monitoring a portfolio. The most common alert is a *price alert:* the stock reaches a new high or low, or it exceeds or falls below some preset level which corresponds to a target or mental stop (which we discuss in Chapter 16). There are also *news alerts* to warn you of a newsworthy event that could affect one of your stocks; *earnings alerts,* which highlight a change in analysts' consensus estimates or buy/hold/sell recommendations or which alert you to the earnings announcement itself and a possible earnings surprise; and, least common of all, *technical alerts,* which notify you of a change in a stock's technical condition.

Here is a sampling of Web sites that offer portfolio trackers and alerts. See the CyberInvesting Guide at the end of this chapter for a feature-by-feature comparison.

DBC Online

http://www.dbc.com

As part of its MarketWatch subscription ($29.95), DBC Online offers real-time updates on as many as six portfolios with 10 securities each (stocks and options). You can update a maximum of 2,500 quotes a day. That means if you have the six portfolios of 10 stocks each, you can update them 41 times a day! DBC has price alerts for a 52-week high and news headlines by industry.

Dow Jones

http://bis.dowjones.com/clipping

Dow Jones' CustomClips service scans thousands of trade and industry publications for your customized list of names. Alerts are delivered either via e-mail or special Dow Jones software, downloadable at the site. (See Exhibit 13.1.)

INVESTools

http://www.investools.com

INVESTools' free Portfolio Workshop allows you to track 10 securities, with three portfolio views: extended quotes, portfolio holdings, and a

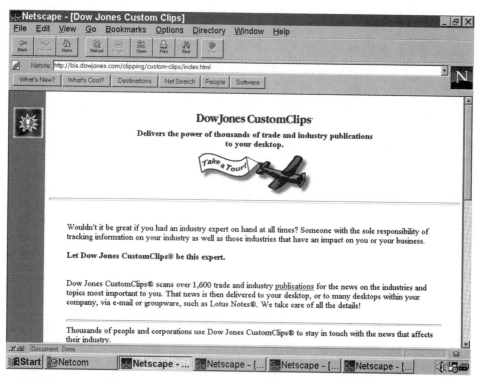

Exhibit 13.1 Dow Jones CustomClips has comprehensive news alerts delivered by e-mail.

summary of fundamental data. Subscribers may track either 20 or 100 securities, depending on the subscription level ($4.95 or $9.95/month). E-mail price alerts and news alerts are available with the subscription package. The news alerts also appear on the portfolio tracker where you can click through to the full-text article.

News alerts include research alerts that announce analysts' changes in their buy/sell recommendations or earnings estimates.

> **FYI** A unique "newsletter alert" offered by INVESTools provides a list of recent articles and reports that match your investing interests. To set up the alerts you must register at the site and select your interests from a list of asset classes, industry sectors, and general investment topics. The alerts are free, but if you care to see more than a headline, the reports or newsletters will cost from $1.25 to $16 each.

Macro*World @ Wall Street City

http://www.wallstreetcity.com

Macro*World portfolios include its Master Rating for each stock in a portfolio, in addition to the regular numbers. (A Master Rating is the combined average rating by all the analysts who follow the stock.) Click on the stock symbol and jump to Macro*World's research section to see the individual analyst ratings, price trends, and fundamentals.

E-mail alerts include five price alerts, two volume alerts, analyst revisions, earnings/dividends news, and company news. (See Exhibit 13.2.) Reports include a daily portfolio summary (by e-mail, if you wish) and an asset-allocation report, as described in Chapter 17. Subscription.

> **FYI** Notable Technologies (http://www.notable.com) marries the Web to an alphanumeric pager for its alerts. Enter your list of stocks at the Notable Web site and its wireless service called Septor will send price updates, high/low alerts, and volume alerts to your alphanumeric pager up to 15 times a day. It will also alert you to news stories by displaying a headline on your pager screen.

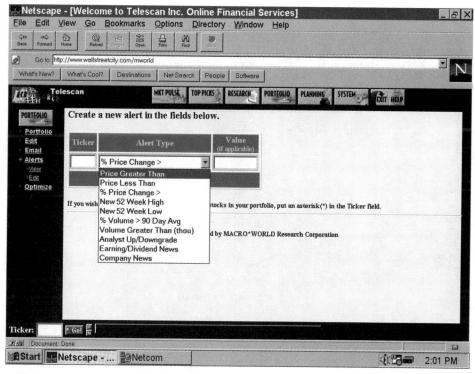

Exhibit 13.2   Portfolio alerts from Macro*World @ Wall Street City.

MarketEdge

http://www.marketedge.com

MarketEdge offers an unlimited number of portfolios with an unlimited number of securities in each (stocks, mutual funds, and bonds). (See Exhibit 13.3.) Stock alerts include expected earnings announcements, revisions in earnings estimates, earnings surprises, upgrades/downgrades in analysts' recommendations, dividend reports, significant insider trading, institutional shareholder activity, short interest ratio, and price changes of more than 3 percent. $7.95/month.

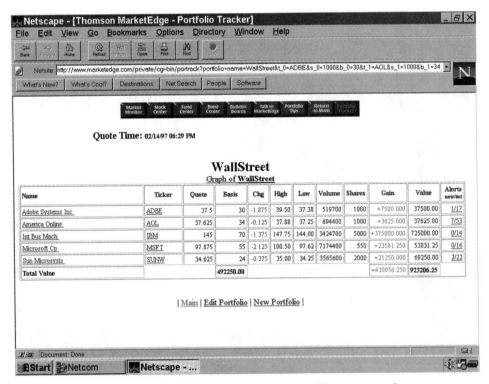

Exhibit 13.3   MarketEdge's portfolio tracker offers news alerts.

NETworth

http://networth.galt.com

At NETworth, you can track up to 50 stocks and funds.

The New York Times on the Web

http://www.nytimes.com

The New York Times offers news alerts by e-mail.

Newspage

http://www.newspage.com

NewsPage, from Individual, Inc., provides free real-time news with a customized NewsPage that tracks topics or companies of your choice. You can also browse the news by industry.

PAWWS Financial Network

http://pawws.com

PAWWS offers a cost-basis, tax-lot portfolio accounting service for $8.95 a month. It includes the PawTrack Stock Monitor which lets you track more than 150 securities, with instantaneous updates of real-time or delayed quotes (depending on the type of account you have). The service accommodates capital adjustments splits, name changes, mergers, distributions, and exchanges. Reports include dividends and interest received, valuation/transaction reports (e-mailed daily), an asset allocation graph, and a Schedule D for filing realized gains and losses with the IRS.

Quote.com

http://www.quote.com

At Quote.com you may track one portfolio with up to seven securities free of charge; subscribers have no limit on the number of portfolios or securities. Portfolio alerts include high- and low-price alerts and news alerts via e-mail. A calendar of expected earnings announcements with forecasted numbers is available to subscribers. Click through for a Zacks earnings estimate report. Portfolio reports include a valuation report, a holdings report, and a fundamental report that shows the EPS, PE, dividend, and 52-week high/low for each stock in the portfolio.

Reuters Money Network

http://www.moneynet.com

Reuters Money Network has a free portfolio tracker that will track up to 10 portfolios with 30 securities each (stocks, mutual funds, and options). Price and news alerts are sent via e-mail as frequently as twice a day. (See Exhibit 13.4.)

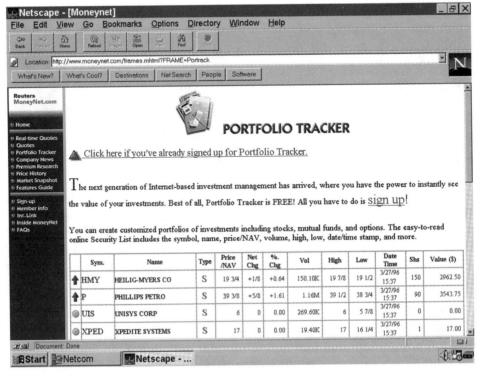

Exhibit 13.4   Reuters' portfolio tracker.

Stock Smart

http://www.stocksmart.com

The free and unlimited portfolio tracker at this site has four price alerts delivered by e-mail or pager. P&L reports are available.

> **FYI**   E-mail alerts can get out of hand if you have a lot of stocks in your portfolio. For a test portfolio of 7 stocks, we received 65 e-mailed headlines in one day. You can, fortunately, turn off the e-mail alerts and still receive the alerts in your portfolio.

Wall Street City

http://www.wallstreetcity.com

Wall Street City offers a unique "Scan My Portfolio" feature at the How Am I Doing? page which will analyze the stocks in your portfolio for technical breakouts, basing-pattern breakouts, and Telescan rankings. (See Exhibit 13.5.) The latter scan ranks your stocks against all other stocks in seven key areas: short-term and long-term technical rank; fundamental rank; volume rank (which measures money flow); analyst rank; momentum rank; and insider rank.

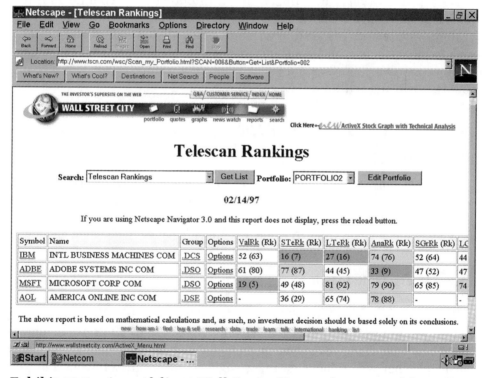

Exhibit 13.5 A portfolio at Wall Street City can be scanned for technical breakouts or for rankings of portfolio stocks against all other stocks, as shown.

You can create up to 7 portfolios with as many as 150 securities in each. Any of the portfolios may be scanned or used in any of the following areas:

1. The scrolling ticker at the home page.
2. To retrieve quotes, along with automatic price and news alerts. (News alerts, by the way, include news; earnings revisions, surprises, and announcements; insider trading reports; and the release of new S&P reports.)
3. At the News Watch page, which offers customized headlines to match your portfolio.

Wall Street City has announced that it intends to incorporate an Internet version of one of the most powerful, professional portfolio tracking systems available. This system will automatically adjust for stock splits, dividend payments, and similar corporate transactions. It will also generate numerous reports, such as transaction summaries of all types and reports for filing with the IRS.

The Wall Street Journal Interactive Edition

http://www.wsj.com

A Personal Journal can be customized to track news on 25 companies. You can also track up to 30 companies or funds in a simple portfolio that shows the last change, number of shares, and current value for each security. Subscription: $49/year.

Zacks Investment Research

http://www.zacks.com

Zacks' e-mail alerts summarize these changes on up to 20 stocks in a portfolio: price changes, revisions in analysts' earnings estimates, earnings surprises, changes in Zacks ranks, changes in buy/hold/sell recommendations, news, expected EPS report dates, and dividend declarations. Alerts can be sent daily or weekly. Multiple portfolios are available if you have multiple e-mail addresses.

FYI   If earnings estimates played an important role in the selection of a stock, don't wait for an alert. Check the Zacks reports (or other earnings estimates) at least monthly and make sure the estimates have not gone down. A downward revision is usually a harbinger of a decrease in stock price.

Monitoring Earnings and Dividends

Stock prices can rise or fall on whether or not a company fulfills the market's earnings expectations. Monitoring earnings releases, therefore, is a very important part of portfolio management. The key is whether the company met or exceeded the estimates reported by services such as Zacks.

You may also wish to monitor dividend announcements, if dividends are important to your portfolio. Dividends have an immediate effect on the price of a stock, because the price is reduced by the approximate amount of the dividend on the ex–dividend date.[1] If a stock you own pays dividends, you'll want to know when that date is and the amount of the dividend when it is announced.

Most news services carry earnings and dividend announcements; Business Wire (http://www.businesswire) and PR Newswire (http://www.prnewswire.com) carry the full news releases written by the company. The following sites are mentioned here because they offer special news categories (free) that make it easy to check on earnings or dividend announcements.

FYI   Astute investors pay attention to earnings expectations and announcements of key companies and leaders in industries in which they own stocks. These announcements can be harbingers of market or industry group action.

---

[1] The *ex–dividend date* is the date on which one must be a shareholder to receive the next dividend. It is the day when the dividend is subtracted from the price of the stock.

The Whisper Numbers

Ever wonder why a stock sometimes plummets when it meets or exceeds its earnings estimates? *Whisper numbers.* These are the numbers that those-in-the-know had expected, the numbers that had been bandied about in coffee rooms in the offices high above Wall Street. Whisper numbers may be several cents higher than the analysts' estimates that are published by firms such as Zacks and First Call. So an earnings announcement that looks like good news to the average investor can be a disappointment to the powers-that-be.

What's the answer to this information gap? Go for the long term. The slippage in stock price that may occur when whisper numbers aren't met is more harmful to the short-term investor. Hang in there for the longer term and give the stock a chance to recover.

Equity Analytics

http://www.e-analytics.com

Equity Analytics has a weekly list of expected earnings reports with the quarterly estimates and actual earnings for the comparable quarter a year ago. It also has a section that explains the significance of stock splits, reverse splits, and cash and stock dividends.

Stock Smart

http://www.stocksmart.com

Stock Smart has corporate earnings reports, announcements of ex–dividend dates, and announcements of dividends, stock splits, and the latest buy/hold/sell ratings by analysts.

Wall Street City

http://www.wallstreetcity.com

Wall Street City will soon offer ex–dividend date estimates and announcements, sponsored jointly by Standard & Poor's and Telescan.

Technical Monitoring

Technical analysis plays an important part in the monitoring process, whether or not you think of yourself as a technician. Many of the positive and negative reasons to sell a stock (recapped in Chapter 16) are prompted by a technical sell signal. It is important, therefore, to monitor your stocks from a technical standpoint.

We suggest that you look at the same technical indicators described in Chapter 10 that you used to buy the stock. When an important technical indicator turns negative, you may want to sell. This can be done weekly, if you're a long-term investor. We prefer to check short-term signals on a daily basis and longer term signals weekly. The ActiveX graphs at Wall Street City are the only technical timing tools we could find on the Internet at this writing. As the Internet matures, this will undoubtedly change.

A portfolio monitoring checklist is provided in Exhibit 13.6.

ACTIVITY	Daily	Weekly	Monthly	Quarterly
Update portfolio & review targets and stops.	✔			
Check out portfolio alerts.	✔			
Review all stock graphs with technical indicators.	✔	✔		
Run searches to generate new prospects.		✔		
Review market conditions and asset allocation.			✔	
Review quarterly earnings report.			✔	
Review new earnings estimates reports.			✔	
Review company reports.			✔	
Review insider trading.			✔	
Review industry group graphs.			✔	
Run industry group search.			✔	
Review annual and quarterly reports.				✔
Evaluate portfolio performance against market indexes or mutual funds.				✔
Review decision-making process to fine-tune investing strategy.				✔

Exhibit 13.6   Checklist for portfolio monitoring.

| Web site | Portfolio Composition | | Alerts
P = Price
E = Earnings
Est = Earnings est.
N = News
T = Technical | Earnings/
Dividend
Monitoring | Technical
Monitoring | Advanced Portfolio Features | | | |
	Number of Portfolios	Number of Securities in Each				Portfolio Analysis	Financial Planning	Asset Allocation	Reports
DBC Online http://www.dbc.com	6	10							
Dow Jones http://bis.dowjones.com			N						
Equity Analytics http://www.e-analytics.com				✓					
INVESTools http://www.investools.com	1	10, 20 or 100	P, N			✓			
Macro*World @ Wall Street City http://www.wallstreetcity.com			P, N, Est	✓		✓	✓	✓	✓
MarketEdge http://www.marketedge.com	UnLtd.	UnLtd.	P, E, Est	✓					
NETworth http://www.networth.galt.com	1	50							
The New York Times http://www.nytimes.com			N						
Newspage http://www.newspage.com			N						
Notable Technologies http://www.notable.com			P, N						
PAWWS Financial Network http://pawws.com		150							✓
Quote.com http://www.quote.com	Free: 1 $: UnLtd.	7 UnLtd.		✓					✓
Reuters Money Network http://www.moneynet.com	10	30	P, N						
Stock Smart http://www.stocksmart.com	UnLtd.	UnLtd.	P	✓					
Wall Street City http://www.wallstreetcity.com	7	150	P, N, E, Est, T	✓	✓	✓			✓
The Wall Street Journal http://www.wsj.com	1	25	N						
Zacks Investment Research http://www.zacks.com	1	20	E, Est	✓					

NOTE: See CyberInvest.Com *(http://www.cyberinvest.com)* for the latest revisions to this Guide.

Exhibit 13.7   The CyberInvesting Guide for Portfolio Monitoring.

FYI   At Wall Street City you can scan your portfolio for technical breakouts (short-term, intermediate-term, and long-term) and for basing-pattern breakouts.

The Last Word

You simply cannot be successful as an investor if you don't monitor your holdings. The market is too dynamic, individual stocks too susceptible, and the process of monitoring too simple not to include alerts and monitoring in your arsenal of Internet investment tools.

CHAPTER FOURTEEN

WINDOWS ON THE MARKET

When the Dow falls, it's time to go shopping.
—The Beardstown Ladies

The Dow is climbing toward 7,000 as we write this chapter. Its latest record-setting level is a staple of the nightly news. It has been the topic of an hour-long special on PBS. It is on everyone's lips at cocktail parties. But keeping up with the market is more than just checking the latest gyrations of the Dow. If you invest in stocks, it is important to do a little bit of market evaluation on a regular basis. Why? Because you may want to adjust your cash position or portfolio composition when the market becomes extended or invest more aggressively when it becomes undervalued.

In this chapter, we'll show you a quick and simple way to evaluate the technical condition of the market and show you where to find market news and commentary. We should point out, however, that regular attention to asset allocation, which we talk about in Chapter 17, may mitigate the need for continuous scrutiny of the market.

Using LSQ Lines to Evaluate the Market

One of the simplest ways to determine whether the market is dangerously extended, from a technical standpoint, is to look at its LSQ trading channels.

An *LSQ line* is based on a mathematical formula called *least squares*. The formula itself is unimportant. What is important is that when drawn on a market index (or stock) graph, an LSQ line roughly divides the price action in half. If you draw parallel lines on either side of the

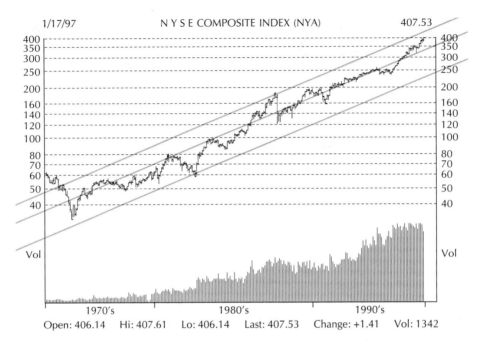

1/17/97   N Y S E COMPOSITE INDEX (NYA)   407.53

Open: 406.14   Hi: 407.61   Lo: 406.14   Last: 407.53   Change: +1.41   Vol: 1342

Exhibit 14.1   The New York Stock Exchange Index was well below the upper boundary of its long-term LSQ channel on 1/17/97. (Graph from Telescan Investment Platform.)

LSQ line, a trading channel is formed, as in Exhibits 14.1 and 14.2. The upper boundary, which should be drawn through at least two tops, shows the potential growth of the index or stock before it reaches long-term resistance (if you're using a long-term graph). The lower boundary shows a major support area. A market index (or stock) that is trading near the top of its long-term LSQ channel is dangerously extended and due for a correction or a trend reversal.[1]

The Dow Jones Industrial Average (the Dow) with its 30 stocks is much too narrow to be used for market analysis. We look at both the New York Stock Exchange (NYSE) index and the Nasdaq index, and we look at long-term and short-term graphs. You could also use the S&P

---

[1] These charts were created with Telescan Investment Platform for Windows because the trendline function (which includes the LSQ line) is not yet available at Wall Street City, although it will be soon.

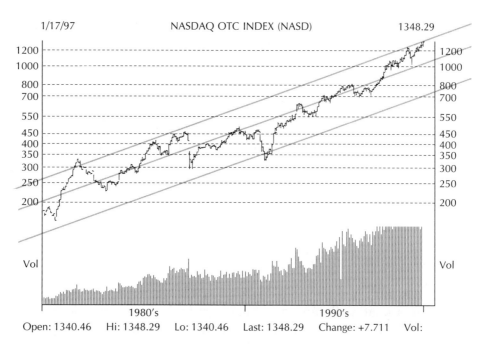

1/17/97   NASDAQ OTC INDEX (NASD)   1348.29

Open: 1340.46   Hi: 1348.29   Lo: 1340.46   Last: 1348.29   Change: +7.711   Vol:

Exhibit 14.2   The Nasdaq Index is at the top of its long-term LSQ channel on 1/17/97. (Graph from Telescan Investment Platform.)

500, which pretty much tracks the NYSE, or the Russell 2000, which represents stocks with smaller capitalization.

FYI   The various Russell indexes are described and tracked at the Russell Web site: http://www.russell.com.

The Dow has broken a succession of barriers in the past two years—4,000, 5,000, and 6,000—but the breaking of a psychological barrier doesn't necessarily mean that the market is extended. As a point of interest, when the Dow was at 4,000 in November 1994, both the NYSE and the Nasdaq were trading just *below* their LSQ lines. Despite the doomsayers who were trembling at the unprecedented level of the market, we believed—and said so in our Cyber-Investing book—that the market had a lot of room to grow before it reached the top of the LSQ channel. And grow it did, as we entered one of the longest bull markets in history. The technical condition of the market, however, was different in January 1997, when the Dow, the NYSE, and the Nasdaq were all near the top of their LSQ channels.

Additional technical evaluation can be done with the MACD (described in Chapter 10) and other technical indicators. If the weekly MACD is negative and the market is extended based on its LSQ line—as it was for both the NYSE and Nasdaq in mid-January 1997—we would consider the market in dangerous territory and due for a correction. What you do about this depends on your risk tolerance and the composition of your portfolio.

Market News and Updates

Many investing sites mentioned in these pages have some sort of market news and updates. Some have tickers showing current prices of the Dow, NYSE, and Nasdaq; others have tables that show the latest trading data for various market indexes. With regard to market news, usually you'll see a list of headlines which are hyperlinked to the full story. Some sites have expert commentary on the direction of the market. Here are a few sites you might want to check out.

Barron's Online

http://www.barrons.com

Barron's Online has several columns of market commentary, including "Up and Down Wall Street" by Alan Abelson; "The Trader" by Andrew Bary; "International Trader" by Neil A. Martin; "Current Yield" by Randall W. Forsyth; "Trading Points" by John Liscio; and others.

Bloomberg Personal

http://www.bloomberg.com

Between its World Markets page and Bloomberg News page, this site has the markets covered. Bloomberg's Snapshot of World Markets includes

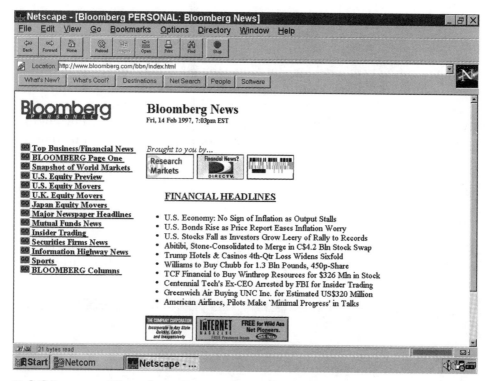

Exhibit 14.3   Bloomberg Personal: Market News.

a summary of activity in the equity, bond, currency, and commodity markets around the world. (See Exhibit 14.3.)

Briefing.com

http://www.briefing.com

Briefing.com provides free-market commentary and sector ratings, but to get its real-time market analysis—including upgrades, earnings reports, economic releases, technical trading points, and other market analysis—you'll need a monthly subscription ($6.95). An in-depth analysis of the fixed-income and FX market, live bond market commentary, and rapid analysis of economic releases will cost you $25.00 a month. The Market Calendar (shown in Exhibit 14.4) is free.

CNN Financial Network

http://www.cnnfn.com

CNN has intraday charts for the Dow, the S&P 500 and Nasdaq, plus details on the NYSE, Nasdaq, AMEX, and S&P 500 that include the most active, gainers, losers, 52-week highs and lows, and volume, high, and low alerts. There are also special pages on world markets, currencies, interest rates, commodities, and technology stocks. There are market news headlines and stories and a Bridge News page that covers the world.

DBC Online

http://mw.dbc.com

DBC Online's MarketWatch offers free market updates (delayed 15 minutes). Market commentary by Frank Barnako ("Online Investor")

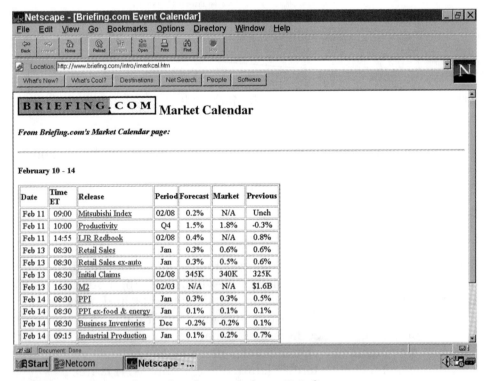

Exhibit 14.4 Market calendar page from Briefing.com.

and Derren Chervitz ("X-Pert Files") is part of its MarketWatch subscription. $29.95/month.

INVESTools

http://www.investools.com

INVESTools has a very thorough and user-friendly Market Update page (under Quotes & News; see Exhibit 14.5). The latest numbers for the Dow, the Nasdaq, and the S&P 500 appear automatically; click on the index name to see the chart. Headlines are shown for the current issues of *The Wall Street Journal* and the business sections of *The New York Times* and *The Washington Post*. Summaries with links to articles are categorized by issues to watch, IPOs, hot news in U.S. equities, Canadian markets, London markets, other foreign markets, U.S. technical trade publications, and press digests. There are company news head-

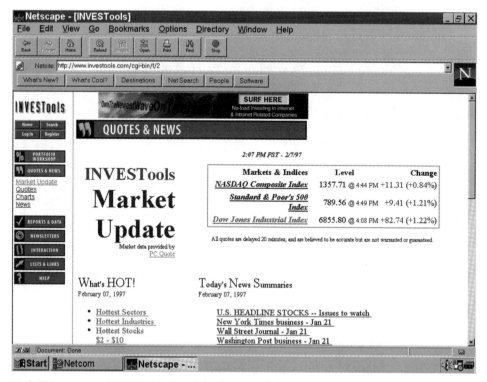

Exhibit 14.5   INVESTools: Market Update.

The Importance of Economic Reports

U.S. Government economic reports can give a B-12 shot to the market or send it reeling with a one-two punch. So it pays to be aware of release dates for the more important reports (especially important if you trade in index options). There are many Web sites that offer a schedule of upcoming economic events and announcements. Here are the few that provide clues to the expected numbers or explain the governmental jargon and acronyms.

Briefing.com (http://www.briefing.com) (See Exhibit 14.4.)

The Cyber-Investing Newsletter (http://www.wallstreetcity/com)

Fidelity Investments (http://personal.fidelity.com)

The Online Investor (http://www.investhelp.com)

lines, with links to articles, and news categorized by industry. Finally, you can customize a stock ticker for up to 20 stocks. Free.

Macro*World @ Wall Street City

http://www.wallstreetcity.com

Macro*World has an informative market wrap-up with a succinct text and graphic overview. A supplemental page recaps industry group performance (click on an industry to see a list of the five top losers and gainers for each industry). A "$flow" page shows the money flow into and out of the top 10 stocks. Other pages recap major world markets and recent stock splits. Short-term traders will appreciate the market timing signal based on the Macro*World forecasting indicators. Subscription.

MarketEdge

http://www.marketedge.com

MarketEdge's Market Monitor is updated four times a day with news affecting the market. The news is categorized by these topics: earnings surprises, mergers and acquisitions, industry news, technology stocks, credit markets, and the economy. There is also an analysis by investment professionals on the stories behind the headlines, a weekly economic calendar of events, and end-of-day market stats.

FYI   For a daily digest of some of the nation's top newspapers, visit the New Century Network at http://www.newcentury.com. This is a consortium of nine major media companies, including Gannett Co., The Hearst Corporation, Knight-Ridder, The New York Times, and The Washington Post.

Quote.com

http://www.quote.com

Quote.com offers real-time market index charts for the Dow, S&P 500, Nasdaq, and S&P 100. Free.

Reuters Money Network

http://www.moneynet.com

Reuters has a customizable Market Snapshot that includes indexes, news headlines, market stats, market commentaries, economic reports, and intraday graphs. (See Exhibit 14.6.) You can delete any of these sections, and you can select which indexes, market stats, and intraday graphs to include.

Stock Smart

http://www.stocksmart.com

The market news here has separate pages for Corporate Ratings (analysts' recommendations); Corporate Earnings; Dividends and Ex–Dividends; Canadian Companies; IPOs, Mergers, and Acquisitions; WEB, Internet, and Intranet; and Stock Splits, Dividends, and Ticker Symbol Changes.

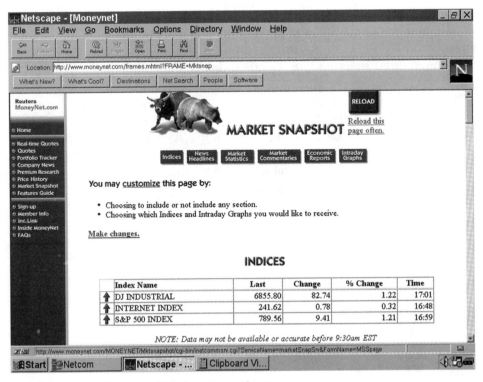

Exhibit 14.6   Reuters Market Snapshot.

USA Today

http://www.usatoday.com

USA Today has a robust Money page with market news from around the world, intraday charts for the Dow, AMEX, NYSE, Nasdaq, and the S&P 500, plus gold, oil, and T-bonds, with updates every two minutes. It also covers 29 major market indexes, plus performance tables for mutual funds, options, futures, and global markets.

Wall Street City

http://www.wallstreetcity.com

Wall Street City has a free Market Snapshot page that shows the quotes for the major market indexes (it can be customized to suit your preferences). Click on an index symbol to see an intraday graph. A news page offers free summaries and stories from Reuters. Market commentary by Mark Draud and Paul Alvim is updated twice a day. All this is free. A "Daily Market Reports" newsletter by Jerry Estill ($8/month) presents a daily poll of market sentiment by compiling opinions expressed in the mainstream financial media.

The Wall Street Journal Interactive Edition

http://www.wsj.com

The Journal has extensive coverage of the market for subscribers:

- ◆ The Marketplace page displays headlines and leading paragraphs of stories that affect the market.
- ◆ At the Money & Investing (M&I) page, click U.S. Stocks to see commentary about specific stocks within the domestic market, plus lists of most active stocks, gainers and losers, and listed options. Click Small U.S. Stocks to see commentary on the small-cap stock sector, with a graph of the Russell 2000 index.
- ◆ The Heard on the Street page has articles by Journal staffers on aspects of the market.

Check the Exchanges

For a market update on a specific exchange, you can go directly to the exchange:

- ◆ The American Stock Exchange (http://www.amex.com)
- ◆ The New York Stock Exchange (http://www.nyse.com)
- ◆ Nasdaq (http://www.nasdaq.com) Nasdaq accompanies its market summary with charts of Nasdaq activity, including the Nasdaq 100.

- ◆ Charts at the M&I page have the Dow Jones averages, with the component stocks listed for each average and hyperlinked to the stock's trading data.
- ◆ Check out the Year-End Reviews and the Market and Financial Scorecard.

If you get lost, the Index to Market Data provides a clean, clear list with hyperlinks to the Journal's market data pages.

When the Gurus Speak, Should We Listen?

Let's face it. Everyone has an opinion on where the market's going: your dentist, your doctor, your golfing buddies. And certainly, market gurus do. That is their stock in trade, so to speak.

Market gurus are yet another potential source of market advice. Typically, they are professionals who make their livelihood studying the market. Their careers depend on their ability to be more right than wrong in forecasting market direction. Thus, they are more aware than the average investor of expectations of the market, what is really news versus what has already been discounted. Have you ever been mystified by the fact that a government release of an important economic statistic seems to be gloom and doom but the market rallies? More often than not, this is because the market had already discounted a worse report than was actually received. Market gurus are generally aware of market expectations, and they know the market will be enthused by the better-than-expected number.

A recent example was the unemployment report. Figures were reported that seemed to be a major negative surprise to the network news anchors. Nonetheless, the market rallied. Why? The bad news was so bad it turned out to be good news. It squelched the idea that the Fed might raise interest rates, and that, it turned out, was more positive to the market than the unemployment figures were negative.

Market gurus devote their lives to trying to understand market expectations and predict its movements. They can gauge with a great deal more accuracy than the average investor, the market's likely reaction to specific news. Moreover, there are many other nuances in market psychology, which is often counterintuitive. You may need guru-reasoning capability to be able to appreciate the underlying causes and expectations of market behavior.

With regard to the direction of the market, however, you'll never find a consensus among the experts. For every three who are bullish, at least two are predicting the market's imminent demise. Even if there appears to be a consensus, many investors will react the opposite because they believe the consensus is wrong. Nevertheless, if you want to give the gurus a whirl, there are many on the Internet to choose from. All offer a free sample of their newsletter that you can view on-line (often requiring the Adobe Acrobat Reader), although many still deliver their subscriptions by fax or U.S. mail. We predict that Internet delivery will become the norm as the World Wide Web continues to grow and mature.

The following newsletters are devoted to market analysis.

Cognotick Market Service

http://www.cognotick.com

Cognotick Market Service is a market-timing newsletter with a daily, weekly, and monthly commentary on market action. It includes daily and weekly resistance and support price targets.

INVESTools

http://www.investools.com

Here are the newsletters at INVESTools which focus on the market.

Hussman Econometrics by Dr. John D. Hussman uses econometric models (based on dividends and interest rates) to forecast the market and the performance of individual stocks.

InvesTech Market Analyst, edited by James Stack, analyzes the Federal Reserve to discern the direction of the market and reviews upcoming economic indicators.

Market Mavens

http://www.tfc.com

Market Maven News & Views at the Financial Center On-Line looks at the financial markets through the eyes of John Bollinger, Bob Gabele,

J. Michael Pinson, Martin Pring, Bernard G. Schaeffer, Jay Taylor, and others. It also provides links to the mavens' home pages.

The Motley Fool

http://www.fool.com

The Motley Fool has irreverent market commentary in its Lunchtime News and Evening News sections.

PAWWS Financial Network

http://pawws.com

Dick Davis' Digest compiles information published by the financial community.

   Systems & Forecasts, published by Gerald Appel who popularized the Moving Average Convergence/Divergence (MACD) system, offers advice on market timing and portfolio management.

Standard & Poor's

https://www.stockinfo.standardpoor.com

Standard & Poor's offers the Standard & Poor's Advisor, a weekly newsletter that provides insight into market trends, among other things. S&P MarketScope at Home also has market commentary.

Wall Street City

http://www.wallstreetcity.com

At Wall Street City, newsletters that focus on market timing or market commentary can be found at the When to Buy and Sell page.

   The Cyber-Investing Newsletter by David Brown, Mark Draud, and Paul Alvim offers market commentary based on the Brown Breakout Ratio, a market-timing indicator that gauges short-term market direction.

   The Inger Letter by Gene Inger is a short-term market timing letter with a focus on technology stocks. Inger also publishes stock, bond, and gold projections for the next day via e-mail. The Inger Letter is also available at the PAWWS Financial Network.

Market Forecast by Keith Moored Jr. forecasts the direction of the stock market based on fundamental economic data, technical data, interest rates, and investor psychology.

Market Line by Steve Naremore distills the market commentary of other investment advisors.

The Wall Street Digest by Don Rowe examines the fundamental and technical influences on the economy in general, and on the stock and bond markets in particular.

The Wall Street SOS by Jerry Gentry features a proprietary timing system called the Bull/Bear Index.

Worth Online

http://www.worth.com

Worth Online offers the advice of Greg Millman in its weekly "The Market Week Ahead." Millman is the author of *The Vandals' Crown: How Rebel Currency Traders Overthrew the World's Central Banks.*

The Last Word

Frankly, market watching is probably an activity on which most investors spend too much time. Studies have repeatedly shown the difficulty of projecting market movements, and many other studies have shown the wisdom of being more or less fully invested at all times. Nonetheless, there are simple tools that allow you at least to be aware of when the market is very extended or has bottomed out. Prudent investors tend to trim their portfolios at extended periods and load up at the bottom, although a reasonable adherence to asset allocation will probably accomplish this task for you.

CHAPTER FIFTEEN

THE RISE AND FALL OF INDUSTRY GROUPS

> *It almost goes without saying that a strong stock in a strong group is going to outperform a strong stock in a weak group. The former is swimming with the tide while the latter goes against it.*
>
> —John Bollinger

Industry groups were invented in order to track and analyze groups of similar stocks. Standard & Poor's started it all, with their breakdown of stocks into about 200 industry groups. Since then, Dow Jones created its own grouping, with about 75 groups, as did Investor's Business Daily, with some 197 groups. More recently, John Bollinger made a statistical study of groups to find those stocks that trend together and came up with 104 groups for his Group Power report. The S&P groups are the standard, however, and the ones used at most Web sites for industry group statistics.

The theory underlying industry groups is that companies in similar businesses are affected in similar ways by various market conditions. High expectations, for example, about the future of microcomputers will cast a rosy glow over all companies that build, service, distribute, or base their businesses on microcomputers. Fears about health care reform will contaminate all companies that have anything to do with the health care field.

All companies within a group will not react the same, of course. Sometimes a company will appear to go counter to the group. But if the group is a cohesive one—that is, if the stocks within the group are strongly correlated on fundamental characteristics—trends will emerge in a clear-cut manner. We now have the tools to analyze such trends.

Industry Group Rotation

Why should you care about industry groups? Because they represent one of the most significant opportunities for the individual investor.

This opportunity is fueled by institutional trading, which accounts for more than 70 percent of all trading. When an industry group begins to edge into the economic limelight, institutions are usually the first to take notice, accumulating shares in the stocks they believe have the best chance for near-term success. However, institutions have one major problem: They are very, very large. They tend to invest millions of dollars in a single stock, and it takes them days, weeks, even months to accumulate a position without causing a precipitous rise in the stock price. Nevertheless, the price inevitably goes up, as one institution builds its position in the same stock. It is as if several leviathans are trying to get into a bathtub without raising the water level.

In fact, the flow of institutional money into an industry group creates a tidal wave. As the number one stock in a group becomes overvalued, comparatively speaking, the institutions turn their attention and dollars to the second-ranked stock, and when that stock becomes overvalued, attention will shift to the next best stock, and so on down the list. When this happens, the industry is said to be rotating upward or into favor.

When a group loses favor with the institutional investors, because of fears about the industry or because another, hotter industry has caught their attention, the reverse process sets in. Institutional money begins to flow out of the stocks in that industry (often much more abruptly than it flowed in). The industry is now said to be rotating downward or out of favor.

Riding the Wave . . .

Industry group rotation isn't this clear-cut, of course. But we now have the tools to analyze industry groups and observe the beginning of the tidal wave as institutions move into a group or a specific stock. And therein lies the unique opportunity for individual investors.

Our relatively small trades give us the nimbleness to jump into a stock in a matter of minutes, enjoy the effect of the institutional tide on the stock price, and take our often handsome profits (using the same tools) before the institutional ardor cools and the tide ebbs.

You can use industry group tools in the first step of the investing process—when you're prospecting for stocks—to be sure the stock you buy is in an upwardly rotating group. You can also use industry group analysis as part of the portfolio management process. When you detect a group beginning to move out of favor, you might want to consider selling the stock, although other factors will play a role, as we will talk about in the next chapter. Search tools can also be used to track the ebb and flow of industry groups.

FYI   Some Web sites track sector performance, as well as industry group performance. A *sector* is a group of industry groups. For example, the automotive sector includes not only automobile manufacturers, but also related industry groups such as parts and service.

What's Rotating on the Web?

The rotation of industry groups can be discerned with technical analysis tools, search tools, ready-made lists, or industry group commentary. These tools are available at the following Web sites.

How Important Are Industry Groups, Really?

Just how important is it to be in the right industry group? Charles Ellis has an interesting take on this question in his book, *Investment Policy: How to Win the Loser's Game.*[1]

  Ellis compares two hypothetical portfolios of $1,000 over a 33-year period from 1940 to 1973, one with perfect market timing and one with perfect industry-group timing. We added a buy-and-hold portfolio for comparison's sake.

[1] Charles D. Ellis, *Investment Policy: How to Win the Loser's Game,* Second Edition (Chicago: Irwin Professional Publishing, 1993).

Continued

Using the Dow Jones Industrial Average as a proxy, the hypothetical portfolio with perfect market timing had 100 percent of the funds invested in all rising markets and 100 percent in cash in all falling markets. The hypothetical portfolio with perfect industry-group timing was always 100 percent invested and always invested in the one best industry group. The hypothetical buy-and-hold portfolio had invested 100 percent of the funds in the Dow 30 and held them for the 33-year period.

The hypothetical results? Over the 33-year period, the $1,000 in the buy-and-hold portfolio would have grown to $34,000. The $1,000 in the portfolio with perfect market timing would have grown to $85,937. The $1,000 in the portfolio with perfect industry group timing would have ballooned into—drumroll please—more than 4.3 billion dollars!

Ellis calls the example absurd, and of course, it is, because no one is likely to invest in the one best industry group all the time. Ellis also pooh-poohs the whole idea of market timing, but we and many, many others side with John Bollinger, whom we quoted at the beginning of this chapter: A strong stock in a strong group is swimming with, rather than against, the tide. Why not take advantage of the group momentum? It can do nothing but buoy the performance of a strong stock.

Briefing.com

http://www.briefing.com

Briefing.com rates 23 sectors on a scale of 1 to 5 (1 = outperform; 5 = underperform) with a ranking of stocks within the sector.

DBC Online

http://www.dbc.com

DBC Online has industry group summaries for more than 30 groups that include the daily trading data for the top stocks in the industry. This is also hyperlinked from *USA Today*'s Money page.

Macro*World @ Wall Street City

http://www.wallstreetcity.com

Macro*World publishes lists of best and worst industries based on its forecasting indicators. It also shows its price forecasts for 97 industry groups for 1, 7, 30, and 90 days and 1 year, along with graphs of the same.

Market Guide

http://www.marketguide.com

Market Guide has a series of "what's hot and what's not" performance charts for sectors, industry groups, and stocks. Start with a sector chart and click on a sector name for a performance chart on industry groups in that sector. (See Exhibit 15.1.) At that chart, click on an industry group to

What's Hot / What's Not
All data as of February 11, 1997
Industry Price Performance

Industry	1 Day Price Chg %	5 Day Price Chg %	P/E	Div. Yield (%)	Price to Book	ROE (%)	Debt to Equity	Rev. Qtr vs Yr Ago	EPS Qtr vs Yr Ago
Oil Well Services & Equipment	3.0	-6.8	28.2	1.7	4.0	15.3	0.4	39.1	48.1
Computer Peripherals	2.2	-10.6	34.9	1.8	9.4	30.6	0.1	67.2	42.6
Printing & Publishing	2.2	4.2	25.5	1.7	4.3	13.0	1.1	7.2	50.6
Computer Hardware	2.0	-3.6	18.6	1.0	4.4	21.9	0.6	11.3	22.0
Waste Management Services	1.6	-2.6	36.0	1.9	4.0	2.9	1.0	4.2	-7.4
Oil & Gas - Integrated	1.5	-1.9	15.8	3.2	2.9	18.5	0.4	21.1	31.9
Beverages (Non-Alcoholic)	1.3	-0.5	43.0	1.0	18.5	46.8	1.0	2.9	-3.9
Oil & Gas Operations	1.1	-3.9	22.2	2.1	3.5	13.5	1.0	41.6	45.6
Airline	1.1	-0.3	17.5	0.4	2.3	20.1	1.3	7.3	13.9
Apparel/Accessories	1.0	1.2	23.3	1.4	3.4	6.4	0.7	11.8	28.9

Exhibit 15.1   A sector price performance chart from Market Guide. A similar chart is available for industries.

see a performance chart for the stocks in that industry group. Finally, at the stock chart, click on a stock symbol to retrieve a Market Guide Snapshot. This "what's hot and what's not" series is also available at the INVESTools Web site (http://www.investools.com). All are free.

Quote.com

http://www.quote.com

Quote.com allows you to access data for major industry groups, including biotechnology, consumer electronics, Internet stocks, and four computer groups (PCS, workstations, networking, software).

Standard & Poor's

http://www.stockinfo.standardpoor.com

S&P provides an in-depth industry analysis as part of its Enhanced Stock Reports. (See Exhibit 15.2.) The analysis looks at the forces affecting the industry's growth and offers a peer comparison for valuing a company relative to other companies in the same industry. The analysis is updated monthly. The report costs $4.95.

FYI   The Stock Room (http://www.stockroom.org) has a cool way of looking at industry sectors. Thumbnail graphs of 35 Fidelity Select Sector Funds are displayed side by side to reveal at a glance the relative performance of each sector over the past six months. Click on a graph to get a full-sized price-and-relative-strength graph for that sector. Even if you're not a Fidelity funds investor, this will give you a quick graphic look at where the action is.

Stock Smart

http://www.stocksmart.com

Stock Smart gives you a quick way to compare the daily performance of different industries or different companies within an industry. It displays the daily percentage change for 29 sectors and 110 industry

STANDARD & POOR'S
STOCK REPORTS

Sun Microsystems

08-FEB-97

INDUSTRY OUTLOOK

Our longer-term investment outlook for the S&P Computers (Hardware) industry remains positive. During 1996, the index gained 35% versus a 20% rise for the S&P 1500. In the month ended January 31, 1997, the index rose 7.4% versus a 5.7% gain for the S&P 1500. Prospects for the industry remain bright led by strenghtening corporate demand for PCs and the continued build-out of the internet/intranet. Nevertheless, we expect shares of companies in this segment to remain extremely volatile near term and we counsel investors to approach these investments with a longer-term perspective.

The fundamentals in the computer industry remain strong, mainly due to a growing global appetite for technology products that increase productivity. Worldwide competition is forcing companies to become more productive, a task being accomplished largely through the employment of technology. While this trend is favorable for computer system vendors, the industry is still dominated by intense competition that can quickly turn today's leaders into tomorrow's losers. The new computing paradigm demands that vendors constantly introduce new, more powerful, and cheaper versions of successful

products, while keeping a tight rein on operating expenses.

A profitable trend in the computer industry through 1997 is expected to be the continued movement toward client-server computing. This model promotes the use of networks of cheap, yet powerful, PCs and servers, versus larger, more expensive, and proprietary mainframe computers. Companies that specialize in migrating customers to this new model -- like Hewlett Packard and Sun Microsystems -- are expected to be key beneficiaries. Another key trend is the growing implementation of corporate "intranets," which are internal corporate networks based on existing Internet technologies. These intranets require high-powered servers that are fueling a new product class for many hardware companies. Fundamentals in the PC industry will remain challenging to all participants, as new competitors and price pressures will challenge profitability. Nevertheless, we expect that strong international growth and a strong upgrade cycle, fueled by a new version of Microsoft's Windows NT operating system, will boost prospects. We view Compaq as a attractive play here, while Dell and Gateway remain core holdings.

Industry Stock Performance

Related S&P 1500 Industry Index

Computer (Hardware)

Month-end Price Performance As of 01/31/97

OTHER INDUSTRY PARTICIPANTS

Principal Peer Group	Stock Symbol	Recent Stock Price	P/E Ratio	12-mth. Trail. EPS	30-day Price Chg %	1-year Price Chg. %	Beta	Yield %	Quality Ranking	Stk. Mkt. Cap. (mil. $)	Ret. on Equity %	Pretax Margin %	LTD to Cap. %
Sun Microsystems	SUNW	34	24	1.44	29%	41%	0.92	Nil	B	12,488	21.8	10.0	2.6
Amdahl Corp.	AMH	11⅛	NM	-2.71	-5%	44%	0.89	Nil	C	1,350	3.2	3.3	11.8
Apple Computer	AAPL	15¾	NM	-6.99	-10%	-43%	1.10	Nil	B	1,969	NM	NM	28.2
Citrix Systems	CTXS	44¼	65	0.68	-4%	141%	NA	Nil	NR	1,176	NM	NM	NA
Comdisco, Inc.	CDO	30⅞	15	2.08	0%	39%	1.28	0.9	B	1,532	15.2	7.6	75.3
Compaq Computer	CPQ	82⅝	18	4.72	13%	62%	1.27	Nil	B	22,375	19.0	8.1	6.1
Concord EFS	CEFT	22¾	51	0.45	-17%	41%	0.15	Nil	B+	1,370	NM	NM	NA
Dell Computer	DELL	65¾	31	2.10	17%	311%	1.12	Nil	B	11,512	36.3	7.2	10.5
Digital Equipment	DEC	35¼	NM	-2.47	-3%	-53%	1.48	Nil	C	5,460	NM	NM	21.7
Gateway 2000, Inc.	GATE	60¾	19	3.21	18%	122%	NA	Nil	NR	4,658	37.2	7.1	1.9
Micron Electronics	MUEI	20	35	0.57	-11%	48%	1.57	Nil	B-	1,849	22.2	4.5	7.3
NCR Corp.	NCR	35⅞	NM	-1.07	4%	NA	NA	Nil	NR	3,633	NM	NM	NA
NEC Corp.	NIPNY	55¾	24	2.37	-12%	-10%	0.64	0.8	NR	17,240	9.2	3.6	51.9
Silicon Graphics	SGI	25¼	NM	-0.17	1%	-13%	0.38	Nil	B	4,417	7.7	6.3	18.5
Stratus Computer	SRA	32⅝	18	1.83	19%	18%	NM	Nil	B	769	3.6	3.7	1.5
Tandem Computers	TDM	13⅝	NM	-0.11	2%	35%	0.92	Nil	B-	1,617	NM	1.2	6.5

Exhibit 15.2   Standard & Poor's Industry Outlook Report for the computer/hardware group.

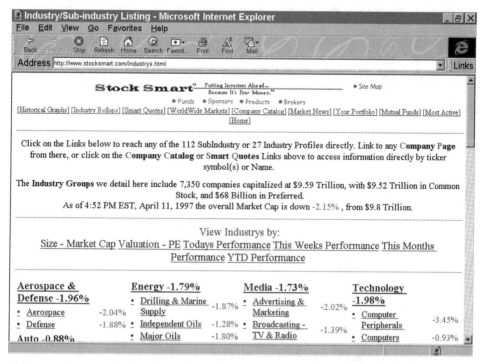

Exhibit 15.3   Stock Smart: Industry Group Performance page.

groups. (See Exhibit 15.3.) Click on a group name and go to an industry profile that lists every company in the industry, with its P/E ratio, market cap, and stock data (price, change, open, high, low, volume). Click on a company name and go to a page of information about the company that includes a graph comparing the stock to its industry and the S&P 500. If there is a "News!" notation for the company, click it and read the full story. All free.

StreetNet

http://www.streetnet.com

StreetNet has in-depth articles on different industries with a list of recommended stocks in the featured industry. (See Exhibit 15.4.)

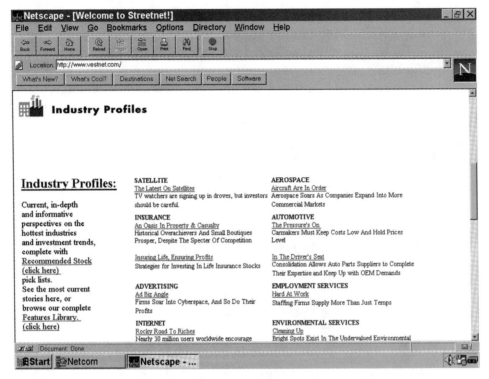

Exhibit 15.4   StreetNet's Industry Profiles.

USA Today

http://www.usatoday.com

USA Today's Money page has trading summaries of stocks by industry groups, which will tell you which stocks in the groups are the best performers.

Wall Street City

http://www.wallstreetcity.com

Wall Street City is in a class by itself when it comes to analyzing industry groups.

Most of the following is at the Research & Info page:

◆ *Industry Group ranking chart.*   Click Industry Group Analysis to display a color-coded bar chart which ranks all 200+ industry groups against all other groups. (See Exhibit 15.5.) The green bars on the right show groups with positive percentile rankings; the red bars on the left show groups with negative percentile rankings. Click on an industry bar to jump to a price-and-volume graph for that industry group.

◆ *Price-and-volume graph.*   The industry group graph is overlaid with a daily advance/decline line and 6-day high-low graph. The time span can be changed to 2, 3, 4, 5, 10, and 15 years or to the maximum span in the database. The group is weighted for capitalization, but you may retrieve a graph of the unweighted group, if you prefer.

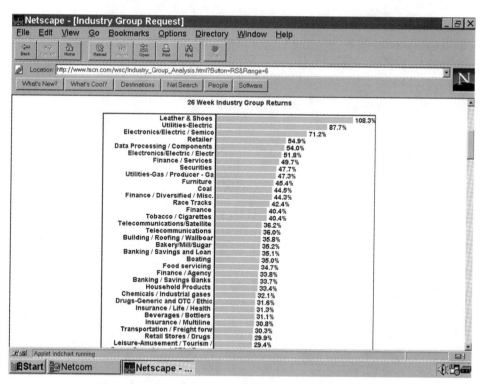

Exhibit 15.5   Wall Street City's Industry Group Rankings. The chart includes all 200+ industry groups in the Telescan database.

Web site	Market Update	Market Commentary	Index Charts Avail.	Index Charts Tech. Analysis	Market News Business	Market News Categories	Market News Global	Economic Calendar	Market Gurus	Industry Group Analysis
American Stock Exchange http://www.amex.com	✔									
Barron's Online http://www.barrons.com	✔	✔			✔	✔	✔		✔	
Bloomberg Personal http://www.bloomberg.com	✔	✔			✔	✔	✔			
Briefing.com http://www.briefing.com	✔	✔			✔	✔	✔	✔		
CNN Financial Network http://www.cnnfn.com	✔				✔	✔	✔			
Cognotick Market Service http://www.cognotick.com		✔							✔	
CyberInvesting Newsletter http://www.wallstreetcity.com		✔						✔	✔	
DBC Online http://www.dbc.com	✔	✔	✔		✔	✔	✔			✔
Fidelity Investments http://personal.fidelity.com	✔									
INVESTools http://www.investools.com	✔	✔	✔	✔	✔	✔	✔		✔	✔
Macro*World @ Wall Street City http://www.wallstreetcity.com	✔		✔	✔	✔	✔	✔			✔
Market Mavens http://www.tfc.com		✔							✔	
MarketGuide http://www.marketguide.com										✔
MarketEdge http://www.marketedge.com	✔	✔	✔		✔	✔	✔	✔		✔
The Motley Fool http://www.fool.com		✔			✔					✔
Nasdaq http://www.nasdaq.com	✔									
The New York Stock Exchange http://www.nyse.com	✔									
The Online Investor http://www.investhelp.com		✔						✔		
PAWWS Financial Network http://pawws.com		✔							✔	
Quote.com http://www.quote.com	✔	✔	✔		✔	✔	✔			✔
Reuters http://www.moneynet.com	✔	✔	✔		✔		✔	✔		
Russell Indexes http://www.russell.com	✔									
Standard & Poor's http://www.stockinfo.standardpoor.com		✔			✔	✔	✔			
The Stock Room http://www.stockroom.org										✔
Stock Smart http://www.stocksmart.com	✔		✔		✔	✔	✔		✔	✔
StreetNET http://www.streetnet.com										✔
USA Today http://www.usatoday.com	✔		✔		✔	✔	✔	✔		
Wall Street City http://www.wallstreetcity.com	✔	✔	✔	✔	✔		✔	✔	✔	✔
The Wall Street Journal http://www.wsj.com	✔	✔	✔		✔		✔		✔	
Worth Online http://www.worth.com		✔							✔	

NOTE: See CyberInvest.Com (http://www.cyberinvest.com) for the latest revisions to this Guide.

Exhibit 15.6 The CyberInvesting Guide for Market/Industry Group Monitors.

- *Stocks in an industry group.*   At the industry group graph is a similar ranking chart for stocks in that group, plus a list of stocks with current trading data. Click on a stock symbol to retrieve a stock graph and list of corporate reports.
- *ActiveX graphs.* With an ActiveX graph, you can plot industry groups for any time span and use the whole array of technical indicators described in Chapter 10. In addition, there are several indicators created for analysis of industry groups or indexes. (At the How Am I Doing? page.)
- *Search tools.*   To search for stocks within a specified industry, click the hyperlink at that industry group graph, which automatically selects that industry group and takes you to a ProSearch screen where you can create the search. Use the Industry Group category search to find the best-performing industry groups.
- *Newsletters.*   John Bollinger's "Group Power" letter (at the When to Buy & Sell page) is a study of the power of industry group rotation.

The Last Word

We know of no better advantage for the individual investor than that presented by industry group rotation. When observed properly, rotating industry groups will tell us where the institutional action is. Those who can move quickly can profit from the upsurge in prices caused by institutional favor. And when it comes to moving quickly, individuals have it all over the institutions.

CHAPTER SIXTEEN

PLANNING THE SELL

No amount of planning will ever replace dumb luck.
—Anonymous

The whole raison d'être of monitoring a portfolio is to determine when to hold on to a stock and when to sell it. Obviously, you don't want to sell too soon and miss a big upsurge in stock price, but you want to sell before the stock reverses direction. Our rule of thumb is to sell when the risk/reward relationship that existed at the time we bought the stock changes significantly. To put it another way, if an event creates a condition that would have prevented us from buying the stock in the first place, we will usually sell it.

For example, if your decision to buy a stock rested on a 20 percent earnings growth forecast, and two months later the company announces earnings growth of only 10 percent, you may want to sell the stock. If you followed the insiders' lead in buying a stock, you may want to follow their lead again if they suddenly start selling the stock en masse. If you bought a stock because eight analysts had given strong buy recommendations and you find out they're now chorusing "sell," you may want to do as they say.

These are what we call "negative reasons to sell," but in the absence of a negative reason, we will still monitor the stock carefully, because the risk/reward ratio changes as a stock moves toward its target. The closer it gets to the target, the more quickly we will use any excuse to sell (which we call "positive reasons to sell"). This becomes clear if you think about the potential upside and downside of the stock when you purchased it.

Let's say, for example, you buy a $12 stock, believing the price will increase to at least $20. The potential upside then is $8, and, for the sake of argument, we'll say you analyzed the downside at about $3. If the stock goes to $18, the remaining upside may now be only $2 or $3 while the downside could be as much as $9. The risk/reward relationship has changed, and it is almost certain there are other stocks with a more favorable risk/reward relationship.

Every situation must be judged individually, however. In the above example, the company's earnings may justify a new, higher target (say, $30) if some time has gone by since the purchase of the stock. If so, we'd hold on to the stock and monitor it as it moved toward the new target.

You can use the same Internet tools for determining this risk/reward relationship that you use in the monitoring process described in Chapter 13. Preliminary to that, however, is planning the sell—setting targets and stops.

Reasons to Sell

There are many reasons to sell a stock. Here are 11 that we've dubbed positive and negative reasons.

The Positive Sell

A *positive sell* can occur when a stock nears its target and one of the following events occurs. These do not always trigger a sell, but we do reassess the situation.

- ◆ A technical indicator gives a short-term sell signal.
- ◆ The stock's P/E ratio nears its high or well exceeds the industry average.
- ◆ The stock falls below the tight stop that we set to protect our profits.
- ◆ We've found another stock with a better risk/reward ratio, which has given a buy signal.

Continued

The Negative Sell

When we buy a stock, we base our decision on certain positive factors, such as strong industry group momentum, strong earnings estimates, high insider buying, and other positive expectations. When one of these factors changes for the worse, we will generally sell the stock. *Negative reasons* to sell, then, include:

- The stock falls and hits a stop.
- There's a significant downward revision in earnings estimates.
- The company has a negative earnings surprise or disappointing earnings.
- The company announces other bad news that could affect the stock's performance.
- There is a large increase in insider selling that we deem significant (such as the chairman selling half his holdings).
- The industry group loses momentum.
- A stock that is far from its target generates a sell signal. We may not act on the signal, but we will closely reassess the situation.

Setting Targets

Setting a target that you expect a stock to reach is an important part of the investing process. Otherwise, you would have no idea of how to gauge the stock's progress. A *target* is not just a number that you pull out of thin air, or at least it shouldn't be. It should have some relation to the past and projected trading pattern of the stock.

There are several technical indicators that can predict a stock's potential upward path, and we've found it convenient to use a series of targets based on several of these indicators. For example, short-term targets can use the upper boundary of a short-term LSQ channel and/or the upper boundary of trading bands. Any strong resistance level is a good intermediate target. The upper channel of a long-term LSQ channel is a good long-term target. (See, for example, Exhibits 16.1 and 16.2.)

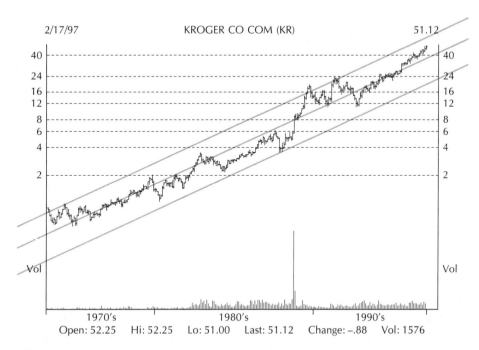

2/17/97   KROGER CO COM (KR)   51.12

Open: 52.25   Hi: 52.25   Lo: 51.00   Last: 51.12   Change: –.88   Vol: 1576

Exhibit 16.1   A long-term target for Kroger based on the LSQ trading channel would be about $60. (Graph from Telescan Investment Platform.)

You may also want to consider targets set by others. Analysts often set price targets for a stock in their research reports. These are sometimes reported as news, especially when the target is a change from a previously announced target. Price targets may also appear in stock reports or company profiles.

FYI   Macro*World @ Wall Street City offers an easy way to set targets and stops. For targets, there are specific price levels forecasted for the Macro*World database of stocks, over various time frames, based on Macro*World economic models. A probability rating tells you their confidence level that the increase or decrease will be achieved. Macro*World also suggests stops for long and short positions in a particular stock. (See Exhibit 16.3.)

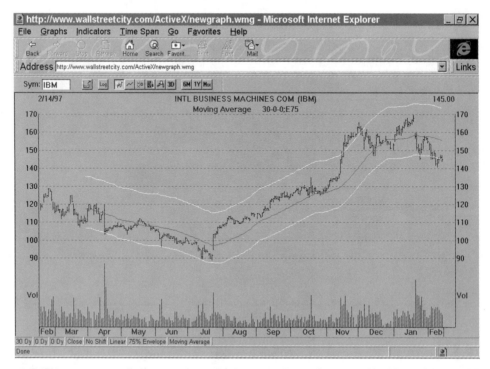

Exhibit 16.2   A short-term target for IBM based on trading bands would be about $160. (Wall Street City.)

Setting Stops

Stops are set to protect profits or minimize losses. We recommend an initial stop and then interim stops that move up as the stock advances.

The Initial Stop

We set an *initial stop* a few points below the purchase price or just below a strong support level. (We set ours 15 to 20 percent below our entry price; others prefer stops as tight as 7 percent.) Initial stops are important because a stock may fall immediately after you purchase it. Then you have to decide whether or not you made a mistake in your evaluation and if and when to cut your losses. It matters at this point what the market is doing. If your stock falls 20 percent and the market has fallen 15 percent, that's not so bad. The time to be alarmed is if your stock falls 20 percent while the market rises 15 percent.

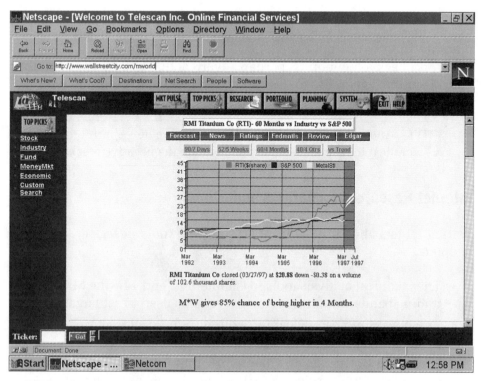

Exhibit 16.3 Using Macro*World's price projections, a four-month target for RMI Titanium would be about $26.

We use mental stops in the early stages as opposed to hard stops. *Mental stops* are simply reminders to ourselves to reassess the conditions surrounding a stock if it falls to a certain level. A *hard stop* is a stop order given to a broker to sell the stock if it falls to a specific price level. The sell is automatic with a hard stop, so we use it only to lock in profits when a stock is nearing its target.

Interim Stops

As a stock advances, we move our stops higher to protect our profits. How much higher is a matter of personal preference. Many investors use support and resistance zones (available on technical charts) to set stops somewhat less arbitrarily.

When a stock nears its target and the risk/reward relationship becomes unattractive, we will switch to a hard stop, because we're looking for any reason to sell. We will enter a formal stop order that instructs the broker to sell the stock if it drops, say, 5 percent below the current price. This is the only time we recommend a hard stop. Why? Because a stock will often pull back a few points, perhaps overreacting to a news event, then begin its climb again, in which case you may wish to continue with it.

FYI   Another way to use mental stops is to review short-term technical indicators each day and sell on the negative breakout.

Internet Resources for Targets and Stops

Setting targets and stops require some of the tools described in earlier chapters.

- The technical analysis tools in Chapters 10 and 14—the MACD, trading bands, and LSQ channels—can be used to set targets.
- The news sources in Chapter 9 often include a target price set by an analyst who is revising an earnings estimate.
- The portfolio tracker in Chapter 13 that updates your stocks can be used to set price alerts that can double as mental stops.
- The broker in Chapter 12 who takes your buy and sell orders can also take your stop orders.

The decision to sell a stock does not take place in a vacuum. The above list clearly shows that the sell decision is part and parcel of the whole portfolio management process. We've given it a separate chapter in order to elaborate on the subject.

The Last Word

You haven't made a profit in a stock until you close the position. *Planning to close*—the setting of targets and stops and monitoring a stock's progress—must be part of the process. Otherwise, it is unlikely that the actual close will be on terms of your choosing.

PART SIX

Investment Strategies

Up to this point, we've concentrated on stocks. But few investors invest only in stocks. Some rarely if ever use stocks, preferring instead mutual funds, bonds, and bank CDs. Others have a portfolio mix that encompasses global securities and even options. This section considers the resources on the Internet for creating a diversified portfolio with some or all of these investment vehicles. First, we talk about how to plan an ideal portfolio. Then we look at the Web sites that offer prospecting and evaluating resources for mutual funds, bonds, bank CDs, global securities, and options.

CHAPTER SEVENTEEN

THE IDEAL PORTFOLIO

Diversification helps spread risk and opportunity.
—NAIC Investment Guideline

One of the most common mistakes investors make is ignoring *asset allocation*—the process of determining the right blend of assets to meet their investment goals and tolerance for risk. Instead, they put all their money in stocks, or in stocks and cash, or in one type of mutual fund. Time has proved this to be a less-than-optimal investing strategy.

An ideal portfolio is a *diversified* one. It is accomplished with asset allocation which takes into consideration market conditions, interest rates, and the risk/reward potential of various asset classes.

An *asset class* is a broad group of similar securities, the major classes being domestic equities (stocks and mutual funds), bonds, cash, and foreign securities. Within these classes, however, are many subgroups. For example, domestic equities include mutual funds and stocks; mutual funds encompass stock funds, bond funds, and money market funds; stocks have subgroups for large-cap stocks, mid-cap stocks, and small-cap stocks, and within each of those subgroups are industry groups. Bonds, cash, and foreign securities also break down into subgroups, each offering different levels of risk and return.

Asset allocation is based on the fact that different asset classes respond differently to major economic factors, thus producing greater or lesser returns as economic conditions change. Past performance is one way to judge the future performance and risk of asset classes, but it is not the only way or the best. The risk/reward relationship of asset classes changes rapidly, sometimes even weekly, and what is prudent in January may not be prudent in July or December of the same year.

For example, in January 1994, a dynamic asset-allocation model would have put next to nothing in long-term bonds for most investors, because at that time they had an extremely unfavorable risk outlook. In fact, long-term bonds declined more than 20 percent that year, but the following year interest rates had once again brightened the outlook for bonds, and long-term bonds were typically allocated to be 20 to 40 percent of a model portfolio.

Because the economy is dynamic, asset-allocation tools should predict the future performance of asset classes based on current and expected economic events. In the past, this kind of asset allocation was the province of professional investors because they were the only ones who could afford the detailed study of macroeconomics that underlies any effective asset allocation program. Now asset allocation is available to the individual investor on the Internet.

The Macro*World Asset-Allocation Plan

Macro*World @ Wall Street City (http://www.wallstreetcity.com) is one of the leading forecasters of economic conditions. Its statistical forecasting models cover all securities, all major market indexes, industry groups, interest rates, commodity prices, and economic factors. Each night the massive Macro*World database is updated with the day's new financial and economic information; then the system re-analyzes all the data and updates its forecasts. This dynamic model assures a timely and historically accurate forecast. Simply put, the system checks through historical data to see what kind of economic conditions were produced by financial and economic events similar to those that exist today. In this way, they can forecast conditions that will be produced by today's financial and economic events.

Happily, these are the same forecasts that form the basis of the investment signals and asset allocations in the newest Macro*World product for the individual investor, the Macro*World Investor available at Wall Street City. Investors can now update their portfolio mix with the very latest forecasts. We should point out that asset allocation should be reviewed three or four times a year, not daily or weekly.

Here's how Macro*World's asset-allocation system works.

FYI   The Macro*World Model Portfolio realized a 37 percent
annualized return over the past 12 years. Lists of stocks with
Macro*World forecasts are available as prospecting tools, as
described in Chapter 3.

Creating a Personal Investment Plan

Identifying your investment objectives is the first step in asset allocation.
You need to assess your current financial profile and determine your
future needs. These, plus your level of tolerance for risk, will help you
decide which assets will meet your needs at this time. Macro*World
takes you through a series of screens that asks questions about the types
of assets you have (or want), your time horizon, and your acceptable risk
level. (See Exhibit 17.1.) Then, based on this information, Macro*World:

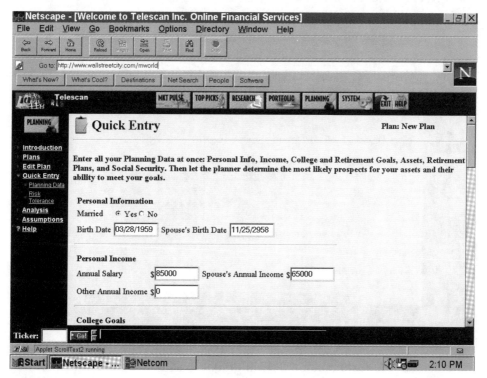

Figure 17.1   A quick entry data screen for Macro*World's Personal
Investment Plan at Wall Street City.

- ◆ Analyzes the expected returns and risk of your current mix of investments
- ◆ Runs a computer simulation of how your investments may behave in the future
- ◆ Compares the results of these simulations with your goals

If there are inconsistencies between your goals and your investment plans, Macro*World presents up to three options to remedy the situation. The summary of the options for our sample portfolio is shown in Exhibit 17.2. If you want to experiment with variables, such as retirement age or retirement goals, use the What If screen shown in Exhibit 17.3.

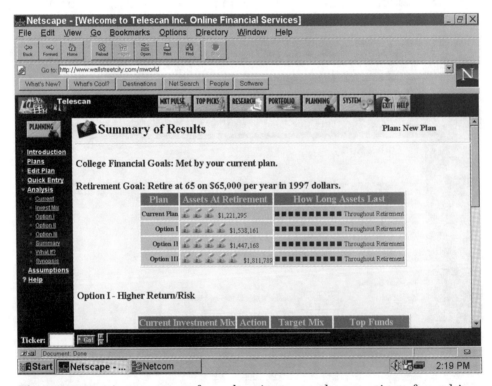

Figure 17.2 A summary of results gives you three options for achieving your Personal Investment Plan. (Macro*World @ Wall Street City.)

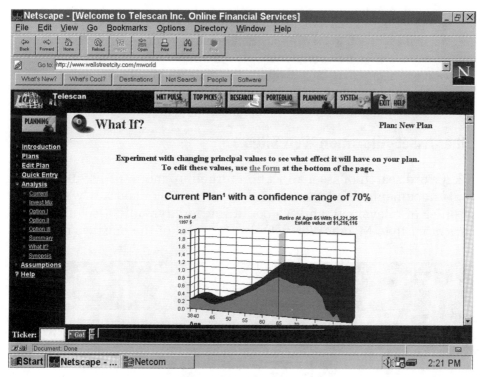

Figure 17.3   A "What If?" screen lets you experiment with variables.
(Macro*World @ Wall Street City.)

Allocating Assets

The second step in Macro*World's asset-allocation system requires a bit
more work on your part. The Personal Investment Plan gave the system
your investment objective, risk tolerance, and time horizon. Now you
have to tell the system which asset classes you are willing to consider. The
Macro*World list includes 97 industry groups, 50 domestic market
indexes, and 15 non-U.S. markets. You must go through the list and check
the ones you are willing to have in your portfolio. Then click the Optimize
button at the bottom of the screen and Macro*World does the rest, dis-
playing the percentage of your portfolio that it suggests be allocated to
each of the asset classes, based on the forecast of each asset's performance. If you're dissatisfied with some of the assets included, simply go
back and remove those asset classes from the system.

FYI   Charles Schwab (http://www.schwab.com) offers a simplified approach to asset allocation. You can complete the Personal Investor Profile, or choose one of five plans that range from conservative to aggressive. (See Exhibit 17.4.) This isn't based on market forecasts, but it's a place to start and it's free.

Other Asset-Allocation Web Sites

A keyword search of asset allocation turned up more than 17,000 "relevant" documents! We looked at only the top 100 or so (they were listed in order of relevancy), and we could find no dynamic asset-allocation sites other than Macro*World. Only a handful of the ones we reviewed

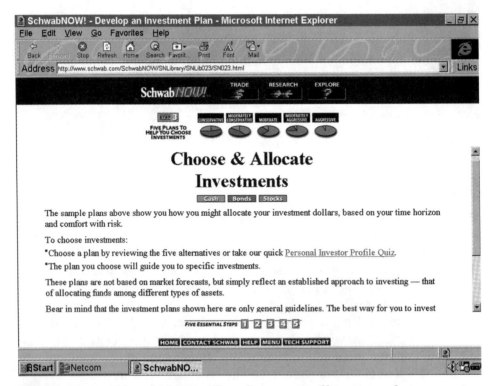

Figure 17.4   SchwabNOW offers five asset allocation plans, ranging from conservative to aggressive.

were truly relevant to the individual investor. They are grouped in this section as advisory sites and software vendor sites.

FYI   Many mutual fund families offer asset allocation among their family of funds. The top 20 fund families are listed in Chapter 18, along with several Web sites that offer links to fund families.

Advisory Sites

Many of the investment advisors offer free educational material which might be of interest to the novice investor.

Cambridge Advisors (http://www.cambridgeadvisors.com) has an article entitled "Asset Allocation: Balancing Your Portfolio." (This is an alliance of "fee-only" personal financial advisors.)

Community Financial Planning Services (http://www.comfin.com) asks you to fill out a free on-line questionnaire to determine your investment objectives and risk tolerances. Then it gives you recommendations for a proper mix of mutual funds. They suggest a follow-up with their asset-allocation service, for a fee.

Interactive Advisors Group (http://www.iadvisor.com) provides asset-allocation services.

InvestorWEB (http://www.investorweb.com/asset1.htm) has a two-part article by Bob Costa entitled "Asset Allocation for the Absolute Beginner."

Karagosian Financial Services, Inc. (http://toinvest.com/assetmix.html) gives you (gratis) its recommendations for the best current asset-allocation mix. We could not determine the type of investor this was meant for, but it looked like a good mix.

LPL Financial Services (http://www.sddt.com/~lplreilly/asset/asset allocation.html) is a fee-based asset management company in San Diego, which may not interest you, but an article by Donald F. Reilly and D. Todd Reilly might. Entitled "A Time-Tested Investment Strategy," it is about strategic asset allocation vs. market timing.

Merrill Lynch's Investor's Handbook at its Investor Learning Center page (http://www.ml.com/investor/assetal.html) has a section on asset allocation that gives you an instantaneous asset mix based on five investment personality types from conservative to risk-taking.

Financial Planning Sites

While not related specifically to investing, the following sites may be worth a look for simplified financial planning:

American Express (http://www.americanexpress.com/advisors)

Fidelity Investments (http://www.fidelity.com)

John Hancock (http://www.jhancock.com)

Massachusetts Mutual Life Insurance (http://www.massmutual.com)

Phoenix Insurance Investments (http://www.phoenixhomelife.com)

Prudential Securities (http://www.prusec.com)

Pioneer National Bank in Duluth, Minnesota (http://www.pioneer-bank.com) offers a personalized asset-allocation analysis free of charge through an independent brokerage service.

Software Vendor Sites

Most asset-allocation software is either too simplistic to be useful or too sophisticated or expensive for the individual investor. We offer the following so you can see for yourself.

Advisor Software, Inc. (http://www.advisorsw.com) is the creator of Windows-based software that shows you how to accomplish asset allocation using mutual funds. Mutual Max is for the individual investor; Mutual Fund Advisor is for the professional.

LaPorte Asset Allocation System (http://www.laportesoft.com) has sophisticated analytical tools for professionals and high net worth investors.

Reuters Money Network (http://www.moneynet.com) offers Wealth-Builder, an all-purpose financial planning program that uses a "Nobel-prize-winning asset allocation model" to develop an optimal investment mix.

The Last Word

Asset allocation is important in the long run, because the market is a kaleidoscope of changes. Interest rates rise and fall, the economic outlook varies, world economies rotate. As the Internet matures, more and more investing sites will no doubt incorporate some form of asset allocation. If you're serious about investing, you will want to become familiar with its basic principles.

Now, let's look at some of the investing vehicles that might be included in an optimum portfolio.

CHAPTER EIGHTEEN

MUTUAL FUND MANIA

If you were permitted to know only three things about a mutual fund before deciding whether to own it, these are the questions you should ask: How well does this fund do in bull markets? How well in bear markets? What does it cost to own it?

—James M. Clash
"How to Rate a Fund"
Forbes 1996 Mutual Fund Survey

The growth of mutual funds over the past 15 years has been nothing less than astonishing. In 1980 there were 564 funds with assets of $135 billion. At the end of 1994, there were 5,371 funds with assets of $1.2 trillion.[1] Since, then, money has continued to pour into this sector at record levels, with new funds being created almost faster than new public companies. The result is a pool of more than 9,500 funds in a mind-numbing array of categories: U.S. stock funds, global stock funds, foreign stock funds, taxable bond funds, municipal bond funds, junk bond funds, global bond funds, index funds, Treasury funds, Ginnie Mae funds, money market funds, sector funds, specialized funds that focus on emerging markets, "ethical" investing, natural resources, precious metals, real estate, short selling, small companies, Internet stocks, and one fund designed to appeal to the youngest investors, our children. Whew!

Finding the fund best suited to your investment goals now takes almost as much effort as finding the right stock. The Internet comes to the rescue with an abundance of Web sites offering aid and assistance to the "mutual-fund-challenged."

---

[1] *Mutual Fund Fact Book* (Investment Company Institute, 1995).

Finding the Right Fund

Finding the right mutual fund in which to invest is a little like searching for the right job or the right spouse. There are a number of ways to pre-qualify the job or the mate of your dreams, but you don't really know if you've made the right decision until you have lived with them a while.

When searching for mutual funds, you should first consider your investment goals, your tolerance for risk, your need for liquidity, and your time horizon. Then look at the fund's characteristics: its objectives, size, risk level, and short-term and long-term performance. Performance, by the way, should be considered in conjunction with a fund's management—historical performance won't mean as much if the fund has a new manager. Finally, you'll want to know the fund's minimum investment requirement, fees and sales charges, if any, and expense ratios.

The Internet offers a variety of tools to help you do this. There are the usual best and worst lists, a few screening tools, and one full-blown search engine for mutual funds. There are Web sites that offer mutual fund profiles and rating systems for evaluating funds. There are market fund gurus eager to share their knowledge and fund selections (for a fee). There is a growing archive of educational material to bring you up to speed on the newest fund types and the latest slant on investing strategies. Give it another year, and a guide to mutual funds on the Web could fill an entire book.

Here are the sites we've found thus far that offer the best information and guidance on mutual funds.

Quotes and Charts

Mutual fund quotes are available from any broker that trades mutual funds (see Chapter 12). Net asset value (NAV) charts can be found at many sites, including:

> MarketEdge (http://www.marketedge.com)
> Mutual Funds Online (http://www.mfmag.com)
> NETworth (http://networth.galt.com) See Exhibit 18.1.
> Wall Street City (http://www.wallstreetcity.com)

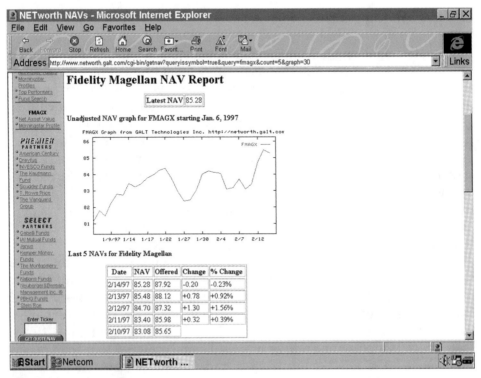

Exhibit 18.1   A NAV chart for Fidelity Magellan from NETworth.

The EDGAR Files

http://www.sec.gov

The EDGAR files at the SEC site includes filings for mutual funds. So do most of the EDGAR-enhanced sites mentioned in Chapter 7.

Forbes Magazine

http://www.forbes.com

In its annual Mutual Fund Survey Forbes rates almost 2,000 funds and presents a searchable database of Best Buy tables for U.S. stock funds, international stock funds, taxable bond funds, and municipal bond funds. A Best Buy table for Fidelity Magellan is shown in Exhibit 18.2. Forbes has a detailed guide on how to use the tables.

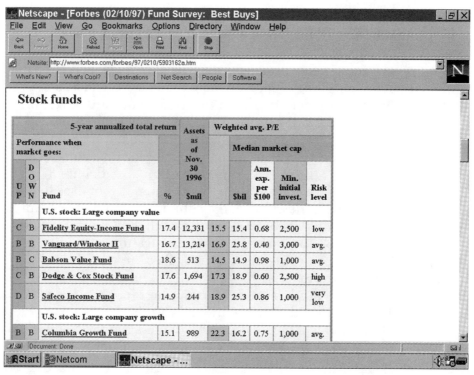

Exhibit 18.2 Forbes' 1996 Best Buy Tables for stock mutual funds.

Fortune Magazine

http://www.fortune.com

Fortune Magazine has a searchable mutual fund database and a ranking of 250 top-performing funds. To find these, click the Investors Guide under Special Issues/Lists.

INVESTools

http://www.investools.com

Morningstar Reports OnDemand is available here. (The Adobe Acrobat Reader is required.) There is also a screening feature that lets you search for funds based on their Morningstar rating, minimum annual return over a specified period, and minimum annual yield.

Morningstar: The Definitive Guide to Mutual Funds

Morningstar, Inc. is the premier rating and analysis service for mutual funds, compiling reports on more than 7,700 funds, such as the one shown in Exhibit 18.3. The report includes a description and analysis of the fund, historical profile, management description, tax analysis, investment style, list of portfolio holdings, evaluation of the fund by a Morningstar analyst, and Morningstar ratings.

Morningstar.Net (http://www.morningstar.net) debuted in March 1997, just as we were editing this chapter. It promises to be a dynamic site, with news, a daily column by publisher John Rekenthaler, planning features, and research and performance data for more than 7,700 funds. A screening feature should be in place by July. The coolest feature is the X-Ray View, at the Monitor Page, where you can enter your portfolio of funds and discover the exact nature of your holdings. Morningstar reports can also be obtained through several sites mentioned in this section, namely INVESTools, NETworth, Quote.com, and Reuters Money Network. They are also available from America Online and CompuServe.

Kiplinger Online

http://www.kiplinger.com

Kiplinger Online has lists of top-performing stock mutual funds and bond mutual funds (by categories) for 1, 3, and 5 years. There are also lists of largest stock funds and bond funds.

Macro*World @ Wall Street City

http://www.wallstreetcity.com

Macro*World has a Master Rating system for mutual funds shown in the Rating and Return chart (Exhibit 18.4). The Master Rating is the overall average rating by analysts who follow the fund. The chart also shows the Morningstar rating, historical ratios for the past 1, 3, 5, and 10 years, and the Macro*World forecasted returns for the next 10 years.

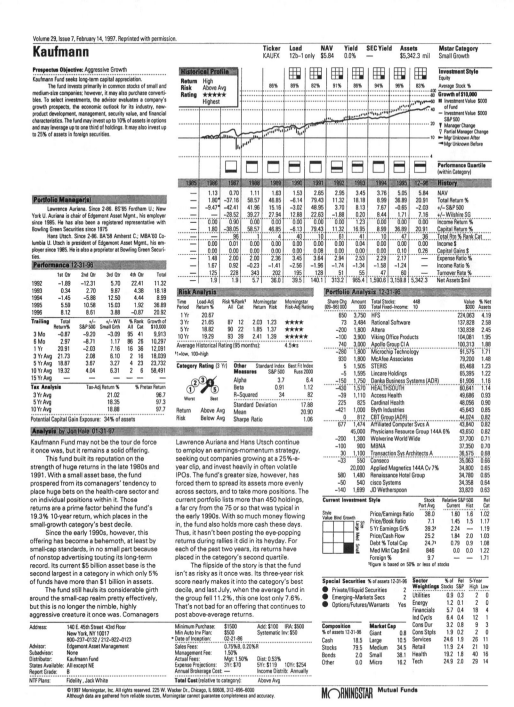

Exhibit 18.3 A Morningstar Report for the Kaufmann Fund. Reprinted with the permission of Morningstar, Inc.

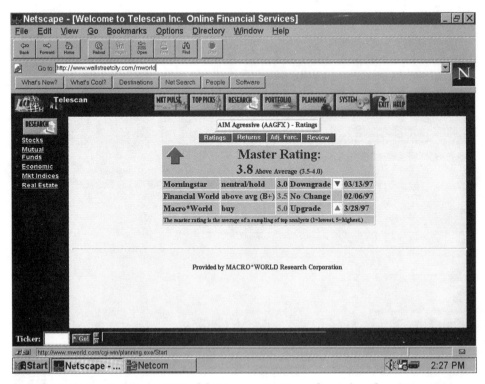

Exhibit 18.4   A Macro*World Master Rating chart for the Aim Aggressive Growth Fund. (Macro*World @ Wall Street City.)

For prospecting, Macro*World has lists of its top-rated stock funds, bond funds, and balanced funds, plus lists of funds with the highest 5-year returns. (Click Research, then Funds.) You can screen the Macro*World database with your own customized criteria, although we found the screen for customizing the criteria a bit complicated.

MarketEdge

http://www.marketedge.com

Thomson Financial Services, the company behind the MarketEdge site, has its own comprehensive reports for over 5,000 mutual funds. The reports include an overall rating by Thomson, plus NAV charts.

The mutual fund database may be screened (by subscribers) with 12 variables based on fund performance, risk categories, age of fund, size of fund, and investment objective. Prospects can also be gleaned from the monthly lists of top-performing funds in two dozen categories, and from the monthly Mutual Fund Overview, which points out emerging trends and funds to watch. (See Exhibit 18.5.) Click on a fund symbol to pull up an NAV chart.

FYI   Want to talk mutual funds with some fund-loving friends? Try the misc.invest.mutual newsgroup. The FAQ for this group can be found at the Syndicate Web site (http://www.moneypages. com/syndicate). Also, Mutual Fund Interactive has a newsgroup monitored by its staff.

Mutual Fund Interactive

http://www.fundsinteractive.com

Mutual Fund Interactive calls itself "*The* mutual fund's home page." It offers news and features on mutual funds and interviews with leading money managers (via link with Bloomberg Personal). There are also links to related funds sites and several links to Canadian funds.

Mutual Funds Online

http://www.mfmag.com

This subscription-based site has a searchable database of some 9,500 mutual fund profiles, which include ratings, key investing information, and charts. Back issues are available through the October/November 1994 issue. There are jumps to fund families and other fund services. For prospecting, check out their annual All-Star Awards (Fund of the Year, Comeback of the Year, Manager of the Year, etc.). There are also the usual performance ranking lists. A personalized page lets you monitor articles and news on funds of your choice.

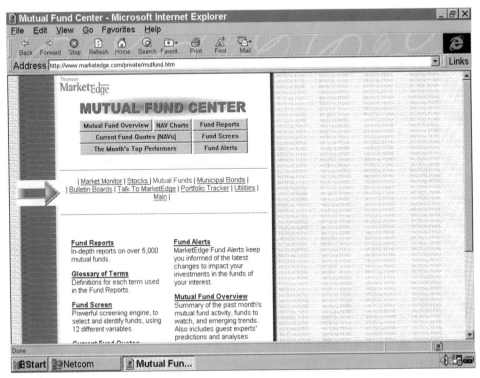

Exhibit 18.5   MarketEdge's Mutual Fund Center.

NETworth

http://networth.galt.com

NETworth has a free list of the 25 top-performing funds for different time frames, with links to each fund's Morningstar profile and NAV chart. For registered users, a screening engine will screen some 7,500 funds by category or by all categories, using a variety of criteria.

PAWWS Financial Network

http://pawws.com

At the PAWWS Mutual Fund Information Center you can order investing kits and prospectuses from various fund families free of charge.

Quote.com

http://www.quote.com

Quote.com has Morningstar reports and ratings for subscribers.

Research:

http://www.researchmag.com

Research: has 2- to 4-page reports on more than 3,000 funds, including profiles, performance, and portfolio analysis. At the Fund Screens page you can select a fund by inserting your own criteria.

Reuters Money Network

http://www.moneynet.com

Reuters Money Network offers 6- to 8-page Morningstar reports on a per-report basis ($4.95 each). To order a report, you must have a First Virtual account (which is described in Chapter 7.)

Stock Smart

http://www.stocksmart.com

Stock Smart has free lists based on a variety of statistics.

- The 20 largest mutual funds with net asset value and percent change in NAV.

- Weekly and monthly lists of best and worst performers in several categories.

- A performance ranking of over 5,000 funds with comparisons to similar fund types and the S&P 500.

- An annual list of the top 50 best performing funds.

Mutual Fund Families

Here are the URLs for the top 20 mutual fund families on the Web. Links to these and other fund families can be found at many sites. Two of the most complete listings are Mutual Funds Online at the Screens, Reports & Tools page (http://www.mfmag.com), and Tradeline Mutual Fund Center (http://nestegg.iddis.com/mutfund). The latter includes a list of the funds within a family.

FUND FAMILY	URL
Aetna Fund Series	http://www.aetna.com
AIM Funds	http://www.aimfunds.com
Alliance Funds	http://www.alliancecapital.com
Dean Witter Funds	http://www.deanwitter.com
Dreyfus Funds	http://www.dreyfus.com
Federated Funds	http://www.fedservco.com
Fidelity Funds	http://www.fidelity.com
John Hancock Funds	http://www.jhancock.com
Kemper Funds	http://www.kemper.com
Merrill Lynch Funds	http://www.ml.com
Nations Funds	http://www.nationsbank.com/mutual_funds
Prudential Funds	http://www.prusec.com
Putnam Funds	http://www.putnminv.com
Salomon Brothers Funds	http://www.salomon.com
Schwab Funds	http://www.schwab.com
Scudder Funds	http://www.scudder.com
Smith Barney Funds	http://www.smithbarnery.com
T. Rowe Price Funds	http://www.troweprice.com
Van Kampen American Capital Funds	http://www.vkac.com
Vanguard Group	http://www.vanguard.com

Tradeline Mutual Fund Center

http://nestegg.iddis.com/mutfund

There are more than 500 fund families listed in the Mutual Fund Directory at this site, with brief descriptions and contact information for each. The site features two weekly focus lists: One is a fund family; the other is a specific investment objective, with a list of representative funds. Click on a fund symbol in one of these lists for an NAV chart and other data.

Wall Street City

http://www.wallstreetcity.com

Wall Street City offers one of the few bona fide search engines for mutual funds, and it's free!

Mutual Fund Search has 82 criteria for designing a search and three different ways of searching (elimination, ranking, or list-only). You can use up to 40 criteria in a single search, and you can search all funds or limit your search to one of 25 different types of funds. The criteria includes all the standard items, plus historical performance in up and down markets, risk-adjusted performance, portfolio composition, and more. Our search, shown in Exhibit 18.6, took about 20 seconds.

If you don't want to build your own search, you can generate 82 different prospecting lists of the top 20 funds using any of the criteria used by the search engine. Actually, there are more than 2,000 possible lists because you can request a list from all funds, or from any of the 25 different categories!

Click on the fund symbol in any list or search report to retrieve an NAV chart. From there, you can go to a fund profile which lists the fund's management, investment objectives, minimum investment requirements, composition of the portfolio, and performance figures.

F^{YI} If you have a sense that the market is at the tail end of a long upward climb (although one never knows for sure), you may want to use the down market premium indicator in Mutual Fund Search at Wall Street City. This will find mutual funds that have done well in down markets.

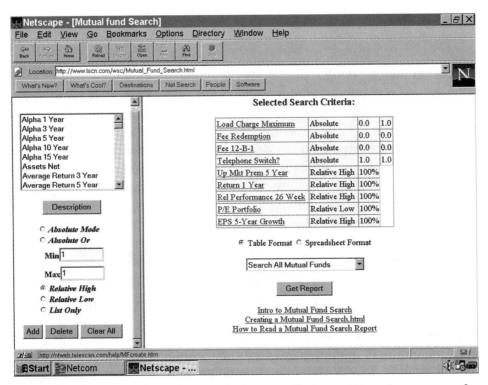

Exhibit 18.6   A mutual fund search at Wall Street City. Seven out of a possible 82 criteria have been selected.

Open-end versus Closed-end Funds

An *open-end fund* is an investment company that pools money from shareholders and invests in a variety of securities. It is open-ended in that the number of shares in the fund is not limited, or closed. An open-end fund continuously offers new shares to investors and buys back shares at their net asset value (NAV), which is the market value of a fund's investment portfolio. When we talk about mutual funds or fund families in this chapter, we're talking about open-end funds.

A *closed-end fund* is an investment company that issues a limited number of shares in its company to the public and trades them over a stock exchange or Nasdaq, just like a stock. The price of such shares, like the price of a stock, is determined by the market.

The Wall Street Journal Interactive Edition

http://www.wsj.com

The Journal's Mutual Fund Scorecards list the top 15 and bottom 10 performing funds in 30 categories, based on their 12-month return. Available to subscribers only at the Personal Finance page.

The Gurus of Mutual Funds

There are many experts on mutual funds who are willing to share their knowledge with you, for a price. If that's where your interest lies, there may be something to learn from such gurus. There is, however, some question as to how much advice a mutual fund investor really needs from outside sources, once a fund has been selected.

By purchasing the fund, you've asked the fund manager to manage the investment. The guru, in effect, is attempting to micromanage the fund manager. Taken to its ridiculous extreme, one could imagine gurus who rate the gurus who rate the fund managers; then someone who rates the gurus who rate the gurus who rate the fund managers; and so on. At some point, you will have to decide that enough is enough.

That said, here are three Web sites that host mutual fund gurus. Subscription prices begin at $89 a year.

INVESTools

http://www.investools.com

All Star Funds, edited by Ron Rowland, is based on strategic concepts of sector rotation and management-style rotation. Published monthly.

Closed-End Fund Digest by Patrick Winton picks the best opportunities from closed-end funds and REITs. Published monthly.

Equity Fund Outlook by Thurman Smith tells you about promising new funds and offers several model portfolios. Published monthly.

InvesTech Mutual Fund Advisor, published by InvesTech Research and edited by James Stack, applies a blend of monetary and technical analysis to mutual fund recommendations and tracks the performance of a select list of funds. It also offers specific switching advice in all major fund categories.

No-Load Fund Analyst offers analysis and research on no-load funds, plus updates on its no-load fund model portfolios.

PAWWS Financial Network

http://pawws.com

Peter Eliades' Stock Market Cycles makes recommendations for two mutual fund groups: Fidelity Select and Rydex.

Fabian Premium Investment Resources covers domestic, international, and gold markets for serious mutual fund investors who want, in their words, "to enhance their profits and control market risk."

Fidelity Monitor by Jack Bowers has four portfolios of Fidelity funds: a conservative income model, a growth and income model, a growth model, and an aggressive model that trades Fidelity Selects.

Jay Schabacker's Mutual Fund Investing tells you which funds to buy and sell, and why. Three portfolios are provided: Growth, Growth with Income, and Long-term Growth.

MoneyLetter by Walter Frank and Ralph Norton is a mutual fund advisory letter with four portfolio strategies based on risk.

Wall Street City

http://www.wallstreetcity.com

The Fund Advisor by Don Rowe publishes a list of the top 50 mutual funds each month. He also lists the top 30 funds in various categories.

Mutual Fund Advisor by Bruce Sankin trades mutual funds using several technical indicators for buy and sell signals and provides the list of funds followed. Updated monthly.

FYI   International funds are discussed in Chapter 21, along with other global securities.

Monitoring Your Funds

It is almost as important to monitor the ongoing performance and changes in mutual funds as it is to monitor stocks. The bottom line is that you're paying someone to manage your money for you, and it makes sense to check up on that person from time to time. The items to watch are the fund's quarterly return, changes in portfolio composition, and changes in management. Doing this quarterly seems reasonable, although a manager should not be judged on just one quarter. In a *Forbes* magazine article, Jason Zweig reminds us: "Short-term results are shockingly poor predictors of long-term performance. So are performance numbers considered in a risk vacuum."

With regard to portfolio composition, make sure the fund remains postured to meet your objectives. If it is a high growth fund, for example, you wouldn't want to see a shift toward established but slow-growth companies. Obviously, you should stay aware of the fees being charged by the fund manager; make sure you know the purpose of each.

The most important change to monitor is a change in fund managers. The investing acumen and skill of the manager is what you buy in a mutual fund. If that changes, the whole ballgame could change.

Here are some sites for monitoring your funds and the mutual fund industry in general.

Barron's Online

http://www.barrons.com

The Traders Column at Barron's Online has general news on the mutual fund industry.

Dow Jones

http://bis.dowjones.com

You can customize Dow Jones CustomClips for news alert on mutual funds.

MarketEdge

http://www.marketedge.com

Fund alerts at MarketEdge inform you of changes in a fund's one-month total return, changes in risk factors as determined by increases or decreases in standard deviation, changes in a fund's asset composition of more than 2 percent, and changes in fee structuring.

Money Talks

http://www.talks.com

Money Talks calls itself the investment magazine for the serious investor. The Portfolio column by John Tompkins focuses on the mutual fund industry. Free.

The Stock Room

http://www.stockroom.org

The Stock Room offers a quick overview of sector performance, of special interest to Fidelity sector fund investors. Thumbnail graphs show the 6-month relative performance for each of the 35 Fidelity sector funds. You can see at a glance where the action is—or is not. (See Exhibit 18.7.)

USA Today

http://www.usatoday.com

USA Today's Money page has general news on the mutual fund industry.

The Wall Street Journal Interactive Edition

http://www.wsj.com

The Journal's Personal Journal can be customized to track news on mutual funds. Be sure to check out the Year-End Review of Mutual Funds for lists of leaders and laggards, and performance numbers by sector.

Learning about Mutual Funds

Many of the Web sites mentioned earlier offer free educational material on mutual funds. Here are some of particular interest to the novice investor.

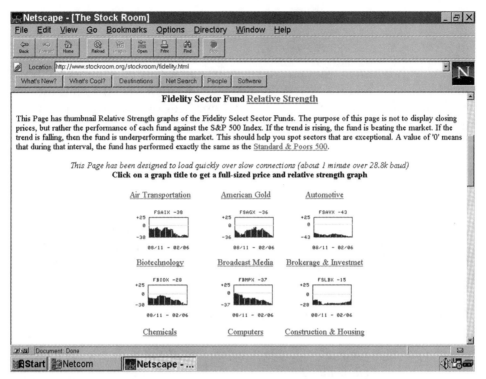

Exhibit 18.7   Thumbnail charts of Fidelity Sector Funds at The Stock Room.

American Association of Individual Investors

http://www.aaii.org

AAII members can access a treasure trove of articles and seminars about mutual funds.

Forbes Magazine

http://www.forbes.com

See the Investment Primer for excellent articles on mutual fund investing and the annual Mutual Fund Survey for articles on fund families.

Mutual Funds Interactive

http://www.fundsinteractive.com

Mutual Funds Interactive has a free monthly newsletter and an educational tool called Funds 101. A good article for novices and a reminder for more seasoned investors is "The 10 Commandments of Mutual Fund Investing".

The Mutual Fund Investor's Center

http://www.mfea.com

The Mutual Fund Investor's Center is a five-star site for mutual fund investors. Presented by the Mutual Fund Education Alliance, the national trade association of direct-marketed funds, the site is brimming with content, all of it free.

- ◆ Fund prices are posted daily on nearly 1,000 no-load and low-load funds.
- ◆ A QuickList feature lets you sort these 1,000 funds by a number of important factors.
- ◆ A news section gives you announcements and commentaries by fund companies.
- ◆ A planning section lets you develop an asset allocation plan, retirement plan, or college savings plan.
- ◆ An educational section presents a mini-course on "The Basics of Mutual Fund Investing." You can download and print the entire course for offline viewing.
- ◆ More than 40 direct-marketed mutual funds have information pages at this site, with links to their own home pages if available. These are mutual funds that sell funds directly to the public without brokers.

A companion educational book to the site, *The Complete Mutual Fund Investor's Kit,* is available through the bookstore at the site.

Web site	NAV Charts	Prospecting		Search Engines	Fund Profiles	Performance Ranking	News or Alerts	Mutual Fund Gurus	Links to Fund Sites & Families	Educational Content
		Lists	Screening							
AAII *http://www.aaii.org*			✓							✓
Barron's Online *http://www.barrons.com*							✓			
DBC Online *http://www.dbc.com*							✓			
Dow Jones *http://bis.dowjones.com*							✓			
EDGAR *http://www.sec.com*					✓					
Forbes *http://www.forbes.com*		✓			✓	✓			✓	✓
Fortune *http://www.fortune.com*		✓	✓			✓				
INVESTools *http://www.investools.com*					✓			✓		✓
Kiplinger Online *http://www.kiplinger.com*		✓								
Macro*World @ Wall Street City *http://www.wallstreetcity.com*		✓	✓			✓				
MarketEdge *http://www.marketedge.com*	✓	✓	✓		✓	✓	✓			
Money Talks *http://www.talks.com*							✓			
Morningstar.Net *http://www.morningstar.net*	✓	✓	✓		✓	✓	✓	✓		✓
Mutual Fund Interactive *http://www.fundsinteractive.com*							✓		✓	✓
The Mutual Fund Investor's Center *http://www.mfea.com*		✓	✓				✓		✓	✓
Mutual Funds Online *http://www.mfmag.com*	✓	✓	✓		✓	✓	✓		✓	✓
NETworth *http://networth.galt.com*	✓	✓	✓		✓					
The Online Investor *http://www.investhelp.com*										✓
PAWWS Financial Network *http://pawws.com*								✓	✓	
Quote.com *http://www.quote.com*					✓					
Research: *http://www.researchmag.com*		✓			✓					✓
Reuters Money Network *http://www.moneynet.com*					✓					
The Stock Room *http://www.stockroom.org*						✓				
Stock Smart *http://www.stocksmart.com*		✓				✓				
Tradeline Mutual Fund Center *http://nestegg.iddis.com/mutfund*	✓	✓							✓	✓
USA Today *http://www.usatoday.com*							✓			
Wall Street City *http://www.wallstreetcity.com*	✓	✓	✓	✓	✓		✓	✓		
The Wall Street Journal *http://www.wsj.com*		✓					✓			

NOTE: See CyberInvest.Com *(http://www.cyberinvest.com)* for the latest revisions to this Guide.

Exhibit 18.8   The CyberInvesting Guide for Mutual Funds.

The Online Investor

http://www.investhelp.com

The Online Investor has several articles on mutual fund investing: "Starting Small," "When Not to Buy a Fund," "Guide to Mutual Funds," and "When to Start Investing in Mutual Funds." The Online Investor is also available at the INVESTools site.

The Last Word

The key to being a happy mutual fund investor is to find funds whose goals and past performance suit your taste and objectives. It is the fund manager, remember, who sets the goals and is responsible for achieving the performance. You can monitor the fund to your heart's content, but you don't need to micromanage your fund manager.

CHAPTER NINETEEN

The Game Is Bonds

Gentlemen prefer bonds.
—Andrew Mellon

Some very conservative investors utilize bonds almost exclusively because of the perceived lower risk. In fact, as we will talk about later, it is a myth that bonds represent little risk—even if they are gilt-edged government bonds—because the value of a bond, particularly a long-term bond, is directly related to interest rates. Nevertheless, at some point, bonds will represent an appropriate and attractive investment vehicle for a portion of any investor's assets, so it is a good idea to know where to find information on bonds.

Searching for Bonds

The first time we searched for bonds on the Internet—in September 1996—we found four Web sites. By late January 1997 the same search turned up more than 40 bond-related sites (although most were investor advisors). In addition, some of the major stocks-and-mutual-fund sites already described offer information on bonds. In this chapter, we'll present the most relevant of those sites we reviewed. No doubt, by the time you read this book, there will be many more.

Bonds Online

http://www.bonds-online.com

Developed by Twenty-first Century Municipals, Inc., Bonds Online is the supersite for bonds, and much of the information is free. Here's a list of some of the features:

- Weekly recaps of the U.S. bond markets and graphs on bond market trends
- A guest market commentary
- Free municipal bond valuations, provided by R. W. Smith & Associates (e-mailed within 48 hours)
- Weekly fixed-income market commentary, provided by Inter-active Data Corp (requires the Adobe Acrobat Reader)
- A daily municipal market digest provided by FGIC AMN, Inc.
- Moody's quarterly outlook on municipal bonds
- Municipal and corporate insights from Fitch Investors Service (requires the Adobe Acrobat Reader)
- Weekly rankings on taxable and tax-free bond funds from IBC Financial Data, Inc.
- Search engine for corporate and municipal bonds from BondTrac
- Calendar of Treasury auctions
- Downloadable demo of the bond calculator CompoundIt!
- Bond Map that presents a listing of municipal bonds and bro-kerage firms dealing in bonds when you click on a state. (See Exhibit 19.1.)

BradyNet

http://www.bradynet.com

In addition to prices and information on a variety of bonds, BradyNet has international credit ratings from Duff & Phelps Credit Rating Company.

DBC Online

http://www.dbc.com

The DBC Newsroom has quotes on selected U.S. Treasuries, corporate bonds, mortgage bonds, and CMO bonds. (See Exhibit 19.2.)

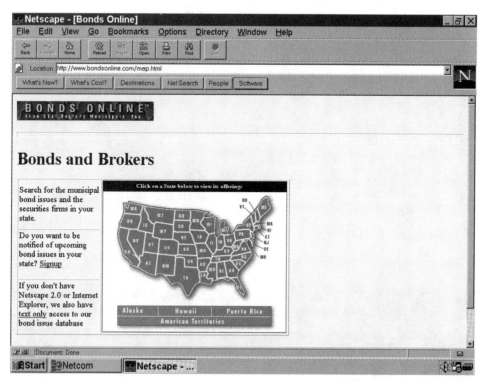

Exhibit 19.1   Bonds Online's map page: Click on a state to view its offerings.

The Bond Professor

One of the most helpful features of Bonds Online is "The Bond Professor," where a gentleman by the name of Richard Wilson will answer any question you want to ask about corporate bonds, municipal bonds, Treasury bonds, and savings bonds. At the time we checked, we found 56 questions and answers. His answers are clear, thorough, and to the point, and if he doesn't have the answer on the tip of his mouse, he refers you to appropriate sources.

Equity Analytics

http://www.e-analytics.com

Equity Analytics has daily closing numbers for U.S. T-notes, T-bonds, and T-bills.

IBC Financial Data

http://www.ibcdata.com

IBC Financial Data, Inc. has weekly ratings of money market and bond mutual funds.

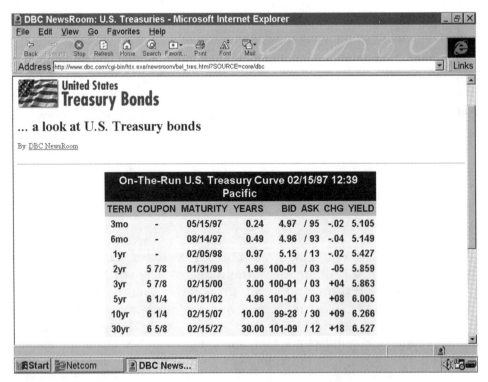

Exhibit 19.2   U.S. Treasury Bond listing from DBC Online.

FYI   Power bond investors should check out the BondVu site (http://www.bondvu.com.) for information on a Windows-based software program (by Capital Management Sciences) that analyzes fixed-income securities and one that uses a fuzzy logic search engine to sift through a database of more than 850,000 securities.

MarketEdge

http://www.marketedge.com

Among bond-related features at the MarketEdge site are news and analysis on municipal bonds from *The Bond Buyer;* news on the debt market, including major government reports; a current calendar of new municipal issues; a tutorial about municipal bonds; and a weekly calendar of upcoming economic events. (See Exhibit 19.3.)

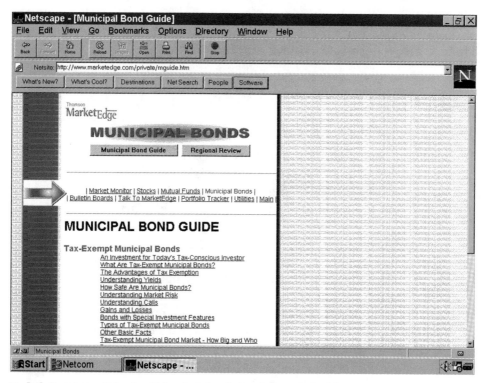

Exhibit 19.3   MarketEdge's Municipal Bond Guide.

F^{YI} Bond quotes are available from some of the investing Web sites mentioned in this chapter, and from several of the on-line trading sites discussed in Chapter 12.

Municipal Resource Center

http://www.municipal.com

Municipal Resource Center has information on municipal issues from R.R. Donnelley, including market analysis and links to related sources.

The Syndicate

http://www.moneypages.com/syndicate

The Syndicate has educational information on bonds, including articles on bond swaps, treasury auctions, and municipal bond terminology. There is also a description of Moody's Bond Ratings.

TradeHistory

http://www.tradehistory.com

TradeHistory is a database of bond price histories aimed at fixed income money managers (bond traders). The data is obtained from bond traders themselves and would be of interest mainly by those who want to study historical bond price trends. This is not a place for current bond quotes.

F^{YI} In wrapping up this section, we ran across an extensive listing of bond-related sites at the links page of Invest-o-rama (http://www.investorama.com/bonds). Many of the links were for bond brokers and investment advisors, but you might want to keep Invest-o-rama in mind as it will surely be a place to find the latest and greatest bond Web sites.

Bonds Can Be Risky, Too!

Despite their reputation as an ultrasafe investment, bonds do have risk. If you purchase a 30-year government bond with the intention of holding it for 30 years, your money's fairly safe. However, most bond purchasers only hold them for a relatively short period. This is where risk can come in. Frequently, when the stock market is extended, bonds have relatively low coupon interest rates, say, in the range of 6 percent. Unfortunately, in an extended market, investors frequently flock to bonds for safety. If long-term interest rates rise to levels of say, 8 percent, which has frequently happened over the past 25 years, those 6-percent bonds could face a loss of 20 to 30 percent due to this increase in interest rates. Sometimes it can take three to five years just to break even, when you purchase bonds with long-term yields below 6 percent.

Of course, the reverse is also true. If you purchase long-term bonds when interest rates are extremely high, say, 10 to 12 percent, you have a significant opportunity to make not only the 10 to 12 percent interest rate but significant appreciation on the bond itself, should interest rates fall back to the 6 to 8 percent range.

The bottom line is this. Over relatively short periods (one to three years), long-term bonds can generate total returns as high as 20 to 30 percent. Just keep in mind that the risk can also be 20 to 30 per cent if rates go the wrong way.

The Last Word

The good news for bond investors is that you finally have a wealth of information at your fingertips. The bad news is, you finally have a wealth of information at your fingertips. Try to find the sites that best suit your needs, and keep in mind that there is more risk in bonds than most investors are aware of.

CHAPTER TWENTY

TAKE IT TO THE BANK

The Internet will redefine banking entirely.
—The Forrester Report
PC Banking Meets the Web

At some point in your investing life, you will surely place some of your funds in a bank certificate of deposit. CDs are the safest, most conservative of investment vehicles, and since deregulation, you no longer have to accept whatever your local banks may deign to offer. There is a competitive climate among banks, and you can now shop the Internet for the best CD interest rates in the country.

Searching for CD Rates

The Internet has created the ideal shopping mall for CD rates. With a click of your mouse, you can visit the home pages of hundreds of banks or search for competitive rates from various commercial sites or from CD brokers. Here are some sites to get you started.

Bank-CD Rate Scanner

http://bankcd.com

Bank-CD Rate Scanner, with its access to over 2,200 U.S. banks, is a good place to start. It claims to deal only with federally insured institutions, and it does not deduct for fees or maintenance charges (except for

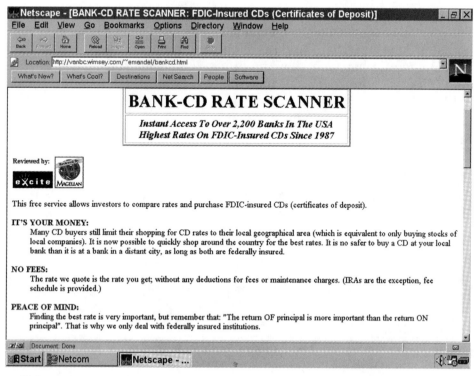

Exhibit 20.1   Bank-CD Rate Scanner.

IRAs). What it offers is a free list of CD rates, like the one in Exhibit 20.1. To receive information on any of the listed CDs, you have to complete a form on-line, and the information will be sent to your e-mail address. There are also hyperlinks to selected banks and tips on long-distance banking.

BanxQuote

http://www.banx.com

BanxQuote offers a comprehensive listing of CD rates across the country, as well as mortgage rates and on-line banking. Click on one of the listings and jump to a list of financial institutions offering that rate, the compounding method, and the minimum deposit. We checked out the listing for high-yield jumbo CDs and received a list of more than 80 institutions. You can click on the name of an institution for a snapshot profile that includes key financials and a telephone number. You'll also find BanxQuote at other Web sites, including The New York Times on the Web, The Wall Street Journal Interactive Edition, Bloomberg Personal, MarketEdge, Quote.com, and others. (See Exhibit 20.2.)

DBC Online

http://www.dbc.com

DBC Online has a Bank Rate Monitor for rates on special high-yielding CDs, as well as rates for home equity loans, credit cards, and con-

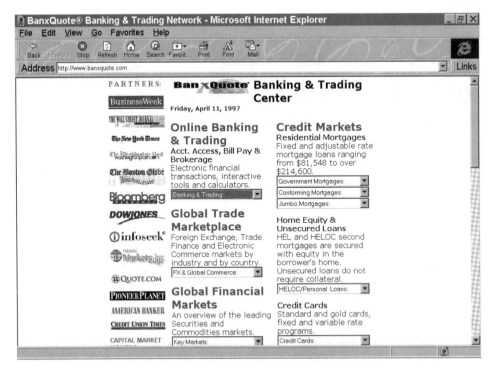

Exhibit 20.2   BanxQuote Banking and Trading Center: home page.

CD Brokers

CD brokers have developed as a specialized business to help investors find the best rates. CD brokers are agents licensed to sell securities, and because they are in the business, they may be aware of higher rates than are being offered locally. (Their services are free to the investor because they make their commissions from the bank, not from the customer.)

Both *Worth* magazine and *The Wall Street Journal* have testified to the credibility of CD brokers, stating that brokers can offer higher yields than CDs purchased directly from banks. As long as you stay with FDIC-insured CDs, buying from a broker should be relatively safe, but check them out.

sumer loans. Its Banking Tips is worth a read if you decide to buy a brokered CD.

FYI   Full service brokerage firms such as Merrill Lynch, Dean Witter Reynolds, and others also act as CD brokers.

Prime Rate

http://www.primerate.com

For smaller CDs, check out the home page of Prime Rate, which offers comparative rates on CDs of any term, often with no minimum deposit (see Exhibit 20.3). Our search retrieved a list of 5 banks offering rates from 5.91 to 6.30 percent for terms of 6 months to 48 months. Some required no minimum balances; others were for jumbo CDs (minimum $99,000). The list includes phone numbers, fax numbers, and e-mail and regular addresses for the participating banks. In some cases, you can also jump to the bank's home page.

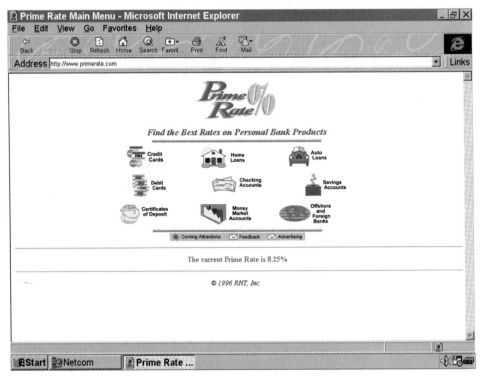

Exhibit 20.3   The home page of Prime Rate.

Bank Home Pages

Most banks on the Web do not publish their CD rates online. That will change in time, perhaps. Nevertheless, several offer online banking over the Internet. Here are the home pages of several nationwide banks; links to others can be found at Wall Street City and the Worldwide Banking Directory at http://www.orcc.com/banks.htm. (See examples in Exhibits 20.4 and 20.5.)

Bank of America	http://www.bankamerica.com
Bank of Boston	http://www.bkb.com
Bank One	http://www.bankone.com
Chase Manhattan Bank	http://www.chase.com

Exhibit 20.4 The home page of BankOne.

Citibank	http://www.citibank.com
First Union National Bank	http://www.firstunion.com
NationsBank	http://www.nationsbank.com
Security First Network Bank	http://www.sfnb.com
U.S. Bank	http://www.usbank.com
Wells Fargo Bank	http://wellsfargo.com

FYI CyberInvest.Com (http://www.cyberinvest.com) maintains an up-to-date comparison of on-line banking features of major U.S. banks on the Web.

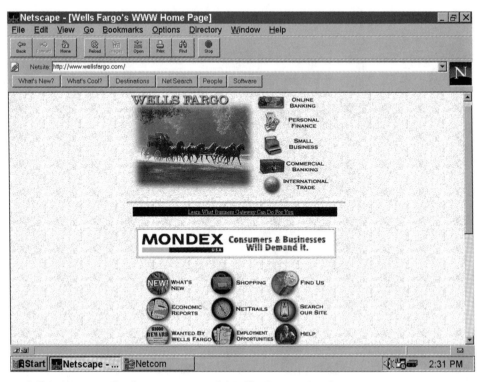

Exhibit 20.5   The home page of Wells Fargo Bank.

The Last Word

There will always be times when bank CDs can play an important role in your investment portfolio. The Internet now provides a way to shop the entire country for the highest possible rates without leaving your desk.

CHAPTER TWENTY-ONE

GLOBAL INVESTING

It doesn't matter how deep the water is if you know how to swim.

—David L. Brown
*Cyber-Investing: Cracking
Wall Street with Your PC*

For most of the twentieth century, the United States dominated world markets in the sheer number of marketable securities. Now, in 1997, it is one player among many, representing less than one third of stocks, funds, and bonds in the world. We now share the stage with Australia, Canada, Europe, Japan, Malaysia, Singapore, Taiwan, and a host of emerging countries. With the expansion of world markets comes unprecedented opportunities for investing in global securities.

The general premise behind international investing is that countries do not necessarily go through their economic cycles in tandem. When there is a bearish market in this country, there is likely to be a bullish market somewhere else in the world. When one country's market is flat, another's may be soaring. What makes global investing possible is the proliferation of electronic data and the increasingly less difficult task—courtesy of the Internet—of obtaining information on international securities.

Global investing is not for the novice or the faint of heart. Information on international securities is sparse, and there is the risk of local currency. Still, it is becoming easier, and the basic investing process is the same.

There are several ways to approach global investing, each increasingly demanding of the investor. The least demanding are *global funds,* which are offered by most of the largest fund families. A global fund diversifies the risk among countries; the fund manager does all the work. More demanding are *global sector funds* where you choose the region or type of fund, such as a European fund, an emerging country fund, or a Pacific Rim fund. If you want to get even more involved, choose the country in which you want to invest with a *country fund.* Country funds are closed-end funds that invest in the stocks of specific countries. (For a detailed look at country funds, read Robert Schwabach's book on global investing, which was published just before the explosion of the Internet.[1])

Most demanding of all for the global investor are international stocks. *American Depository Receipts* (ADRs) are the easiest international stocks to buy, although you still must select the country and the stock. An ADR is a receipt issued by a U.S. depository bank, which represents shares of a non-U.S. company. ADRs are traded in U.S. dollars on domestic exchanges, just like domestic stocks, and therefore have no direct currency risk. Keep in mind, however, that currency risk exists *indirectly* in any foreign investment, even in U.S. companies that do business on an international scale. Finally, if you want the whole enchilada, you can invest directly in *foreign stocks* and shoulder the responsibility for selecting both the country and the stock.

The Internet offers resources for each approach, although not to the same extent as for domestic securities. Global sites are multiplying at an astonishing rate, however, so there is little doubt that the global sector will catch up. In this chapter we'll show you some of the current international ports of call.

Choosing the Right Country

According to Morgan Stanley research, about 75 percent of a global investor's gains come from selecting the right country. It would behoove you, then, to research the country along with the security and then stay on top of what's happening in the country of your choice. Specifically, you need to be aware of the economic outlook and currency risk of that country.

---

[1] Schwabach, Robert. *The Business Week Guide to Global Investments Using Electronic Tools* (New York: Osborne McGraw-Hill, 1994).

On the Internet, you can get global economic outlooks straight from the *caballo*'s mouth. Many international banks and research institutions offer economic outlooks, investment data, or commentary on their own countries. So do some international publications. Most of the sites are bilingual, with usually one of the languages being English. The following is just a sample of what is likely to be a deluge of global investing sites on the World Wide Web.

FYI   It does not cost any more to visit an international site than a domestic one, except, of course, for any subscription fees charged by the site itself.

Master Resources

The following sites offer a variety of information for selecting a country. They are not linked to a specific country or else they offer information for more than one international region.

Foreign Markets Advisory (http://www.investools.com) by David G. Mullen, Jr., highlights the opportunities and risks in the economies of 42 countries and regions. It provides two-year market charts on each country, comparative key statistics on each country, identification of bull and bear markets, and those that are topping or bottoming. Subscription-based.

Fortune Magazine (http://www.fortune.com). Fortune's special reports on the Pacific Rim tell you the opportunities and pitfalls of investing in Asia. (Look under Special Issues/Lists.)

I.D.E.A. A currency and economic outlook on a country-by-country basis will soon be offered by Wall Street City as a result of its agreement with Independent Economic Analysis (I.D.E.A.) of London. I.D.E.A., which collaborates with the London School of Economics to produce reports on the emerging markets of Asia and Latin America, is a world leader in currency and economic forecasts. Its services were previously available only to the world's highest-volume trading rooms.

M.A.I.D./Profound (http://www.maid-plc.com). In its Countryline database, M.A.I.D. has comprehensive country reports, economic forecasts, and analyses from international publishers covering every established and emerging market, with special coverage of the Asia-Pacific Rim, the Middle East, and Africa. (See Exhibit 21.1.)

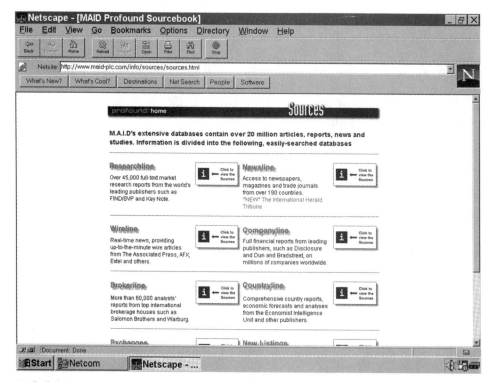

Exhibit 21.1   M.A.I.D./Profound offers six searchable databases from worldwide sources.

Wall Street City (http://www.wallstreetcity.com) has a solid international section. In addition to the stock quotes and the unique presentation of foreign exchange rates, mentioned elsewhere, there are market snapshots of 37 world markets. (See Exhibit 21.2.) Each includes a graph of the major market index, plus end-of-day quotes for major indexes and industry groups of that country, along with symbols that can be used to retrieve individual graphs. For each country, there is also market commentary and news. In addition, you can plot a graph on any foreign index or security (there's a symbol look-up at the International page).

F**YI**   The MacroWorld section of Wall Street City has outlooks for countries and industries within countries.

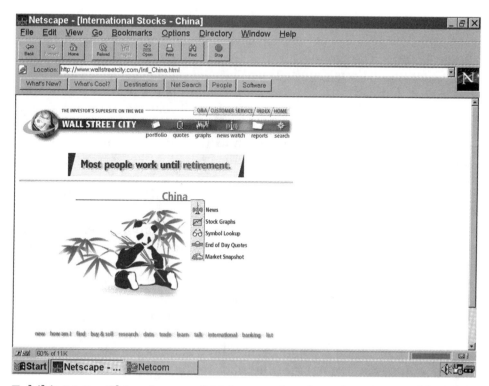

Exhibit 21.2 China is one of 37 international markets covered by Wall Street City's International section.

FYI New international sites are multiplying rapidly. To keep up with them, see the CyberInvesting Guide at CyberInvest.Com (http://www.cyberinvest.com). Yahoo! also has country-by-country listing (http://www.yahoo.com/Regional/Countries).

Asia

The Asia Business Connection (http://www.asiabiz.com). This is a business mall with links to home pages of banks, financial institutions, and other companies in Australia, Cambodia, China, Hong Kong, India, Indonesia, Japan, Korea, Malaysia, New Zealand, Philippines, Singapore, Taiwan, Thailand, and Vietnam.

Asia Business News (http://www.abn.com.sg) offers quotes on Asian market indexes and links to Asian exchanges. It also offers news, market updates, and exchange rates. (This site is sponsored by Dow Jones and Tele-Communications, International.)

Asia Inc. Online (http://www.asia-inc.com) is the on-line publication of *Asia Times*, a daily business newspaper. It focuses its search engine on the Pacific Rim and maintains a directory of Asian Resources on the Internet by country (from Bangladesh to Thailand) and by subject (from databases to travel). They claim to have visited and assessed every site. It also has Bridge financial summaries of London, New York, and Tokyo markets, plus stock reviews for Australia, Hong Kong, Japan, Malaysia, South Korea, and Taiwan.

AsiaOne (http://www.asia1.com.sg), from Singapore Press Holdings Ltd., is the on-line site for Singapore's *Business Times.* It has extensive trading information for stocks, funds, and commodities. See the Business Centre section for company research, fund reports, and other research information. (See Exhibit 21.3.)

Singapore Business Times Online (http://biztimes.asia1.com) is an English language newspaper about news and trends in Singapore and Asia. (It is part of the AsiaOne family.) It has a searchable index of Singapore companies, plus real-time data from the Singapore and Kuala Lumpur stock markets.

Australia

The Privateer (http://www.the-privateer.com) is an Australian-based newsletter on the principles of global economics, politics, and finance.

Canada

Canada's Department of Foreign Affairs and International Trade (http://www.dfait-maeci.gc.ca) has an information-packed site about investing and doing business in Canada.

Canada Trust (http://www.canadatrust.com) offers various investment services for mutual funds.

The Investment Reporter is a newsletter at the INVESTools site (http://www.investools.com) which has a long-term fundamental approach to Canadian stocks and indexes.

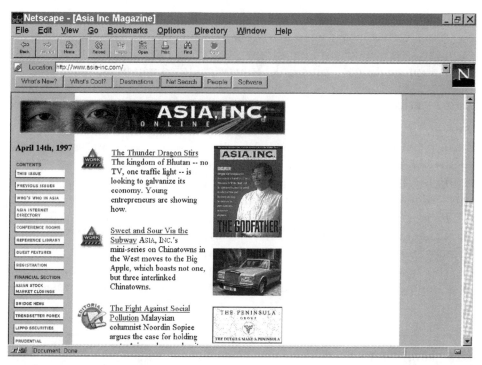

Exhibit 21.3 The home page of Asia Inc. Online.

StreetNet (http://www.streetnet.com) has Market West fact sheets on companies listed on the Vancouver and Alberta, Canada exchanges.

Europe

The Bank of England (http://www.bankofengland.co.uk) provides quarterly and annual economic reports on specific sectors of the British economy.

FT.com (http://www.ft.com) is the web site of *The Financial Times,* which is the leading international English language business newspaper (it is published in the United Kingdom). It offers coverage of the Americas, Asia-Pacific Rim, Europe, and the United Kingdom. There are some 200 surveys each year on countries, regions, industries, and other topics. You can search the site with one or more keywords.

The *French Finance Ministry* (http://www.tresor.finances.fr/oat) extols the virtues of French government securities.

The Institute of Finance and Banking at the University of Goettingen, Germany (http://www.wiso.gwdg.de/ifbg/stock1.htm) disseminates information on finance and banking on the World Wide Web (both domestic and international), plus links to worldwide exchanges.

Latin America

Argentina's Ministry of Economy and Public Works and Services (http://www.mecon.ar) publishes annual and quarterly economic reports and reports on specific sectors of the economy.

Infosel (http://www.infosel.com.mx) publishes electronic versions of the newspapers *Reforma* and *El Norte.*

Mexican Commentary (http://www.investorweb.com/NEWSLTRS/mexicancommentary/intro.htm) is a newsletter at InvestorWEB which briefs you on what to expect if you invest in Mexico.

The Mexican Consulate (http://www.quicklink.com/mexico) has lists of economic indicators and links to the finance ministry and president's office.

Foreign Exchange Rates

The currency risk is very real if you're trading stocks in a different country. You need a place to quickly convert the currency of your country into dollars, pounds, lire, francs, marks, yen, or other less familiar currencies. Several Web sites offer conversion tables:

Bloomberg Personal (http://www.bloomberg.com) has a table of cross currency rates for 11 major currencies.

DBC Online (http://www.dbc.com) has foreign exchange rate tables that convert U.S. dollars into more than 100 worldwide currencies.

Wall Street City (http://www.wallstreetcity.com) has a conversion table that lets you convert U.S. dollars, pounds, German marks, and Swiss francs into more than 70 currencies. Market commentary comes with each currency conversion table. (See Exhibit 21.4.) In addition, you can perform technical analysis of currencies, with the ActiveX graph feature using Microsoft Internet

Continued

Investor's World by John Dessauer publishes commentary on international funds. Dessauer is a regular panelist on PBS's "Wall Street Week With Louis Rukeyser."

M.A.I.D./Profound

http://www.maid-plc.com

M.A.I.D./Profound has more than 45,000 full-text market research reports (the Researchline database), more than 60,000 analyst reports (the Brokerline database), full financial reports on millions of companies worldwide (the Companyline database), and two news databases that cover current newswire articles and newspapers, magazines, and trade journals from more than 190 countries (the Wireline and Newsline databases). All databases are searchable.

The PIPEX Worldserver Business Park

http://www.worldserver.pipex.com

This Web site has a hyperlinked list of international corporate sites.

Standard & Poor's

http://www.stockinfo.standardpoor.com

S&P offers free profiles of Israeli public companies traded on the Tel Aviv and U.S. stock exchanges. It also has background information on Israel's economy.

Stock Smart

http://www.stocksmart.com

Stock Smart has announced it will soon offer profiles on more than 9,000 worldwide stocks in 40 countries.

Wall Street City

http://www.wallstreetcity.com

The Telescan Ranking Snapshot, described in Chapter 7, can be used with ADRs, if you know the name or symbol. The snapshot gives an overview of the ADR's technical condition, compared with all other stocks. The fundamental rankings on the snapshot may not be available, since fundamental data is harder to come by. Corporate reports, such as the Zacks earnings estimates and S&P Stock Report, are available for many ADRs.

ActiveX graphs can be used for technical analysis of ADRs, as well as for foreign stocks. ADRs, by the way, are treated just like any domestic stock; it is not necessary to go to the International page to obtain quotes, graphs, or company reports.

The Wall Street Journal Interactive Edition

http://www.wsj.com

The Journal's "Heard in Asia" and "Heard in Europe" columns are sources for international stock tips.

The Vanguard Group

http://www.vanguard.com

Vanguard has a broad selection of funds for investing overseas, including a European portfolio, a Pacific Rim portfolio, an emerging markets portfolio, and others.

Keeping Up with Global Markets

After you've added global securities to your portfolio, it is important to stay abreast of news and events in the countries involved. The following Web sites offer global market updates, along with news and charts of international market indexes.

Trading International Stocks

Few discount brokers trade international stocks over the Web. So if you're into global investing *and* you want to trade stocks over the Internet, you should choose a broker that offers both traditional brokerage and Web-based trading. You might want to ask your broker if they can handle trades in specific countries or trades of specific types of international securities. Most will handle country funds and ADRs, but will they handle your trade on the Kuala Lumpur exchange?

Bloomberg Personal

http://www.bloomberg.com

Bloomberg has on its home page the closing prices for these foreign indexes: the FT-SE 100, the DAX, Hang Seng, and the NIKKEI 225 index. There is also extensive news coverage of world markets.

FYI   Asia Inc. On-Line offers a weekly worldwide financial calendar of release dates for economic reports in Asia, Europe, and the Americas. To go directly to that page, use this URL: http://www.asia inc.com/knight/calendar.html.

Macro*World @ Wall Street City

http://www.wallstreetcity.com

Macro*World offers charts based on its forecasts for several world markets, including Frankfurt, Hong Kong, London, Mexico, Milan, Netherlands, Paris, Stockholm, Sydney, Toronto, and the Nikkei Dow.

The New York Times on the Web

http://www.nytimes.com

The New York Times has basic international news at its News by Category page.

Stock Smart

http://www.stocksmart.com

Stock Smart monitors more than 500 global market indexes. It also has financial news on international markets, including the Canadian, Mexican, European, and Asian exchanges.

The Times of London

http://www.the-times.co.uk

You can read the news update, browse back issues, and search the archives of *The Times* and *The Sunday Times*.

FYI   Fidelity Investments at http://www.fidelity.com has a color-coded ticker that displays the closing prices for major international exchanges.

Wall Street City

http://www.wallstreetcity.com

Wall Street City has extensive coverage for 37 countries. (See page 282.)

The Wall Street Journal Interactive Edition

http://www.wsj.com

The Journal's Money & Investing page has market news on the Americas, Asia, and Europe, plus coverage of global indexes. Also, check out the year-end reviews from the European and Asian Journals.

Links to International Exchanges

Most Web sites for international exchanges are either in English or offer an English version. (Click on the British or American flag icon to get the English version.) In addition to free quotes for their own indexes and stocks, these exchanges sometimes offer market commentary and economic information about their countries. Here is a partial listing. To find other exchanges, check the links at Wall Street Research Net (http://www.wsrn.com); The Financial Center On-Line (http://www.tfc.com), or Asia Business News (http://www.abn.com.sg).

Africa

Johannesburg   http://www.jse.co.za

Asia

Indonesia	http://www.indoexchange.com
Korea	http://www.kse.or.kr
Singapore	http://www.ses.com.sg
Taiwan	http://www.tse.com.tw
Thailand	http://www.set.or.th
Tokyo	http://www.tse.or.jp

Australia/New Zealand

Australia	http://www.asx.com.au
New Zealand	http://www.nzse.co.nz

Canada

Alberta Stock Database, Ltd.	http://www.altastock.com
Montreal Stock Exchange	http://www.me.org
Vancouver Stock Exchange	http://www.vse.ca

Caribbean

Bermuda	http://www.bsx.com
Jamaica	http://www.infochan.com/jamex/jam-lite/ts970206.htm

Europe

Amsterdam	http://www.financeweb.ase.nl
Athens	http://www.ase.gr
Budapest	http://www.fornax.hu/fmon
Helsinki	http://www.hse.fi
Istanbul	http://www.medyatext.com.tr/imkb
Italy	http://www.borsaitalia.it
Lisbon	http://www.bvl.pt
London (AIM)	http://www.stockex.co.uk.
Madrid	http://www.bolsamadrid.es
Paris	http://www.bourse-de-paris.fr
Prague	stock.eunet.cz
Stockholm	http://www.xsse.se
Switzerland	http://www.bourse.ch
Zagreb, Croatia	http://www.zse.com.hr

India

Bombay (Invest-India)	http://quark.kode.net/india/home.html
National Stock Exchange of India	http://www.nseindia.com.

Latin America

Bogota, Colombia	http://www.bolsabogota.com.co
Caracas, Venezuela	http://www.caracasstock.com

Lima, Peru	http://www.bvl.com.pe
Mexico	http://www.bmv.com.mx
Rio de Janeiro, Brazil	http://www.bvrj.com.br
Santiago, Chili	http://www.bolsasantiago.cl
São Paulo, Brazil	http://bovespa.com.br

Middle East

| Beirut | http://www.lebanon.com/financial/stocks |
| Tel Aviv | http://www.tase.co.il |

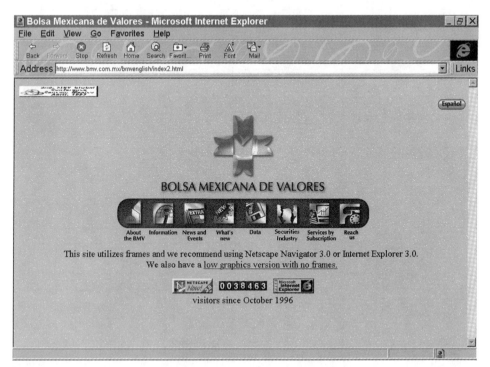

Exhibit 21.5   The home page Stock Exchange of Mexico.

Web site	Quotes (stocks, ADRs, funds)	Market Update	World News	Country: Economic Condition/ Outlook	Prospecting Tools	Co./ Fund Research	Technical Analysis of Stocks/ Indexes	Foreign Exchange Rates	Links to Int'l Sites
Argentina's Ministry of Economy http://www.mecon.ar				✓					
The Asia Business Connection http://www.asiabiz.com									✓
Asia Business News http://www.abn.com.sg		✓	✓						✓
Asia Inc. Online http://www.asia-inc.com		✓		✓				✓	✓
AsiaOne http://www.asia1.com.sg	✓					✓			
The Bank of England http://www.bankofengland.com				✓					
Bloomberg Personal http://www.bloomberg.com		✓	✓					✓	
Canada's Department of Foreign Affairs http://www.dfait-maeci.gc.ca				✓					
Canada Trust http://www.canadatrust.com						✓			
CyberInvest.Com http://www.cyberinvest.com									✓
DBC Online http://www.dbc.com	✓		✓					✓	
Fidelity Investments http://www.fidelity.com		✓							
The Financial Center Online http://www.tfc.com	✓				✓				✓
Foreign Markets Advisory http://www.investools.com				✓	✓		✓		
Fortune Magazine http://www.fortune.com				✓	✓				
FT.com http://www.ft.com			✓	✓					
French Finance Ministry http://www.tresor.finances.fr/oat				✓					
Global Investing Newsletter http://www.investools.com					✓				
I/B/E/S Financial Network http://www.ibes.com						✓			
I.D.E.A. http://www.wallstreetcity.com				✓					
InfoSel http://www.infosel.com.mx			✓						
The Institute of Finance and Banking University of Goettingen, Germany http://www.wiso.gwdg.de/ifbg/stock1.htm				✓					✓
The Investment Reporter http://www.investools.com				✓					
Investor's World Newsletter http://www.investools.com					✓	✓			
INVESTools http://www.investools.com						✓			
Macro*World @ Wall Street City http://www.wallstreetcity.com		✓		✓					
M.A.I.D./Profound http://www.maid-plc.com			✓	✓		✓			
Mexican Commentary http://www.investorweb.com/NEWSLTRS				✓					
The Mexican Consulate http://www.quicklink.com/mexico				✓					
The New York Times on the Web http://www.nytimes.com			✓						
The PIPEX Worldserver Business Park http://www.worldserver.pipex.com									✓
The Privateer http://www.the-privateer.comCy				✓					
Singapore Business Times Online http://biztimes.asia1.com		✓	✓			✓			
Standard & Poor's http://www.stockinfo.standardpoor.com				✓		✓			
Stock Smart http://www.stocksmart.com		✓	✓			✓			
StreetNet http://www.streetnet.com	✓				✓	✓			
The Times of London http://www.the-times.co.uk			✓						
Wall Street City http://www.wallstreetcity.com	✓	✓	✓	✓	✓		✓	✓	
The Wall Street Journal Interactive Edition http://interactive6.wsj.com		✓	✓	✓					
The Vanguard Group http://www.vanguard.com				✓					

NOTE: See CyberInvest.Com (http://www.cyberinvest.com) for the latest revisions to this Guide.

Exhibit 21.6   The CyberInvesting Guide for Global Investing.

The Last Word

If you are interested in global investing, be prepared for change. This is clearly the most rapidly evolving arena in the world of investing. Your reward for persevering will be virtually limitless opportunities in the years to come.

CHAPTER TWENTY-TWO

Option Trading

A speculator is a man who observes the future, and acts before it occurs.

—Bernard M. Baruch

At the opposite end of the investment risk spectrum from bank CDs are options. *Options* are basically speculative, with the investor betting on an anticipated move in the price of the underlying stock, often within a very short time frame.

There are dozens of rationales for buying and selling options. You can trade options as a hedging device or speculate on unusual moves. You can trade options based on their discount from theoretical value or on the deviation of their implied volatility from statistical volatility. You can use a mind-boggling array of spreads and straddles to accomplish specific risk/reward goals.

Option strategies are so varied and so complex that a single strategy is frequently the subject of an entire book—but not this book. We just want to point you to the Web sites that can be of value to option traders. Before we do, let us mention a few simple ways to trade options that might appeal to the novice or conservative investor.

A Simple Use of Options

Option trading doesn't have to be complex or unnecessarily risky. Here are three simple ways to get your feet wet in the option game—without undue risk.

Accumulating the Underlying Stock

Some investors use options to minimize potential risk while accumulating a position in a stock. For example, if you think AOL's chances for gain are significant, but you don't want to buy 100 shares and risk $3,500, you can very likely find an option for 100 shares that costs a couple hundred dollars. You might even find one that's somewhat out of the money for as little as $100. If the stock goes up, you have almost the same potential for gain; if it goes down, you're risking only the amount you paid for the option.

The downside to this strategy is the time horizon. The stock must move in the one or two months before the option expires. If it takes too long to make the expected move, you're left holding a worthless option.

Trading Options on Stocks You Own

There are two other simple ways to trade options to decrease your risk: sell a call or buy a put on stock that you own. The former increases your income but limits your upside; the latter limits your risk.

Selling a call on your stocks. Let's say you own 100 shares of IBM which, in late January 1997, was trading at $157. You could sell a 160 call that expires April 19 for $8 a share or $800 for one contract. You would be betting that IBM won't exceed $160 before April 19. If you're right, you get to keep the $800 option premium and any quarterly dividend paid by IBM, and you still own the stock. You're $800 better off than if you'd simply held the stock without selling the option.

The worst that could happen is the stock would be called away from you, should it go to $160 or higher by April 19. If that were to happen, you'd still have the $800 option premium, plus the $3-per-share gain from the current price, and, hopefully, the quarterly dividend as well. If the stock goes to $180, well, you've lost the bet but still made money.

In effect, this kind of option trading limits your upside but reduces your downside and puts a little cash in your pocket if the stock isn't called away.

Buying a put on your stocks. If you really believe that a stock you own is ready to make a big upward move but you want some insurance against a downside loss, you can buy a put on the stock.

Let's say you own 100 shares of Wal-Mart which, in late January 1997, is selling for $23¼. You could buy a 22½ put that expires March 22 for only about ⅝ or about $65 plus commission. If there is a big upward movement in Wal-Mart by late March, you'll have the benefit of the increased stock price, and the option will expire worthless. But you will have had a little insurance policy for just $65.

In this scenario, the worst that could happen is the stock would fall below the strike price of $22½. Because of the put, you could sell your stock to the purchaser of the put for 22½ a share. You would have limited your downside to $0.75 a share, plus the $65 option premium, while retaining all of the upside potential.

If you're new to options you may want to try one of these simple trades before venturing further into the option game. Once you're ready to speculate a little, we'll show you a fun and potentially rewarding strategy that doesn't risk a lot of dollars.

Low-Risk Speculation in Options?

There *is* a way to speculate with options without risking a great deal of money. It is based on the fact that those-in-the-know often speculate on options when they become aware of an impending event that might cause a sharp rise in the price of the underlying stock. This could be a rumored merger or acquisition; it could be a new product release; it could be FDA approval of a new drug or anything that could positively affect earnings. It is a lot cheaper to buy options than the same amount of the underlying stock.

Let's say there is a sudden, major surge in Microsoft options, and you believe there may be a positive event for Microsoft in the wings. You could try to get in on the action by buying Microsoft stock, for which you'd spend $10,000 for 100 shares (in late January 1997). Or, you could buy an in-the-money option to purchase 100 shares of Microsoft (one contract) for as little as $500. With the option purchase, you'd lose a relatively small sum if the speculative event falls through, but if it indeed materializes you could make a handsome profit.

How do you find such opportunities for speculation? Use an option search program and look for options with unusual volume activity, for example, a high 1-day-to-14-day volume ratio with a reasonable current volume (say, more than 100 contracts). Keep in mind, we're talking about a sudden surge of unusual volume, not simply high volume. The option search is shown in Exhibit 22.1. Details appear in our *Cyber-Investing* book.

Searching for Options

All options are time-sensitive. If the underlying stock doesn't move to the anticipated level before the expiration date of the option, its entire value evaporates. Due to their leverage, options exhibit extraordinary volatility. In addition, their time-sensitive nature generates a steady time-decay effect. As a result of all this, timely information is absolutely critical for properly evaluating options. Fortunately, the Internet offers a number of sources for this information, along with other essential information for evaluating an option.

CyberBrokers

Any on-line broker that accepts option trades will have option quotes. Most of the brokers reviewed in Chapter 12 accept Web-based option trades. See the CyberInvesting Guide at the end of that chapter.

DBC Online

http://www.dbc.com

DBC Online offers top 10 option lists of volume leaders, percentage gainers, and percentage losers (at the Financial Markets page).

OptionVue Systems International

http://www.optionvue.com

OptionVue Systems International is the developer of the options analysis program, OptionVue IV. (See Exhibit 22.2.) You can use two of its analysis tools free of charge at the OptionVue Web site. A probability calculator will give you the probability of a stock being above, below, or between two price targets; an options calculator gives you the fair mar-

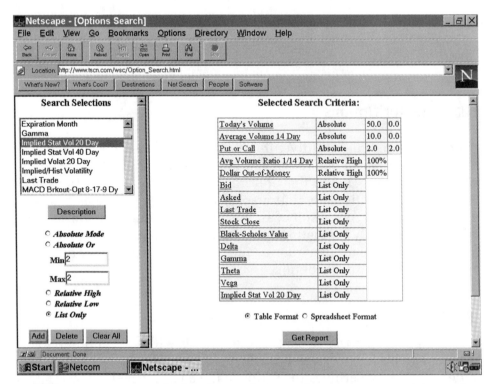

Exhibit 22.1 A search for low-risk speculative opportunities using Telescan's Option Search at Wall Street City. Fifteen out of a possible 120+ search criteria have been selected.

ket value of an option, using the Black/Scholes formula. There are also several free articles on option trading strategies at the site, written by Len Yates, president of OptionVue, and a bimonthly newsletter ($39/year) that focuses on using trading strategies with the OptionVue analysis program.

Wall Street City

http://www.wallstreetcity.com

The only true search engine for options on the Internet is, again, Wall Street City. It uses the basic Telescan search engine, but this one has over 100 criteria designed especially for options, and it uses Telescan's database of some 300,000 options and spreads. You can obtain option quotes and price-and-volume graphs here. The graphs, by the way, are critical for analyzing the unusual volume activity described in the previous section. There is also an options glossary at this site. (See Exhibit 22.2.)

The Wall Street Journal Interactive Edition

http://www.wsj.com

The Journal's Money & Investing page (U.S. stocks) has volume, close, and open interest for all listed options. The option database is updated every trading day at about 9 P.M. (See Exhibit 22.3.)

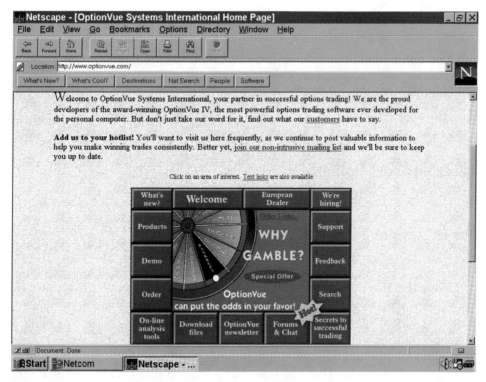

Exhibit 22.2   The home page of OptionVue Systems International.

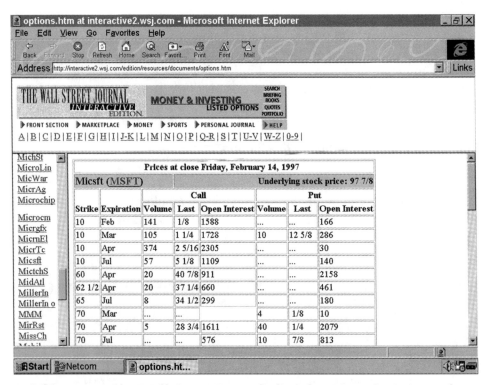

Exhibit 22.3 *The Wall Street Journal*'s listed options for Microsoft on 2/14/97.

Learning about Options

The best place to learn about options are the various option exchanges.

The Chicago Board Options Exchange

http://www.cboe.com

CBOE is the world's largest options exchange where you'll find, among other educational material, an options symbol guide, glossary of options terms, a list of recommended reading, and frequently asked questions. Novice option traders will appreciate the succinct and to-the-point overview of options called "The Language of Options" (in the CBOE Background section). There is also a schedule of classes across the country sponsored by the Options Institute and the Options Industry Council.

The Chicago Mercantile Exchange

http://www.cme.com

If you want to learn about options futures trading, check out the CME Education Center Courses. There are introductory courses, such as Pit Trading 101; intermediate courses on options, fundamental and technical analysis, and the market; and advanced courses on technical analysis, options, Japanese candlesticks, and the market.

Other Options and Futures Exchanges

You may want to check these out while you're at it:

> *The Chicago Board of Trade* (http://www.cbot.com)
> *The Chicago Stock Exchange* (http://www.chicagostockex.com
> *The Kansas City Board of Trade* (http://www.kcbt.com)
> *The Minneapolis Grain Exchange* (http://www.mgex.com)
> *The New York Cotton Exchange* (http://www.nyce.com)
> *The New York Mercantile Exchange* (http://www.nymex.com)
> *The Philadelphia Stock Exchange* (http://www.phlx.com)

The Option Gurus

How options relate to the volatility of the underlying stock has much to do with their pricing and the opportunities in option trading. Conversely, the implied volatility of options can be used to determine likely stock behavior. But this is a difficult, highly technical subject, one in which it would behoove the novice to seek the wisdom of a market guru. Here are a few we found on the Internet.

DBC Newsletter Network

http://www.margin.com/cbn/newsletters

DBC Newsletter Network is a joint effort of DBC Online and Network Technologies, Inc. (At DBC Online, you'll find it at the Financial Store page.) There are four option-related letters, ranging from $196 to over $3,000 a year. Each offers a free trial.

The Bedford Option Review is a real-time stock and index option trading advisory service, with four intraday reports and a nightly report.

The OEX Advantage, also by the Bedford folks, is a daily index option advisory with two intraday updates and a nightly update.

Opportunities in Options by David L. Caplan gives you a comprehensive look at options through market analysis, educational strategies, volatility composite index and charts, book reviews, guest columns, and special reports. Published monthly.

Trade Like a Bookie, also by David L. Caplan, is based on the trading methods described in the book of the same name, in which "aspects of gaming theory and probability analysis are combined with the advantages of selling overvalued options."

Wall Street City

http://www.wallstreetcity.com

The following newsletters are found at the Find an Investment page (Options). Subscriptions start at $228/year.

The Alpha Options Newsletter by Luiz Alvim and Paul Alvim use the Alpha Trading System to recommend options that appear poised for sudden moves. This is the same trading system they use for picking stocks in Chapter 5. Updated weekly.

The Wall Street SOS Options Alert by Jerry Gentry features trend analysis and recommendations for index options and stock options. Updated daily.

The Last Word

Speculative options are not for the faint of heart. The rewards can be extremely large, but so can the risks. On the other hand, options can be used to hedge your bets, so to speak. We consider this an area suitable for dabbling. At present, the Internet does not offer all that an option trader might wish. Given the trend of the past few months, it undoubtedly will soon.

PART SEVEN

Wall Street U

The Internet offers an enormous amount of educational material for investors, and most of it is free. Many of the commercial investing Web sites have some complimentary educational features; so do the exchanges and investor associations, such as the AAII and the NAIC, which are free to members. Others sources are not free, namely some educational newsletters and bookstores, which are in the business of selling books. In this section we tell you what we've found to be the best educational sites for the investor and discuss electronic magazines, which are a rich source of educational articles on investing.

CHAPTER TWENTY-THREE

Continuing Education

Keep pressing to learn more and more. The more you learn the more you will realize there is to learn.
—Charles J. Kaplan
President, Equity Analytics, Ltd.

Becoming a knowledgeable investor is a lifelong educational process. No matter how good you become, there is always more to learn. Investing seminars are filled with investors who already make good returns but are eager to expand their investing horizons. They know that an improvement of even one percent can add a substantial amount to their returns.

The Internet offers an enormous amount of educational material for both novice and seasonal investors. We'll point you to a number of rewarding Web sites in this chapter.

Come into My Web Site . . .

Commercial enterprises want to sell you their proprietary products or services, there is no doubt about that. (And nothing wrong with it.) But as denizens of the World Wide Web they know they must provide as much free material as possible to keep the lookers happy and to tempt the serious surfers to give them a try. The free stuff is frequently in the form of educational materials. Here is a sampling.

Barron's Online

http://www.barrons.com

Barron's has a column called "The Electronic Investor" which features Internet-related articles.

CyberInvest.Com

http://www.cyberinvest.com

CyberInvest.Com features a review of the five-step cyber-investing process, along with links to Web sites that offer resources for each of the five steps.

Equity Analytics

http://www.e-analytics.com

Equity Analytics has educational information on stocks, bonds, mutual funds, options, futures, and financial planning, all written, it appears, by its president, Charles J. Kaplan.

Investor's Business Daily

http://www.investors.com

IBD's Investment Education Course includes publisher William J. O'Neil's C-A-N-S-L-I-M strategy, which is based on seven characteristics found in the top performing stocks of the last forty years. (See Exhibit 23.1.)

InvestorWEB

http://www.investorweb.com

There are several educational articles for the beginning investor at this site, many of them written by the webmaster Bob Costa. Some of the titles include "Money and Investing," "Investment Style," "Asset Allocation for the Absolute Beginner," and "Individual Stock Investing for the Small Investor." His tips on using newsletters are excellent.

The Online Investor

http://www.investhelp.com

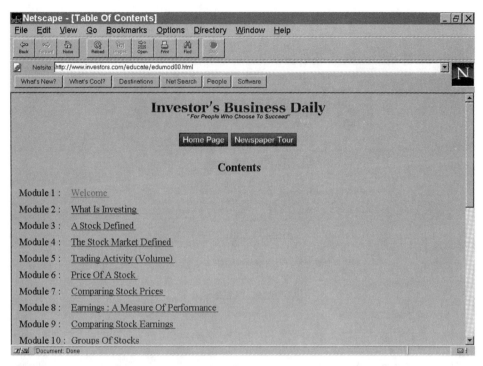

Exhibit 23.1   The contents page for *Investor's Business Daily*'s Investment Education Course.

This education-rich site is the product of Ted Allrich (author of *The On-Line Investor,* St. Martin's Press) and James C. Hale, a former bond market analyst. Their goal, in their own words, is "to explain in terms everyone can understand: investing in stocks, the stock market, the economy, and mutual funds." To that end, they write columns on various aspects of equity investing and mutual funds. They also have a good article on the "Ingredients of Investment Success." (See Exhibit 23.2.)

Research:

http://www.researchmag.com

Research: has several articles that deal with the basics of investing, including ways to figure out how your portfolio is doing.

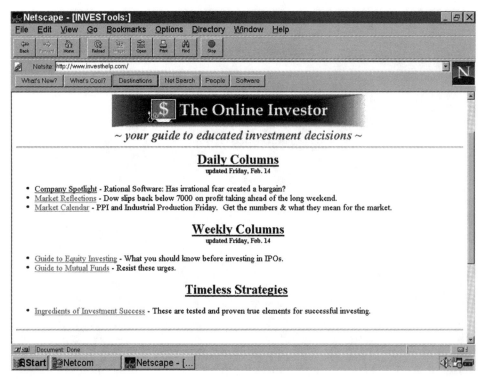

Exhibit 23.2   The Online Investor offers help for the beginning investor.

Standard & Poor's

http://www.stockinfo.standardpoor.com

Standard & Poor's has an excellent guide for the novice investor entitled "How to Invest: A Guide to Buying Stocks, Bonds and Mutual Funds." This is also available at the PC Financial Network (http://www.pcfn.com).

The Syndicate

http://www.moneypages.com/syndicate

The Syndicate is a good educational site, with information on stocks, bonds, mutual funds, and brokers. You'll find Warren Buffett's top holdings and a definition of William O'Neil's C-A-N-S-L-I-M method of picking stocks. There are also articles that sum up the world of investing in a few succinct "rules," if you like that sort of thing: "Fourteen Investment Tenets that Could Improve Your Investment Performance" by Jeff Weiss; "Trading Rules—Strategies for Success" by William F. Eng; and Jessie Livermore's "Rules for Capital Gains." The Syndicate also lists stock symbols for foreign stocks.

The Vanguard Group

http://www.vanguard.com

Vanguard has what it calls the Vanguard Online University which offers a series of free on-line seminars, including "The Fundamentals of Mutual Funds" and "Facing Your Retirement."

FYI Web sites that offer educational material specific to mutual funds, bonds, options, and global investing may appear in those specific chapters.

Wall Street City

http://www.wallstreetcity.com

At its Learn About Investing page, Wall Street City has a number of items of special interest to cyber-investors:

- Several articles on technical indicators are written by investing professionals. Topics include industry group analysis, MACD indicators, relative strength as an analytical tool, stochastics, trading band theory, and the Wilder Relative Strength Index.
- Free educational newsletters (at the When to Buy and Sell page) include John Bollinger's Capital Growth Topics and Telescan's Newsletters (the Adobe Acrobat Reader is required for the latter).
- Telescan sponsors investing seminars throughout the country on cyber-investing, high-growth stocks (a workshop hosted by Ian Woodward), and other topics. There are beginning and advanced levels. Check the current schedule here.

- ◆ On-line forums and roundtables are held on a variety of investing topics at the Talk to Investors page.
- ◆ Wall Street City has announced a series of Web-based training programs that will begin in 1997. They will be aimed at all levels of investors and contain both technical and fundamental courses.

The Wall Street Journal Interactive Edition

http://www.wsj.com

The Journal has a weekly column called "Getting Going" by Jonathan Clements, author of *Funding Your Future: The Only Guide to Mutual Funds You'll Ever Need* (Warner Books). (You'll find it at the Money & Investing page.) Other columns and articles on investing are archived in the Journal's Personal Finance Center, including a year-end review of mutual funds and global markets.

The Woodward Investment Newsletter

http://www.wallstreetcity.com

Author Ian Woodward attempts to educate his readers about high growth stock investing and the ERG Factor, a screening strategy that he codeveloped. To this end, he discusses in "Ian's Corner" each month some aspect of the ERG process. This is a subscription-based newsletter.

Exchange-ing Information

The exchanges offer a broad array of educational material, and regulatory agencies such as the SEC and NASD are also doing their part to educate the investor. Here is a sampling of the current offerings which can only get better.

The American Stock Exchange

http://www.amex.com

Of interest at this site is the AMEX Newsmaker Exchange, a recap of interviews by business journalists with business leaders. For the sophisticated investor, the Dictionary of Financial Risk Management offers graduate-school-level definitions of risk management terminology. Its "Essential Tips" is a studious analysis of financial risk management.

Nasdaq

http://www.nasdaq.com

Nasdaq has a cool site with colorful charts and lots of market information, but the only educational material at this time appears to be a glossary. Enhancements are underway, however. Read about them in Nasdaq's FAQ.

NASDR

http://www.nasdr.com

The National Association of Security Dealers has a regulatory arm which offers several articles about using the Internet as an investing tool (under "How Secure are your Trades?"). The NASDR site offers a toll-free hotline (1-800-289-9999) for information on disciplinary actions taken against brokerage firms and securities representatives.

The New York Stock Exchange

http://www.nyse.com

The NYSE was designed, so it says, as an educational tool for investors, students, and teachers. Currently, it has a free monthly newsletter and a list of publications that include research papers on financial and trading concepts, pamphlets, and information kits about the equities market, updates on technical and trading-related issues, and more. Some are downloadable at the site; others can be ordered for delivery by mail.

FYI   If you want to know which stocks make up the Dow Industrial Average, the Dow Transportation Average, and the Dow Utilities Average, you'll find the lists at Investor's Galleria (http://www.centrex.com/stocks.html).

Birds of a Feather Learn Together

One of the main purposes of an association is to educate its members. Investor associations, such as the AAII and the NAIC, do a good job, and now offer some of their educational tools on the Internet.

The American Association of Individual Investors

http://www.aaii.org

The AAII Web site has many free articles in numerous categories, some of which are Investing Basics, Computers, Financial Planning, Portfolio Management, Brokers, Mutual Funds, Stocks, Bonds, and International. They also have a comprehensive glossary of investing terms. Most of these are available only to members. Membership in the AAII currently costs $49 a year. (See Exhibit 23.3.)

The National Association of Investors Corporation

http://www.better-investing.org

Membership in the NAIC currently costs $39 a year and includes a subscription to *Better Investing,* which offers educational material, free seminars, workshops, and investors' fairs to aid the individual investor. Members also receive discounts on investment books and magazines, and free access to the Research: site (http://www.researchmag.com), mentioned several times in these pages.

Bookstores on the Net

The largest bookstore in the world (Amazon.com) is located on the World Wide Web. So are many smaller ones and some that specialize in investing-related books. The trend seems to be a bookstore at every investing site. You can browse the "stacks" and place books in a virtual shopping cart or bag, then pay for them at the end of your shopping spree.

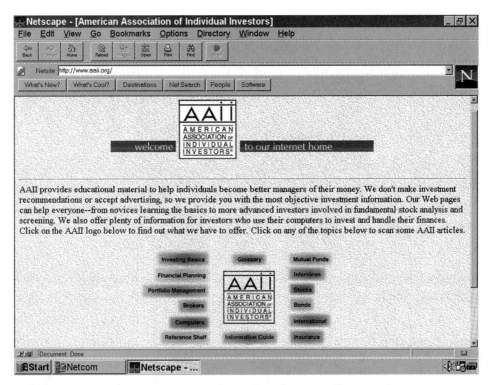

Exhibit 23.3   The AAII is an educational mecca for members.

The Amazon Bookstore

http://www.amazon.com

The Amazon Bookstore claims to have over 2.5 million titles, searchable by keyword, author, title, or subject. They list the books on *The New York Times Book Review*, along with a synopsis of the review, plus reviews from *The New Yorker, Atlantic Monthly,* and others. Amazon.com allows readers to add their own reviews.

Booksite

http://www.booksite.com

In addition to its "hundreds of thousands of titles discounted and available immediately," a BookWatch feature at Booksite will keep an eye out for books in which you're interested and e-mail you when the book comes in.

The Equis Online Bookstore

http://www.equis.com

The Equis Online Bookstore has an extensive offering of investment and financial books searchable by author, title, and subject. You can view jacket descriptions, table of contents, and comments by reviewers and readers (you can add your comments, if you wish).

Traders Library

http://www.traderslibrary.com

Traders Library is devoted to financial and investing books, with a heavy emphasis on those about technical analysis, futures, and options.

Wall Street City

http://www.wallstreetcity.com

At its Learn about Investing Page, the Wall Street City bookstore has a listing of mostly technical titles.

Look It Up on Your Web-ster's

Glossaries are indispensable when you're learning about a new field, and they are free at dozens of investing Web sites. If you stumble upon a term you don't understand, just jump to one of these sites.

Cyberspace Terms

Learn the latest cyberspeak in these glossaries.

The CyberDictionary (http://www.cyberstocks.com) is *the* reference tool for Web surfers. Published by Knowledge Exchange, it has definitions of such cyberspeak as *big iron, dark fiber, eyeball tracking, jaggies,*

Moore's Law, vaporware, WANs, LANs, and *Xanadu,* to name a very, very few. (See Exhibit 23.4.)

The New York Times on the Web (http://www.nytimes.com) has a glossary of Internet terms at its CyberTimes page.

General Investing Terms

There are a number of general glossaries on the Net.

AAII (http://www.aaii.org)
Kiplinger Online (http://www.kiplinger.com)
Lombard Securities (http://www.lombard.com)
New York Stock Exchange (http://www.nyse.com)
Wall Street Directory (http://www.wsdinc.com)
The Wall Street Journal Interactive Edition (http://www.wsj.com)

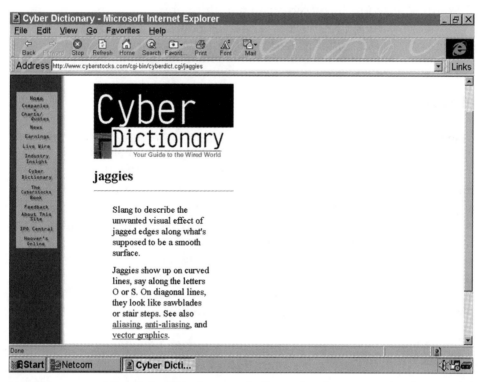

Exhibit 23.4 The CyberDictionary defines the daemons of cyberspace.

Mutual Fund Terms

Talk the mutual fund talk with these glossaries.
  e.Schwab (http://www.eschwab.com)
  Mutual Funds Online (http://www.mfmag.com)

Options Terms

A beginning options trader might want to check out these glossaries.
  Equity Analytics (http://www.e-analytics.com)
  Wall Street City (http://www.wallstreetcity.com)

Technical Analysis Terms

Technical indicators and theories are defined in these glossaries.
  Equity Analytics (http://www.e-analytics.com)
  Investor's Galleria (http://www.centrex.com)
  Stocks & Commodities Magazine (http://www.traders.com)

Magazines on the Web

Magazines on the Web are called *e-zines* (for electronic magazines), *Webzines,* or just *zines.* True zines, according to the CyberTimes dictionary, have a narrower focus and a stronger personality than traditional magazines. Those are the zines that were spawned on the Web without a previous hard-copy existence. But many traditional business and finance magazines have a zine counterpart that transforms their print images—in whole or in part—into the electronic medium. Usually, you cannot access anything more than headlines or leading paragraphs in the current issue without a subscription, but most archive past issues, which are a rich source of free educational material. Here is a sampling, some of which have been mentioned in previous chapters.

Business Week Online

(http://www.businessweek.com)

The Economist

(http://www.economist.com)

Forbes

(http://www.forbes.com)

Fortune

(http://www.fortune.com)

Inc. Magazine

(http://www.inc.com)

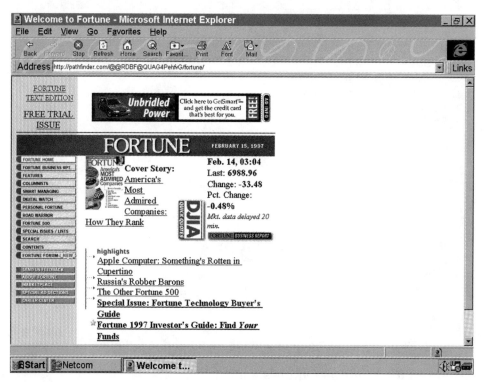

Exhibit 23.5   *Fortune* magazine's home page.

Internet World Online

(http://www.iw.com)

InvestorGuide Weekly

(http://www.investorguide.com)

Kiplinger Online

(http://www.kiplinger.com)

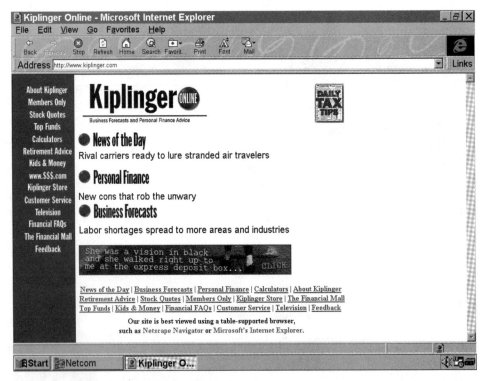

Exhibit 23.6   *Kiplinger* Online's home page.

Money Magazine

(http://pathfinder.com/money)

Money Talks

(http://www.talks.com)

Nest Egg Magazine

(http://nestegg.iddis.com/nestegg)

Exhibit 23.7 Money Online, the Web-based counterpart of *Money* magazine, offers a tool kit for financial planning.

The Red Herring Magazine

(http://www.herring.com)

Stocks & Commodities

(http://www.traders.com)

Time Magazine

(http://www.time.com)

Upside Magazine

(http://www.upside.com)

U.S. News Online

(http://www.usnews.com)

Worth Online

(http://www.worth.com)

The Last Word

The interactive nature of the Internet and the wealth of information it offers makes it an ideal educational medium. We've barely scratched the surface of what it currently has to offer for the investor. The future, no doubt, will increase these offerings manyfold.

WHERE DO WE GO FROM HERE?

I think there is a world market for about five computers.
—Thomas J. Watson, Sr.
Former chairman of IBM

Now that you've read this far, we are tempted to say, forget everything you've read. We don't really mean that, of course, but the fact is, the World Wide Web is in its infancy, and it is changing at an astonishing rate. By the time you read this, there will be more of everything we have discussed, plus new Web sites and new features at existing Web sites.

Even as we were writing this book, Web sites shed their old images and donned new ones. In mid-December of 1996, as we were writing the final chapters, Wall Street City introduced a new version of its Web site. So did Stock Smart, INVESTools, and American Express. In fact, in an apparent attempt to greet the new year with a fresh face, half the Web sites mentioned in these pages underwent complete makeovers, which entailed complete rewrites of related sections. We continued to update references to the sites until the manuscript left our hands, but there will be changes that didn't get in. It will always be impossible to pin the Internet down in a print medium.

The key to using the vast kaleidoscope of investing resources on the Internet will be to adhere to the investing process we have introduced—or to another process more to your liking—and try to stay informed on the investing content and tools on the Web. For starters, our own Web site—CyberInvest.Com at http://www.cyberinvest.com—is designed to keep

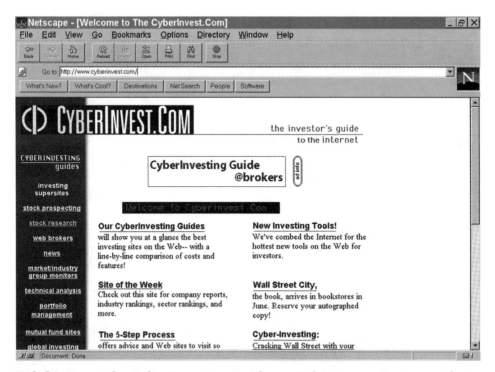

Exhibit E.1   The CyberInvesting Guides at CyberInvest.Com provide an up-to-date comparative look at investing Web sites.

investors up to date on new Web sites that have content or tools for any of the five steps of the cyber-investing process. (See Exhibit E.1.) Whoever you choose as a guide—we mention several in the sidebar—you'll need one to stay on top of this explosive medium.

How explosive is it? Forrester Research projects that the current one million on-line brokerage accounts will grow to 10 million by 2001. You can bet that every brokerage firm, every mutual fund family, every data provider, every information vendor that serves this burgeoning market has seen those same projections. And they will not ignore them. This fertile area could see 1,000 percent growth over the next three or four years.

The good news is that you, the individual investor, can only benefit from this growth, because costs should fall and the quality and quantity of content should increase. Specifically, the cost of trading stocks and other securities will undoubtedly decrease. The breadth and depth of content offerings of each Web site should significantly increase, and it is possible their costs will fall as well. Offerings of financial instruments themselves will proliferate. We've already seen the emergence of DPOs, which may become the initial public offering of choice for many companies. No doubt new types of mutual funds will continue to be introduced. Global investing opportunities should grow from their current embryonic stage to the full maturity of domestic markets. Other innovations that we cannot even foresee will undoubtedly emerge.

A Few Predictions

Just for fun, here are our uncensored predictions about investing on the World Wide Web in the twenty-first century.

- ◆ Videoconferencing will allow public companies to make their earnings announcement on the Web, opening up this important event to individual investors.
- ◆ Alert technology and push technology will become more intelligent, more customized, and more pervasive.
- ◆ Software agents will automate and customize the entire prospecting and research process, surfing the Net while you sleep, gathering investment prospects and research materials. Even better, they will learn from their mistakes!
- ◆ The investment newsletter will cease to exist as printed epistle delivered by snail mail, e-mail, or fax, and become wholly a child of the Internet.
- ◆ Electronic newspages will grow more customized, setting the standard for obtaining daily news—not a stretch, since they're already being offered. But newspages of the future will keep track of your Web-surfing activity and automatically incorporate your new interests.
- ◆ Brokers as we know them now will change dramatically, as the majority acclimate to the Internet and provide value-added services to Internet-literate customers.
- ◆ Mutual funds will be sold directly to the investor over the Web, mostly by fund families.

- The so-called whisper numbers described in Chapter 13 will be published on the Internet by some daring entrepreneur.
- DPOs will proliferate, as they become a standard way of raising capital for small companies.

Will all this really happen? Probably this and more than we can possibly dream.

Keeping Up with the Web

On the Internet, Web sites materialize, merge, or sometimes disappear between one visit and the next. Even at a stable site, whole sections can be added, deleted, or revised between one visit and the next.

Here are few Web sites to help you stay on top of this dynamic, ever changing medium.

- CyberInvest.Com (http://www.cyberinvest.com)
- *Invest$Link* (http://www.imfnet.com)
- *Investor's Galleria* (http://www.centrex.com)
- *InvestorWEB* (http://www.investorweb.com)
- *The New York Times'* CyberTimes Navigator (http:/www.nytimes.com/library)
- *Wall Street Directory* (http://www.wsdinc.com)

This is not, by any means, a complete list of sites that offer hyperlinks to new Web sites. *Netscape* and *Microsoft Internet Explorer* both have finance sections on their home pages where you can find lists of investing-related sites. Yahoo and the other Internet search engines have lists and links. In addition, virtually all the sites mentioned in these pages offer links to related sites. There are a few annotated lists, however, so you don't know what a site is about until you jump there. That's why we offer a comparative analysis at CyberInvest.Com.

The Last Word

If you have not yet joined the throng of cyber-investors, this is the time to start. You have everything to gain—more prospecting tools, more research data, lower commissions—and, if you're good, higher returns in your portfolio.

Now if the markets will just hold up. . . .

APPENDIX

Alphabetical Listing of URLs

AAII
http://www.aaii.org

Accutrade
http://www.accutrade.com

Advisor Software, Inc.
http://www.advisorsw.com

Aetna Fund Series
http://www.aetna.com

AIM Funds
http://www.aimfunds.com

AIQ MarketExpert
http://www.aiq.com

Alliance Funds
http://www.alliancecapital.com

AlphaChart
http://www.techcharts.com

Amazon Bookstore
http://www.amazon.com

American City Business Journals
http://www.amcity.com

American Express Financial Direct
*http//www.americanexpress.com/
direct*

American Stock Exchange
http://www.amex.com

America Online
http://www.aol.com

Anderson Investor's Software, Inc.
http://www.invest-soft.com

Argentina's Ministry of Economy
and Public Works and Services
http://www.mecon.ar

Asia Business Connection, The
http://www.asiabiz.com

Asia Business News
http://www.abn.com.sg

Asia Inc. Online
http://www.asia-inc.com

AsiaOne
http://www.asia1.com.sg

Ask Research
http://www.askresearch.com

K. Aufhauser
http://www.aufhauser.com

Avid Trading Co.
http://avidinfo.com

Bank-CD Rate Scanner
http://bankcd.com

Bank of America
http://www.bankamerica.com

Bank of Boston
http://www.bkb.com

Bank of England, The
http://www.bankofengland.com

Bank One
http://www.bankone.com

BanxQuote
http://www.banx.com

Barron's Online
http://www.barrons.com

Bloomberg Personal
http://www.bloomberg.com

Bonds Online
http://www.bonds-online.com

BondVu
http://www.bondvu.com

Booksite
http://www.booksite.com

BradyNet
http://www.bradynet.com

Bridge News
http://news.bridge.com

Briefing.com
http://www.briefing.com

Business Week Online
http://www.businessweek.com

Business Wire
http://www.businesswire.com

Cambridge Advisors
http://www.cambridgeadvisors.com

Canada Trust
http//www.canadatrust.com

Canada's Department of Foreign
Affairs and International Trade
http://www.dfait-maeci.gc.ca

Ceres Securities
http://www.ceres.com

Charts by CPCUG InvestSIG
http://cpcug.org

Chase Manhattan Bank
http://www.chase.com

Chicago Board of Trade
http://www.cbot.com

Chicago Board Options Exchange
http://www.cboe.com

Chicago Mercantile Exchange
http://www.cme.com

Chicago Stock Exchange
http://www.chicagostockex.com

Citibank
http://www.citibank.com

CNN Financial Network
http://www.cnnfn.com

Cognotick Market Service
http://www.cognotick.com

Commodities Futures Trading
Commission
http://www.cftc.com

Communities Financial Planning
Services
http://www.comfin.com

Companies Online
http://www.companiesonline.com

CompuServe
http://world.compuserve.com

CompuTEL
http://www.rapidtrade.com

Cutter & Co., Inc.
http://www.stocktrader.com

CyberCash Wallet
http://www.cybercash.com

CyberInvest.com
http://www.cyberinvest.com

CyberInvesting Newsletter
http://www.wallstreetcity.com

Cyberstocks.com
http://www.cyberstocks.com

Datek
http://www.datek.com

DBC Newsletter Network
http://www.margin.com/cbn/ newsletters

DBC Online
http://www.dbc.com

Dean Witter Funds
http://www.deanwitter.com

Delphi Software
http://www.delphi-software.com

Direct Stock Market
http://www.direct-stock-market .com

Disclosure
http://www.disclosure.com

Dow Jones
http://bis.dowjones.com

Dreyfus Funds
http://www.dreyfus.com

EBN Interactive
http://www.ebn.co.uk

eBroker
http://www.ebroker.com

The Economist
http://www.economist.com

EDGAR
http://www.sec.com

EDGAR-Online
http://www.edgar-online.com

A. G. Edwards & Sons
http://www.agedwards.com

Emerging Companies Network
http://www.capitol-network.com

Equis International
http://www.equis.com

Equity Analytics
http://www.e-analytics.com

E*Trade
http://www.etrade.com

Ezy Group
http://www.ezygroup.net.au

Falkor Technologies
http://www.falkor.com

Federated Funds
http://www.fedservco.com

Fidelity Funds
http://www.fidelity.com

Fidelity Investments
http://personal.fidelity.com

Final Bell
http://www.finalbell.com

The Financial Center Online
http://www.tfc.com

First Call
http://www.firstcall.com

First Union National Bank
http://www.firstunion.com

First Virtual Accounts
http://www.fv.com

Flexsoft
http://www.flexsoft.com

Forbes
http:/www.forbes.com

Foreign Markets Advisory
http://www.investools.com

Fortune Magazine
http://www.fortune.com

Fox News
http://www.foxnews.com

French Finance Ministry
http://www.tresor.finances.fr/oat

FT.com
http://www.ft.com

Gold Newsletter
*http://www.investorweb.com/
NEWSLTRS*

Griffin Capital Management Corp.
http://pawws.com/Grif phtml

Growth Lists
http://www.growthlist.com

John Hancock Funds
http://www.jhancock.com

Holt Report
*http://metro.turnpike.net/
holt/curr.htm*

Hoover's Online
http://www.hoovers.com

IBC Financial Data
http://www.ibcdata.com

I/B/E/S
http://www.ibes.com

IBM Infomarket
http://www.infomarket.ibm.com

I.D.E.A.
http://www.wallstreetcity.com

Inc. Online
http://www.inc.com

Info-Mine
http://www.info-mine.com

InfoSel
http://www.infosel.com.mx

INO
http://www.ino.com

Insider Chronicle
*http://www.marketedge.com/
chronicle*

Insider Trader
http://www.insidertrader.com

Institute of Finance and
Banking, The
University of Goettingen, Germany
*http://www.wiso.gwdg.de/ifbg/
stock1.htm*

Interactive Advisors Group
http://www.iadvisor.com

Interactive Quote
http://www.iqc.com

Internet World Online
http://www.iw.com

InvestEXpress Online
http://www.investexpress.com

Investext
http://www.investext.com

InvestLink
http://www.investlink.com

Investment Reporter, The
http://www.investools.com

INVESTools
http://www.investools.com

Invest-o-rama
http://www.investorama.com

InvestorGuide
http://www.investorguide.com

Investor's Business Daily
http://www.investors.com

Investor's Galleria
http://www.centrex.com

Investor's Hotline
http://www.investorshotline.com

InvestorsEdge
http://www.irnet.com

InvestorWEB
http://www.investorweb.com

InvestQuest
http://invest.quest.columbus.oh.us

IPO Center
http://nestegg.iddis.com/ipo

IPO Central
http://www.ipocentral.com

IPO Network
http://www.iponetwork.com

IPO Online
http://www.ipo-source.com

ISDEX
http://www.iworld.com

Kansas City Board of Trade
http://www.kcbt.com

Karagosian Financial Services, Inc.
http://toinvest.com/assetmix.html

Kemper Funds
http://www.kemper.com

Tom Kinakin's Stockline
http://www.stockline.com

Kiplinger Online
http://www.kiplinger.com

LaPorte Asset Allocation System
http://www.laportesoft.com

Lombard
http://www.lombard.com

LPL Financial Services
http://www.sddt.com/~lplreilly/
asset/assetallocation.htm

Lycos
http://www.lycos.com

M.A.I.D./Profound
http://www.maid-plc.com

Macro*World @ Wall Street City
http://www.wallstreetcity.com

Market Guide
http://www.marketguide.com

Market Mavens
http://www.tfc.com

Market Technicians Assn.
http://www.teleport.com/~lensmith

MarketPlayer
http://www.marketplayer.com/
sponsor/investorama

Massachusetts Mutual Life
http://www.massmutual.com

Merrill Lynch
http://www.ml.com

MetaStock
http://www.equis.com

Mexican Commentary
http://www.investorweb.com/
NEWSLTRS/mexicancommentary/
intro.htm

Mexican Consulate
http://www.quicklink.com/mexico

Microsoft Internet Explorer
http://home.microsoft

Microsoft Network
http://www.msn.com

Minneapolis Grain Exchange
http://www.mgex.com

Money Magazine
http://pathfinder.com/money

Money Talks
http://www.talks.com

J. P. Morgan
http://www.jpmorgan.com

Morningstar.Net
http://www.morningstar.net

Motley Fool, The
http://www.fool.com

Multex
http://www.multex.com

Municipal Resource Center
http://www.municipal.com

Mutual Fund Interactive
http://www.fundsinteractive.com

Mutual Fund Investor's Center, The
http://www.mfea.com

Mutual Funds Online
http://www.mfmag.com

My Yahoo!
http://my.yahoo.com/ticker.html

MyBank
http://www.mybank.com

NASD Regulation
http://www.nasdr.com

Nasdaq
http://www.nasdaq.com

National Association of Investors
Corporation (NAIC)
http://www.better-investing.org

NationsBank
http://www.nationsbank.com

Nations Funds
*http://www.nationsbank.com/
mutual funds*

NDB Online
http://pawws.com/Ndb

NestEgg Magazine
http://nestegg.iddis.com/nestegg

Net Capital Communications
http://www.netcapital.com

The Net Investor
http://netinvestor.com

Netscape
http://home.netscape.com

NETworth
http://networth.galt.com

New Century Network
http://www.newcentury.com

New York Cotton Exchange
http://www.nyce.com

New York Mercantile Exchange
http://www.nymex.com

New York Stock Exchange
http://www.nyse.com

The New York Times on the Web
http://www.nytimes.com

Newspage
http://www.newspage.com

Notable Technologies
http://www.notable.com

NYU
http://edgar.stern.nyu.edu

The Online Investor
http://www.investhelp.com

Onramp Access
http://www.onr.com

Oppenheimer & Co.
http://www.oppenheimer.com

OptionVue Systems International
http://www.optionvue.com

J. B. Oxford & Co.
http://www.jboxford.com

Pacific Brokerage
http://www.tradepbs.com

PaineWebber
http://www.painewebber.com

PAWWS Financial Network
http://pawws.com

PC Financial Network
http://www.pcfn.com

PC Magazine Online
http://www.pcmag.com

PC Quote
http://www.pcquote.com

PC Week Online
http://www.pcweek.com

PC World Online
http://www.pcworld.com

Philadelphia Stock Exchange
http://www.phlx.com

Phoenix Insurance Investments
http://www.phoenixhomelife.com

Pioneer National Bank
http://www.pioneer-bank.com

PIPEX Worldserver Business Park
http://www.worldserver.pipex.com

PR Newswire
http://www.prnewswire.com

PRARS
http://www.prars.com

T. Rowe Price Funds
http://www.troweprice.com

Primark
http://www.pirc.com

Prime Rate
http://www.primerate.com

Pristine Day Trader
http://www.pristine.com

Privateer, The
http://www.the-privateer.com

Prodigy
http://www.prodigy.com

Prudential Securities
http://www.prusec.com

Putnam Funds
http://www.putnminv.com

Quick & Reilly
http://www.quick-reilly.com

Quote.com
http://www.quote.com

Red Chip Review
http://www.redchip.com

The Red Herring Magazine
http://www.herring.com

Research:
http://www.researchmag.com

Reuters Money Network
http://www.moneynet.com

Robert-Slade, Inc.
http://www.itsnet.com/~rsi

Russell Indexes
http://www.russell.com

Salomon Brothers Funds
http://www.salomon.com

Schwab Funds
http://www.schwab.com

SchwabNOW
http://www.eschwab.com

Scudder Funds
http://www.scudder.com

Securities & Exchange Commission
http://www.sec.gov

Security APL
http://www.secapl.com

Security First Network Bank
http://www.sfnb.com

Silicon Investor
http://www.techstocks.com

Singapore Business Times Online
http://biztimes.asia1.com

Small Cap Investor, The
http://www.financialweb.com

Smart EDGAR
http://dbc.smart-edgar.com

Smith Barney
http://www.smithbarney.com

Standard & Poor's
http://www.stockinfo.standardpoor
.com

Stock Blocks
http://www.stockblocks.com

Stock Chat
http://www.stockchat.com

The Stock Manager's Investment
Report
http://www.lbfinc.com

Stock Smart
http://www.stocksmart.com

The Stock Room
http://www.stockroom.org

StockMaster
http://www.stockmaster.com

Stocks & Commodities Magazine
http://www.traders.com

StreetNet
http://www.streetnet.com

SuperCharts
http://www.omegaresearch.com

The Syndicate
http://www.moneypages.com/
syndicate

Technical Tools
http://www.techtool.com

Telescan, Inc.
http//www.telescan.com

Time Magazine
http://www.time.com

Times of London, The
http://www.the-times.co.uk

The Total Investor
http://ourworld.compuserve.com

TradeAlerts
http://www.tradealert.com

TradeHistory
http://www.tradehistory.com

Tradeline Mutual Fund Center
http://nestegg.iddis.com/mutfund

Traders Library
http://www.traderslibrary.com

Trading Techniques, Inc.
http://www.tradingtech.com

Upside Magazine
http://www.upside.com

U.S. Bank
http://www.usbank.com

U.S. News Online
http://www.usnews.com

USA Today
http://www.usatoday.com

Van Kampen American Capital
Funds
http://www.vkac.com

The Vanguard Group
http://www.vanguard.com

Wall Street City
http://www.wallstreetcity.com

The Wall Street Directory
http://www.wsdinc.com

Wall Street Journal Interactive
Edition
http://www.wsj.com

Wall Street Research Net
http://www.wsrn.com

Web 100, The
http://www.w100.com

Wells Fargo Bank
http://wellsfargo.com

Westergaard
http://www.westergaard.com

Jack White & Co.
http://www.jackwhiteco.com

Window on Wall Street
http://www.wallstreet.com

Winterra Software Group, Inc.
http://www.winterra.com

Worden Brothers Online
http://www.worden.com

Worldwide Banking Directory
http://www.orcc.com/banks.htm

Worth Online
http://www.worth.com

WWW Internet Fund
http://www.inetfund.com

Zacks Investment Research
http://www.zacks.com

INDEX

Page numbers for exhibits, or text that is boxed and highlighted for emphasis, are in italic type.

ABOUT THE CD-ROM

Welcome to Sprint Internet Passport and Wall Street City

What you get with the Sprint Internet Passport:

- 30 days of on-line time with Sprint
- Free Netscape Navigator browser
- Automatic default to the Wall Street City home page with the following:

  - 30 days of free access to Wall Street City (WSC)
  - Bookmarks at WSC for the major Web sites in this book
  - A special on-line guide to the investing tools at WSC

- Special browser buttons on the Sprint Internet Passport for quick links to important investing sites:

  - CyberInvest.Com links to the Web site that offers up-to-date comparisons of the Web sites in this book.
  - Trade Now! links to selected Web brokers
  - Bank Now! links to selected banks which offer on-line banking.

WARNING: If you currently use Netscape Navigator as your Internet browser, installing the Sprint Internet Passport will automatically overwrite that software.

SOLUTION: To install the Sprint CD so that it coexists with your current software configuration, follow the steps found at http://www.sprint.com/passport or call Sprint at 1-800-786-1400.

Users With Current Internet Access: If you do not wish to install the Sprint Internet Passport, you may go directly to the Wall Street City home page at http://www.wallstreetcity.com for the bookmarks and on-line guide.

Getting Started with Sprint Internet Passport:

1. Install the browser software per the following instructions.
2. Set up your Sprint Internet Passport account per the following instructions.
3. Launch the browser and connect to the Internet, as described later.
4. The Wall Street City home page will appear as your default home page.
5. Click Subscribe to set up your account for your 30-day free trial with Wall Street City.
6. **On-line Guide** and **Bookmarks:** Click How to Use Wall Street City; then click Special Guide for Book Purchasers and follow the instructions at that page.

Special Browser Buttons:

Any time you are connected to the Internet, you can click one of the special browser buttons to link to these special services.

1. **CyberInvest.Com:** This is the authors' Web site which maintains more than 20 CyberInvesting Guides to give you up-to-date comparisons of investing Web sites, *plus* highlights on the latest and hottest investing tools on the Web.
2. **Trade Now!** Click this button to go to a page that features four of the best brokerage firms on the Web.

   ◆ Click one of the broker names to see a recap of commissions and features.
   ◆ Click the broker name on that page to jump to the broker's home page.

3. **Bank Now!** Click this button to go to a page that features four of the best on-line banks on the Web.

   ◆ Click one of the bank names to see a recap of on-line banking features.
   ◆ Click the bank name on that page to jump to the bank's home page.

Setting up your Sprint Internet Passport Account:

Installing Sprint Internet Passport (Netscape browser):

WARNING: If you currently have Netscape Navigator installed on your computer, installing Sprint Internet Passport will automatically overwrite that software.

- **Windows 3.1 users:** Insert the CD-ROM. From the File Menu in Program Manager, select Run. Type **D:\install** (where D:\ is the letter of your CD-ROM drive). Press Enter.

- **Windows 95 users:** Insert the CD-ROM. The setup program should launch automatically. If the setup program does not launch automatically, select Run from the Start Menu. Type **D:\install** (where D:\ is the letter of your CD-ROM drive). Press Enter.

- **Macintosh users:** Insert the CD-ROM. Double click on the Installer icon.

NOTE: Dial-up access numbers can be found at Sprint's home page: http://www.sprintsite.com or Sprint Customer Service at 1-800-786-1400.

Sprint README file: D:\WIN.31\DISK5\README.TXT; D:\WIN.95\DISK5\README.TXT; or the Read Me! file in the Macintosh Sprint Internet folder.

Account Setup Procedures for Windows 3.1, Windows95, and Macintosh users:

1. After installing the Sprint CD, restart your computer and double-click on the *Sprint Account Setup* icon in the *Sprint* program group or *Navigator* window.

   Macintosh users: Click on the Next arrow in the Account Setup window.

2. Follow the on-screen prompts to set up your account. *The first 30 days are FREE,* but the account must be set up in order to use the program.

3. Then registration is complete:

   Windows 3.1 users: Double-click on the *Sprint* icon in the Sprint program group and click Dial.

   Windows 95 users: Double-click on the *Dial Sprint* icon on your desktop (Note: If the password field is blank (no stars), enter your password and click Connect.) Then double-click the Sprint icon on your desktop to launch the browser.

Macintosh System 7.1 users: At the prompt, click on Restart. When restart is complete, click on the Connect Now arrow in the Account Setup window to continue with Account Setup.

You're ready to begin!

Notes:

◆ When exiting Sprint Internet Passport, be sure to close modem connections, if they do not close automatically.

◆ Be sure to record in a safe place your Dial Access Number, Sprint Password, Sprint log-in ID, and e-mail address.

◆ If setup encounters difficulties in identifying your modem, you may need to do so manually. See the README file for more information.

◆ Be sure to verify your pricing plan selection.

◆ Be sure your registration address matches your credit card billing address. If your credit card company uses ZIP+4, it is important that you include the extra 4 digits.

◆ If you live in an area where local calls can span two or more area codes, you may want to modify the 1+Area Code settings in your dialer. See the README file for more information.

◆ Please review all numbers available to be sure your modem dialer is set for a local call. If you're unsure, check with your local telephone company. NOTE: In some areas, a call may be considered long distance even though it does not require dialing a "1" or "0".

Minimum System Requirements:

Windows Users:

◆ CD-ROM drive

◆ IBM-compatible computer with 386sx or higher processor (486 or higher recommended)

◆ 8MB RAM and 11MB free hard disk space

◆ 14.4 Kbps or faster modem (28.8 Kbps recommended)

◆ Windows®3.1 or Windows95®

Macintosh Users:

- ◆ CD-ROM drive
- ◆ Macintosh Operating System 7.1 up to 7.5.5
- ◆ 16MB RAM and 12MB free hard disk space
- ◆ Macintosh TCP 2.0.6 (or higher) or Open Transport 1.1 (or higher)
- ◆ FreePPP 2.5 (or higher)—included on the Sprint CD
- ◆ 14.4 Kbps or faster modem (28.8 Kbps recommended)

Customer Service:

For Sprint Customer Service call 1-800-786-1400.

For information on how to use the CD-ROM, refer to the **About the CD-ROM** section on pages 347–351.

WILEY
Publishers Since 1807